Texts and Monographs in Computer Science

F. L. Bauer
David Gries

editors

Automata-Theoretic Aspects of Formal Power Series

Arto Salomaa
Matti Soittola

Springer-Verlag
New York Heidelberg Berlin

Arto Salomaa

University of Turku
Department of Mathematics
20500 Turku 50
Finland

Matti Soittola

University of Turku
Department of Mathematics
20500 Turku 50
Finland

editors

F. L. Bauer

Mathematisches Institut der
  Technischen Hochschule
8000 München
Arcisstrasse 21
West Germany

David Gries

Cornell University
Department of Computer Science
Upson Hall
Ithaca, New York 14859
USA

AMS Subject Classifications: 02F10, 30A10, 68A25, 68A30, 94A30
(C.R.) Computing Classifications: 5.22, 5.23

Library of Congress Cataloging in Publication Data

Salomaa, Arto.
  Automata-theoretic aspects of formal power series.

  (Texts and monographs in computer science)
  Bibliography: p.
  Includes index.
  1. Sequential machine theory. 2. Formal languages. 3. Power series. I. Soittola, Matti,
1945 –   joint author. II. Bauer, Friedrich Ludwig, 1924 –   III. Gries, David, 1939 –
IV. Title.
QA267.5.S4S29   629.8′91   78-2214

ISBN 0-387-90282-1   Springer-Verlag   New York

ISBN 3-540-90282-1   Springer-Verlag   Berlin Heidelberg

Preface

This book develops a theory of formal power series in noncommuting variables, the main emphasis being on results applicable to automata and formal language theory. This theory was initiated around 1960—apart from some scattered work done earlier in connection with free groups—by M. P. Schützenberger to whom also belong some of the main results.

So far there is no book in existence concerning this theory. This lack has had the unfortunate effect that formal power series have not been known and used by theoretical computer scientists to the extent they in our estimation should have been. As with most mathematical formalisms, the formalism of power series is capable of unifying and generalizing known results. However, it is also capable of establishing specific results which are difficult if not impossible to establish by other means. This is a point we hope to be able to make in this book. That formal power series constitute a powerful tool in automata and language theory depends on the fact that they in a sense lead to the arithmetization of automata and language theory. We invite the reader to prove, for instance, Theorem IV.5.3 or Corollaries III.7.8 and III.7.9— all specific results in language theory—by some other means.

Although this book is mostly self-contained, the reader is assumed to have some background in algebra and analysis, as well as in automata and formal language theory. The level of presentation corresponds to that of beginning graduate or advanced undergraduate work. We give an overview of the most important background material in Sections I.1 and I.2. It is suggested that these first two sections are consulted only when need arises and that the actual reading is begun from Section I.3.

Acknowledgments

We want to express our gratitude to the Academy of Finland for good working conditions during the writing of this book. We have (or at least one of us has) benefited from discussions with Jean Berstel, Hermann Maurer, Eli Shamir, Paavo Turakainen, Derick Wood, and our colleagues at the University of Turku, in particular, Juhani Karhumäki and Keijo Ruohonen. Special thanks are due to Leena Leppänen for the excellent typing of the script. Finally, we want to thank Springer-Verlag for very good and timely editorial work.

Turku, November 1977   Arto Salomaa
                                                             Matti Soittola

Contents

I
Introduction

I.1 Preliminaries from algebra and analysis

The central algebraic concepts in the theory of formal series are those of a monoid and a semiring.

A *monoid* consists of a set M, an associative binary operation $*$ on M and of a neutral element 1 such that $1 * a = a * 1 = a$ for every a. A monoid is called *commutative* if $a * b = b * a$ for every a and b. The binary operation is usually denoted by juxtaposition and the neutral element by λ.

Note that the familiar system called a group might be defined as a monoid where every element has an inverse.

The most important type of a monoid in our theory is the *free monoid* X^* generated by a finite set X. It has all the finite strings

$$x_1 x_2 \cdots x_n \quad (x_i \in X)$$

as its elements and the product $a * b$ is formed by writing the string b immediately after the string a.

The direct product $M_1 \otimes \cdots \otimes M_k$ of given monoids $M_1, \ldots, M_k$ means the monoid whose underlying set is the Cartesian product

$$M_1 \times \cdots \times M_k = \{(a_1, \ldots, a_k) \mid a_i \in M_i\}$$

and whose operation is defined by the equation

$$(a_1, \ldots, a_k) * (b_1, \ldots, b_k) = (a_1 * b_1, \ldots, a_k * b_k).$$

Note that the direct product is commutative if $M_i = \{x_i\}^*$ $(i = 1, \ldots, k)$.

By a *semiring* we mean a set A together with two binary operations $+$ and $\cdot$ and two constant elements 0 and 1 such that

(i) $\langle A, +, 0 \rangle$ is a commutative monoid,

1

(ii) $\langle A, \cdot, 1 \rangle$ is a monoid,

(iii) the distribution laws $a \cdot (b + c) = a \cdot b + a \cdot c$ and $(a + b) \cdot c = a \cdot c + b \cdot c$ hold,

(iv) $0 \cdot a = a \cdot 0 = 0$ for every a.

A semiring is called *commutative* if $a \cdot b = b \cdot a$ for every a and b.

Note again that a ring (with unity) might be defined as a semiring where $\langle A, +, 0 \rangle$ is a commutative group.

The semirings most used in this book are the Boolean semiring $\mathbb{B} = \{0, 1\}$ where $1 + 1 = 1 \cdot 1 = 1$, the semiring $\mathbb{N}$ of natural numbers, the ring $\mathbb{Z}$ of integers, the rational number field $\mathbb{Q}$, the real number field $\mathbb{R}$ and the complex number field $\mathbb{C}$.

Let A be semiring. Then a commutative monoid V is called an A-*semimodule* if there is an operation $\cdot$ from $A \times V$ into V such that

(i) $(ab) \cdot v = a \cdot (b \cdot v)$,

(ii) $(a + b) \cdot v = a \cdot v + b \cdot v$ and $a \cdot (v + w) = a \cdot v + a \cdot w$,

(iii) $1 \cdot v = v$ and $0 \cdot v = 0$.

We observe that the familiar modules and vector spaces are special cases of a semimodule.

As an example of an A-semimodule we mention the set A^S of all functions $f: S \to A$ (S a set) where $(f_1 + f_2)(s) = f_1(s) + f_2(s)$ and $(a \cdot f)(s) = af(s)$.

The general algebraic concepts of a *substructure* generated by a set and a *homomorphism* should be well known. In spite of that we write here the definitions in the case of A-semimodules.

If S is a subset of an A-semimodule V then the subsemimodule $[S]$ generated by S is the smallest of all subsemimodules of V containing S. It is easy to show that

$$[S] = \{a_1 s_1 + \cdots + a_n s_n \mid a_i \in A, s_i \in S\}.$$

If U and V are A-semimodules then a mapping $f: U \to V$ is a homomorphism, if

$$f(u_1 + u_2) = f(u_1) + f(u_2)$$

and

$$f(a \cdot u) = a \cdot f(u).$$

This kind of a homomorphism is usually called a linear mapping.

We consider also vectors and matrices whose elements belong to a semiring. The operations used are the classical ones. We note that the set $A^{m \times m}$ of $m \times m$ square matrices forms a semiring. Very important will be the multiplicative homomorphisms $\mu: M \to A^{m \times m}$ (M a monoid) which are usually called *representations*.

The *Kronecker product* of two matrices $B \in A^{m \times m}$ and $C \in A^{m \times n}$ is defined as the matrix

$$\begin{bmatrix} B_{11}C & B_{12}C & \cdots & B_{1m}C \\ B_{21}C & B_{22}C & \cdots & B_{2m}C \\ . & . & \cdots & . \\ B_{m1}C & B_{m2}C & \cdots & B_{mm}C \end{bmatrix} \in A^{mn \times mn}$$

where the B_{ij}'s are the entries of B.

We shall also need some other notions and results concerning matrices, vector spaces, rings and fields, algebraic numbers, etc. Since these matters belong to the realm of standard algebra, we only refer to [La].

In the proof of Theorem 6.3 we need two special results found in [ES]. We cite these theorems here in a simplified form. We call a semimodule *cancellative* if $x + y = x + z$ implies $y = z$.

Let V_1 and V_2 be finitely generated subsemimodules of the cancellative $\mathbb{N}$-semimodule V. Then $V_1 \cap V_2$ is finitely generated.

Let V be a finitely generated cancellative $\mathbb{N}$-semimodule. If T is a finitely generated subsemimodule of V then

$$\mathbb{N}^{-1}T = \{v \in V \mid \exists n \in \mathbb{N} \setminus \{0\}: nv \in T\}$$

is a finitely generated $\mathbb{N}$-semimodule.

The classical analysis in this book should cause no difficulties.

When dealing with projections we have to use semirings where limit notions are at hand. Exactly defined, a *topological semiring* is a semiring which is also a topological space in such a way that the operations $+$ and $\cdot$ are continuous functions of two variables.

The simplest case of a topological semiring is a semiring with a metric d such that $d(x_n, x) \to 0$ and $d(y_n, y) \to 0$ implies $d(x_n + y_n, x + y) \to 0$ and $d(x_n y_n, xy) \to 0$. (The reader not familiar with metric spaces should now consult a textbook of modern analysis.)

Every semiring becomes topological if we define $d(x, y) = 1$ ($x \ne y$) and $d(x, x) = 0$. The topology in question is called *discrete*.

A *valued field* is a field whose topology is given by an absolute value function (see e.g. [La]). And as usual the adjective "complete" in this context means that every Cauchy sequence has a limit.

We say that a denumerable family $F = \{a_0, a_1, \ldots\}$ of a topological semiring is *summable* if for every bijection $g: \mathbb{N} \to \mathbb{N}$ the series $\sum_i a_{g(i)}$ converges and its sum does not depend on g.

Note that the concept of a complete semiring (due to Eilenberg) is based on summability conditions and has nothing to do with metric spaces.

3

I.2 Preliminaries from automata and formal language theory

An *alphabet* is a finite nonempty set. The elements of an alphabet V are called *letters*. A *word* over an alphabet V is a finite string consisting of zero or more letters of V, whereby the same letter may occur several times. The string consisting of zero letters is called the *empty word*, written λ. The set of all words (respectively all nonempty words) over an alphabet V is denoted by V^* resp. (V^+). (Thus, algebraically, V^* and V^+ are the free monoid and free semigroup generated by the finite set V.) For words w_1 and w_2, the juxtaposition $w_1 w_2$ is called the *catenation* of w_1 and w_2. The empty word λ is an identity with respect to catenation. Catenation being associative, the notation w^i, where i is a nonnegative integer, is used in the customary sense, and w^0 denotes the empty word. The *length* of a word w, in symbols $\lg(w)$, means the number of letters in w when each letter is counted as many times as it occurs. A word w is a *subword* of a word u iff there are words w_1 and w_2 such that $u = w_1 w w_2$. Subsets of V^* are referred to as (*formal*) *languages* over the alphabet V.

Various unary and binary *operations* defined for languages will be considered in the sequel. Regarding languages as sets, we may immediately define the Boolean operations of union, intersection, complementation (the complement of a language L is denoted by L^C), difference and symmetric difference in the usual fashion. The *catenation* (or *product*) of two languages L_1 and L_2, in symbols $L_1 L_2$ is defined by

$$L_1 L_2 = \{w_1 w_2 \mid w_1 \in L_1 \text{ and } w_2 \in L_2\}.$$

The notation L^i is extended to concern the catenation of languages. By definition, $L^0 = \{\lambda\}$. The *catenation closure* or *Kleene star* (respectively *λ-free catenation closure*) of a language L, in symbols L^* (respectively L^+) is defined to be the union of all nonnegative powers of L (respectively the union of all positive powers of L). We now define the operation of *substitution*. For each letter a of an alphabet V, let $\sigma(a)$ be a language (possibly over a different alphabet). Define, furthermore,

$$\sigma(\lambda) = \{\lambda\}, \qquad \sigma(w_1 w_2) = \sigma(w_1)\sigma(w_2), \quad \text{for } w_1, w_2 \in V^*.$$

For a language L over V, we define

$$\sigma(L) = \{u \mid u \in \sigma(w) \text{ for some } w \in L\}.$$

Such a mapping σ is called a *substitution*. A substitution σ is *λ-free* iff none of the languages $\sigma(a)$ contains the empty word. A substitution σ such that each $\sigma(a)$ consists of a single word is called a *homomorphism*. (Algebraically, a homomorphism of languages is a monoid homomorphism linearly extended to subsets of monoids.) In connection with homomorphisms (and also often elsewhere) we identify a word w with the singleton set $\{w\}$, writing $\sigma(a) = w$ rather than $\sigma(a) = \{w\}$. A letter-to-letter homomorphism will often in the sequel be called a *coding*. Another operation for languages which we will occasionally need is the *shuffle product*:

$$L \amalg L' = \{w_1 w_1', \ldots, w_n w_n' \mid n \geq 1, w_1, \ldots, w_n \in L, w_1', \ldots, w_n' \in L'\}.$$

Consider an alphabet $V = \{a_1, \ldots, a_m\}$, and denote by $\lg_i(w)$, $i = 1, \ldots, m$, the number of occurrences of a_i in the word w. The mapping ψ of V into the set of ordered m-tuples of nonnegative integers defined by

$$\psi(w) = (\lg_1(w), \ldots, \lg_m(w))$$

is termed the *Parikh mapping* and its values *Parikh vectors*. The Parikh mapping is extended to languages by

$$\psi(L) = \{\psi(w) \mid w \in L\}.$$

The main objects of study in formal language theory are finitary specifications of infinite languages. Most of such specifications are obtained as special cases from the notion of a rewriting system. By definition, a *rewriting system* is an ordered pair (V, P), where V is an alphabet and P a finite set of ordered pairs of words over V. The elements (w, u) of P are referred to as *rewriting rules* or *productions* and denoted by $w \rightarrow u$. Given a rewriting system, the *yield relation* $\Rightarrow$ in the set V^* is defined as follows. For any words w and u, $w \Rightarrow u$ holds iff there are words w', w_1, w'', u_1 such that $w = w' w_1 w''$, $u = w' u_1 w''$, and $w_1 \rightarrow u_1$ is a production in the system. The *reflexive transitive closure* (respectively transitive closure) of the relation $\Rightarrow$ is denoted by $\Rightarrow^*$ (respectively $\Rightarrow^+$).

A *phrase structure grammar* is an ordered quadruple $G = (V_N, V_T, S, P)$, where V_N and V_T are disjoint alphabets (the alphabets of *nonterminals* and *terminals*), $S \in V_N$ (the *initial* letter) and P is a finite set of ordered pairs (w, u) such that u is a word over the alphabet $V = V_N \cup V_T$ and w is a word over V containing at least one letter of V_N. Again, the elements of P are referred to as rewriting rules or productions and written $w \rightarrow u$. A phrase structure grammar G as above defines a rewriting system (V, P). Let $\Rightarrow$ and $\Rightarrow^*$ be the relations determined by this rewriting system. Then the language $L(G)$ *generated* by G is defined by

$$L(G) = \{w \in V_T^* \mid S \Rightarrow^* w\}.$$

Two grammars G and G_1 are termed *equivalent* iff $L(G) = L(G_1)$. For $i = 0, 1, 2, 3$, a grammar $G = (V_N, V_T, S, P)$ is of the *type i* iff the restrictions (i) on P, as given below, are satisfied:

0. No restrictions.
1. Each production in P is of the form $w_1 A w_2 \rightarrow w_1 w w_2$, where w_1 and w_2 are arbitrary words, $A \in V_N$, and w is a nonempty word (with the possible exception of the production $S \rightarrow \lambda$ whose occurrence in P implies, however, that S does not occur on the right side of any production).
2. Each production in P is of the form $A \rightarrow w$, where $A \in V_N$.
3. Each production is of one of the two forms $A \rightarrow Bw$ or $A \rightarrow w$, where $A, B \in V_N$ and $w \in V_T^*$.

5

A language is of type i iff it is generated by a grammar of type i. Type 0 languages are also called *recursively enumerable*. Type 1 grammars and languages are also called *context-sensitive*. Type 2 grammars and languages are also called *context-free*. Type 3 grammars and languages are also referred to as *finite-state* or *regular*. We shall in this book be mainly interested in the latter two language classes.

A specific context-free language over an alphabet with $2t$ letters, $V_t = \{a_1, \ldots, a_t, \bar{a}_1, \ldots, \bar{a}_t\}$, $t \geq 1$, needed often in the sequel, is the *Dyck language* generated by the grammar

$$(\{S\}, V_t, S, \{S \rightarrow SS, S \rightarrow \lambda, S \rightarrow a_1 S \bar{a}_1, \ldots, S \rightarrow a_t S \bar{a}_t\}).$$

The Dyck language consists of all words over V_t which can be reduced to λ using the relations $a_i \bar{a}_i = \lambda$, $i = 1, \ldots, t$. If the pairs $(a_i, \bar{a}_i)$, $i = 1, \ldots, t$, are viewed as parentheses of different types then the Dyck language consists of all sequences of correctly nested parentheses.

The family of regular languages over an alphabet V equals the family of languages obtained from "atomic languages" $\{\lambda\}$ and $\{a\}$, where $a \in V$, by a finite number of applications of "regular operations": union, catenation and catenation closure. (For the proof of this and other results mentioned in this section, cf. [Sa1].) The formula expressing how a specific regular language is obtained from atomic languages by regular operations is termed a *regular expression*.

Every context-free language which is λ-free (i.e., does not contain the empty word) is generated by a grammar in *Chomsky normal form*, as well as by a grammar in *Greibach normal form*. In the former, all productions are of the types $A \rightarrow BC$, $A \rightarrow a$ and, in the latter, of the types $A \rightarrow aBC$, $A \rightarrow aB$, $A \rightarrow a$, where capital letters are nonterminals and a is a terminal letter. According to the Theorem of Chomsky–Schützenberger, every context-free language L can be expressed as

$$L = h(D \cap R),$$

for some regular language R, Dyck language D and homomorphism h. According to the Lemma of Bar-Hillel (also called the Pumping Lemma), every sufficiently long word w in a context-free language L can be written in the form

$$w = u_1 w_1 u_2 w_2 u_3, \qquad w_1 w_2 \neq \lambda,$$

where for every $i \geq 0$, the word $u_1 w_1^i u_2 w_2^i u_3$ belongs to L. For regular languages, the corresponding result reads as follows. Every sufficiently long word w in a regular language L can be written in the form $w = u_1 w_1 u_2$, $w_1 \neq \lambda$, where for every $i \geq 0$, the word $u_1 w_1^i u_2$ belongs to L.

Derivations according to a context-free grammar (i.e., finite sequences of words where every two consecutive words are in the relation $\Rightarrow$) can in a natural way be visualized by labeled trees, the so-called *derivation trees*. A context-free grammar G is termed *ambiguous* iff some word in $L(G)$ has two derivation trees. Otherwise, G is termed *unambiguous*. A context-free language L is unambiguous iff $L = L(G)$, for some unambiguous grammar G. Otherwise, L is termed (inherently) ambiguous. We speak also of *degrees* of ambiguity. A context-free grammar G is ambiguous of degree k (a natural number or ∞) iff every word in $L(G)$ possesses at most k derivation trees and some word in $L(G)$ possesses exactly k derivation trees. A language L is ambiguous of degree k iff $L = L(G)$, for some G ambiguous of degree k, but there is no G_1 ambiguous of degree less than k such that $L = L(G_1)$.

In a *weighted* context-free grammar G a nonnegative real number is assigned to each production (the *weight* of the production). The weight of a derivation is obtained by multiplying the weights of the productions applied in the derivation (each production being taken as many times as it is applied in the derivation). The weight of a word w in $L(G)$ is obtained by summing up the weights of all derivations of w according to G. (Note that infinite weights may occur.)

The families of type i languages, $i = 0, 1, 2, 3$, defined above using generative devices can be obtained also by recognition devices. A recognition device defining a language L receives arbitrary words as inputs and "accepts" exactly the words belonging to L. The recognition devices, *finite and pushdown automata*, corresponding to type 3 and type 2 languages, will be defined below. The definitions of the recognition devices, *linear bounded automata and Turing machines*, corresponding to type 1 and type 0 languages, will be omitted because these devices do not enter the discussions in this book.

A rewriting system (V, P) is called a *finite deterministic automaton* iff (i) V is divided into two disjoint alphabets V_S and V_I (the *state* and the *input* alphabet), (ii) an element $s_0 \in V_S$ and a subset $S_1 \subseteq V_S$ are specified (*initial state* and *final state set*), and (iii) the productions in P are of the form

$$s_i a_k \to s_j, \qquad s_i, s_j \in V_S; a_k \in V_I,$$

and for each pair (s_i, a_k), there is exactly one such production in P.

A finite deterministic automaton over an input alphabet V_I is usually defined by specifying an ordered quadruple (s_0, V_S, f, S_1), where f is a mapping of $V_S \times V_I$ into V_S, the other items being as above. (Clearly, the values of f are obtained from the right sides of the productions listed above.)

The language *accepted* or *recognized* by a finite deterministic automaton FDA is defined by

$$L(FDA) = \{w \in V_I^* \mid s_0 w \Rightarrow^* s_1 \text{ for some } s_1 \in S_1\}.$$

A finite *nondeterministic* automaton FNA is defined as a deterministic one with the following two exceptions. In (ii) s_0 is replaced by a subset $S_0 \subseteq V_S$. In (iii) the second sentence (beginning with "and") is omitted. The language accepted by an FNA is defined by

$$L(FNA) = \{w \in V_I^* \mid s_0 w \Rightarrow^* s_1 \text{ for some } s_0 \in S_0 \text{ and } s_1 \in S_1\}.$$

A language is of type 3 iff it is accepted by some finite deterministic automaton iff it is accepted by some finite nondeterministic automaton.

7

A rewriting system (V, P) is called a *pushdown automaton* iff each of the following conditions (i)–(iii) is satisfied.

(i) V is divided into two disjoint alphabets V_S and $V_I \cup V_Z$. The sets V_S, V_I, and V_Z are called the *state, input*, and *pushdown* alphabet, respectively. The sets V_I and V_Z are nonempty but not necessarily disjoint.

(ii) Elements $s_0 \in V_S$, $z_0 \in V_Z$, and a subset $S_1 \subseteq V_S$ are specified, namely, the so-called *initial state, start letter*, and *final state set*.

(iii) The productions in P are of the two forms

(1) $\qquad zs_i \to ws_j, \qquad z \in V_Z; \qquad w \in V_Z^*; \qquad s_i, s_j \in V_S,$

(2) $\qquad zs_i a \to ws_j, \qquad z \in V_Z; \qquad w \in V_Z^*; \qquad a \in V_I; \qquad s_i, s_j \in V_S.$

The language accepted by a pushdown automaton is defined by

$$L(PDA) = \{w \in V_I^* \mid z_0 s_0 w \Rightarrow^* us_1 \text{ for some } u \in V_Z^*, s_1 \in S_1\}.$$

A pushdown automaton is *deterministic* iff, for every pair (s_i, z), P contains either exactly one production (1) and no productions (2), or no productions (1) and exactly one production (2) for every $a \in V_I$.

The family of context-free languages equals the family of languages acceptable by pushdown automata. Languages acceptable by deterministic pushdown automata are referred to as *deterministic* (context-free) languages. The role of determinism is different in connection with pushdown and finite automata: the family of deterministic languages is a proper subfamily of the family of context-free languages.

The automata considered above have no other output facilities than being or not being in a final state, i.e., they are only capable of accepting or rejecting inputs. Occasionally devices (*transducers*) capable of having words as outputs, i.e., capable of translating words into words, are considered. We give a formal definition only for the transducer corresponding to a finite automaton. A pushdown transducer is defined analogously.

A rewriting system (V, P) is called a *sequential transducer* iff each of the following conditions (i)–(iii) is satisfied.

(i) V is divided into two disjoint alphabets V_S and $V_I \cup V_O$. (The sets V_S, V_I, V_O are called the *state, input*, and *output* alphabet, respectively. The two latter ones are nonempty but not necessarily disjoint.)

(ii) An element $s_0 \in V_S$ and a subset $S_1 \subseteq V_S$ are specified (*initial state* and *final state set*).

(iii) The productions in P are of the form

$$s_i w \to us_j, \qquad s_i, s_j \in V_S, w \in V_I^*, u \in V_O^*.$$

If, in addition, $w \neq \lambda$ in all productions then the rewriting system is called a *generalized sequential machine* (*gsm*).

For a sequential transducer ST, words $w_1 \in V_I^*$ and $w_2 \in V_O^*$, and languages $L_1 \subseteq V_I^*$ and $L_2 \subseteq V_O^*$, we define

$$ST(w_1) = \{w \mid s_0 w_1 \Rightarrow^* w s_1 \text{ for some } s_1 \in S_1\},$$
$$ST(L_1) = \{u \mid u \in ST(w) \text{ for some } w \in L_1\},$$
$$ST^{-1}(w_2) = \{u \mid w_2 \in ST(u)\},$$
$$ST^{-1}(L_2) = \{u \mid u \in ST^{-1}(w) \text{ for some } w \in L_2\}.$$

Mappings of languages thus defined are referred to as (*rational*) *transductions* and *inverse* (*rational*) *transductions*. If ST is also a gsm, we speak of *gsm mappings* and *inverse gsm mappings*.

Homomorphism, inverse homomorphism and the mapping $\tau(L) = L \cap R$, where R is a fixed regular language, are all rational transductions, the first and the last being also gsm mappings. The composition of two rational transductions (respectively gsm mappings) is again a rational transduction (respectively a gsm mapping). Every rational transduction τ can be expressed in the form

$$\tau(L) = h_1(h_2^{-1}(L) \cap R),$$

where h_1 and h_2 are homomorphisms and R is a regular language. These results show that a language family is closed under rational transductions iff it is closed under homomorphisms, inverse homomorphisms and intersections with regular languages.

We shall also, mainly in Chapter III, consider some types of automata and grammars which are more convenient to define directly rather than using the notion of a rewriting system.

A *finite probabilistic automaton* (or *stochastic automaton*) is an ordered quintuple

$$PA = (V_I, V_S, s_0, S_1, H),$$

where V_I and $V_S = \{s_0, \ldots, s_{n-1}\}$ are disjoint alphabets (inputs and states), $s_0 \in V_S$ and $S_1 \subseteq V_S$ (initial state and final state set), and H is a mapping of V_I into the set of n-dimensional stochastic matrices. (A stochastic matrix is a square matrix with nonnegative real entries and with row sums equal to 1.) The mapping H is extended to a homomorphism of V_I^* into the monoid of n-dimensional stochastic matrices. Consider V_S to be an ordered set as indicated, let π be the n-dimensional stochastic row vector whose first component equals 1, and let η be the n-dimensional column vector consisting of 0's and 1's such that the ith component of η equals 1 iff the ith element of V_S belongs to S_1. The language accepted by a PA with *cut-point* α, where α is a real number satisfying $0 \leq \alpha < 1$, is defined by

$$L(PA, \alpha) = \{w \in V_I^* \mid \pi H(w) \eta > \alpha\}.$$

Languages obtained in this fashion are referred to as *stochastic* languages and their complements as *costochastic* languages. We shall also speak of subclasses of this language family, for instance $\mathbb{Q}$-*stochastic* languages, indicating that all of the real numbers involved (all entries in all matrices and the cut-point) belong to $\mathbb{Q}$.

A stochastic automaton is *actual* iff all entries in all matrices are positive. It is *double stochastic* iff all matrices are double stochastic (i.e., the column sums also equal to 1).

Contrary to the "sequential" rewriting discussed above, the rewriting process according to an *L system* is parallel in nature: at each step of the process all letters in the word considered have to be rewritten. By definition, an *OL system* is an ordered triple $G = (V, w_0, P)$, where V is an alphabet, $w_0 \in V^*$ (the *axiom* or *initial word*), and P is a finite set of productions $a \to w$ with $a \in V$ and $w \in V^*$ such that, for each $a \in V$, there is at least one such production in P. The binary relation $\Rightarrow$ on V^* is now defined as follows. For any w and u, $w \Rightarrow u$ iff there is an $n \geq 1$, letters a_i and words w_i, $1 \leq i \leq n$, such that $w = a_1 \cdots a_n$, $u = w_1 \cdots w_n$, and $a_i \to w_i$ is in P for each $i = 1, \ldots, n$. Again, $\Rightarrow^*$ is the reflexive transitive closure of $\Rightarrow$. The language generated by the OL system is defined by

$$L(G) = \{w \mid w_0 \Rightarrow^* w\}.$$

An OL system with *tables* or, shortly, a *TOL system* differs from an OL system in that, instead of P, it has a finite number k of sets of productions $P_1, \ldots, P_k$ such that each triple $G_i = (V, w_0, P_i)$ is an OL system. The relation $\Rightarrow$ associated with a TOL system equals the union of the relations $\Rightarrow_i$, $i = 1, \ldots, k$, associated to systems G_i. The generated language is defined exactly as above.

An OL system (respectively a TOL system) is *propagating* iff no production in P (respectively no production in any of the sets P_i) has the empty word on its right side. It is *deterministic* iff the set P (respectively each of the sets P_i) has exactly one production for each letter $a \in V$. These two notions are abbreviated by the letters P and D, respectively. Thus, we speak of DOL and PDTOL systems. A DOL system G can be defined by specifying an alphabet V, an element w_0 of V^*, and an endomorphism h of V^*. We often define DOL systems in this way in the sequel. Then the generated language consists of all words $h^n(w_0)$, $n = 0, 1, 2, \ldots$. This induces a total order for the language, i.e., the language is given as a sequence. Analogously, we can also define a DTOL system as a $(k + 2)$-tuple

$$(V, w_0, h_1, \ldots, h_k),$$

where each h_i is an endomorphism of V^*.

The meaning of the letters F, E, H, C appearing in the names of L systems will now be briefly explained. The letter F indicates that, instead of just one axiom, we may have an arbitrary finite number of axioms. The letter E (coming from "extension") means that we may specify a subalphabet V_T of the alphabet V such that only words over V_T are considered to be in the language generated by the system. (This is in analogy with the definition of the language generated by a grammar.) The letter H (respectively C) indicates that we take a homomorphic (respectively letter-to-letter homomorphic) image of the language generated by the system. Whenever we say that a language is of certain type (say, DTOL or EOL language), we mean that it is generated by a system of this type (DTOL or EOL system).

In all of the L systems defined above, rewriting is context-free. (This is indicated by the letter O in the name of the system.) Context-sensitive L systems, usually called systems with *interactions,* are not discussed in this book.

Several *decision problems* will be met in the sequel. The usual method of proving that a problem is undecidable is to reduce it to some problem whose undecidability is known. The most useful tool for problems in language theory is in this respect the *Post Correspondence Problem.* By definition, a Post correspondence problem is an ordered quadruple $\text{PCP} = (V, n, \alpha, \beta)$, where V is an alphabet, $n \geq 1$, and $\alpha = (\alpha_1, \ldots, \alpha_n)$, $\beta = (\beta_1, \ldots, \beta_n)$ are ordered n-tuples of elements of V^+. A *solution* to the PCP is a nonempty finite sequence of indices $i_1, \ldots, i_k$ such that

$$\alpha_{i_1} \cdots \alpha_{i_k} = \beta_{i_1} \cdots \beta_{i_k}.$$

It is undecidable whether an arbitrary given PCP (or an arbitrary given PCP over the alphabet $V = \{a_1, a_2\}$) has a solution.

Also the following problem—an equivalent version of the so-called *Hilbert's Tenth Problem*—is undecidable. Given a polynomial $P(x_1, \ldots, x_k)$ with integer coefficients, one has to decide whether or not there are non-negative integers x_i, $i = 1, \ldots, k$, satisfying the equation

$$P(x_1, \ldots, x_k) = 0.$$

I.3 Formal power series in noncommuting variables

This section contains the very basic notions and definitions only. Further material will be given when needed in appropriate places.

Let M be a monoid and A a semiring. Mappings r of M into A are called *formal power series.* The values of r are denoted by (r, w), where $w \in M$, and r itself is written as a formal sum

$$r = \sum_{w \in M} (r, w)w.$$

The values (r, w) are also referred to as the *coefficients* of the series. We shall be mostly interested in the case where M is the free monoid X^* generated by an alphabet X. Then we say also that r is a series with (noncommuting) *variables* in X.

This terminology reflects the intuitive ideas connected with power series. We call the power series "formal" to indicate that we are not interested in summing up the series but rather, for instance, in various operations defined for series. The power series notation makes it very convenient to discuss such operations. The difference between our formal power series and the ones studied in combinatorics is that in the latter the variables commute. Both approaches have in common the basic idea to view the collection of all power series as an algebraic structure.

The collection of all formal power series r as defined above is denoted by $A\langle\langle M\rangle\rangle$. Given r, the subset of M defined by

$$\{w \mid (r, w) \neq 0\}$$

is termed the *support* of r and denoted by $\text{supp}(r)$. The subset of $A\langle\langle M\rangle\rangle$ consisting of all series with a finite support is denoted by $A\langle M\rangle$. Elements of $A\langle M\rangle$ are referred to as *polynomials*.

We denote by 0 also the series all of whose coefficients equal 0. Let λ be the unit element of M. (This is in accordance with the notation for the empty word in the case $M = X^*$.) For $a \in A$, $a \neq 0$, we denote by $a \cdot \lambda$ (or shortly by a) the series whose coefficient for λ equals a, the remaining coefficients being equal to 0. For an arbitrary element w of M, we denote by aw (respectively w) the series whose coefficient for w equals a (respectively equals 1), the remaining coefficients being 0. Such series aw belong to $A\langle M\rangle$ and are referred to as *monomials*.

The support of a series belonging to $A\langle\langle X^*\rangle\rangle$ is a language over the alphabet X. A series r in $A\langle\langle X^*\rangle\rangle$, where every coefficient equals 0 or 1, is termed the *characteristic series* of its support L, in symbols,

$$r = \text{char}(L).$$

We next define some algebraic operations in $A\langle\langle M\rangle\rangle$. The *sum* of two series r and r' in $A\langle\langle M\rangle\rangle$ is defined by

$$r + r' = \sum_{w \in M} ((r, w) + (r', w))w.$$

The multiplication of a series $r \in A\langle\langle M\rangle\rangle$ by a "scalar" $a \in A$ is defined by

$$ar = \sum_{w \in M} (a(r, w))w.$$

Assume that the monoid M possesses the property that each $w \in M$ has only finitely many factorizations $w = w_1 w_2$. (This condition will be satisfied by all monoids M considered in the sequel.) Then the *(Cauchy) product* of two series r and r' in $A\langle\langle M\rangle\rangle$ is defined by

$$rr' = \sum_{w \in M} \left(\sum_{w_1 w_2 = w} (r, w_1)(r', w_2) \right)w.$$

Note that the (scalar) product ar coincides with the Cauchy product of the series $a \cdot \lambda$ and r. The operations defined furnish $A\langle\langle M\rangle\rangle$ with the structure of a semiring with $A\langle M\rangle$ as a subsemiring. If A is a ring, then so are $A\langle\langle M\rangle\rangle$ and $A\langle M\rangle$.

Also various topological structures can be associated with $A\langle\langle M\rangle\rangle$. We need just the following simple notion. A sequence $r_1, r_2, \ldots$ of elements of

$A\langle\langle X^* \rangle\rangle$ *converges* to the limit r, in symbols $\lim_{n \to \infty} r_n = r$, iff for all k there exists an m such that the conditions $\lg(w) \le k$ and $j > m$ imply the condition

$$(r_j, w) = (r, w).$$

The reader will notice that this notion of convergence conforms with the metric topology obtained when defining the distance of two series r and r' in $A\langle\langle M \rangle\rangle$ by

$$d(r, r') = \begin{cases} 0 & \text{for } r = r', \\ 2^{-\min\{\lg(w) \mid (r,w) \ne (r',w)\}} & \text{for } r \ne r'. \end{cases}$$

The notion of convergence introduced above is needed in connection with algebraic series studied in Chapter IV. A weaker notion, meaningful for semirings A in which convergence is defined, is obtained by requiring that, for all w, the sequence $(r_1, w), (r_2, w), \dots$ converges to (r, w).

An element r of $A\langle\langle M \rangle\rangle$ is termed *quasiregular* iff $(r, \lambda) = 0$. Quasi-regular series r have the property, desirable in many respects, that the sequence $r, r^2, r^3, \dots$ converges to the limit 0 (providing $M = X^*$).

Various other operations for series will be considered in the sequel. Here we define a few of these operations, the others will be given in their appropriate places. The *Hadamard product* of two series r and r' belonging to $A\langle\langle M \rangle\rangle$ is defined by

$$r \odot r' = \sum_{w \in M} (r, w)(r', w)w.$$

Consider a *homomorphism* h of M_1 into M_2. It can be extended to a semiring homomorphism of $A\langle\langle M_1 \rangle\rangle$ into $A\langle\langle M_2 \rangle\rangle$ by defining

$$h(r) = \sum_{w \in M} (r, w)h(w),$$

under the assumption that the right side is well defined. (Note that this is not necessarily the case, for instance, if $A = \mathbb{N}$, $M_1 = M_2 = X^*$, and h is erasing, i.e., maps some letters into the empty word. In this case infinite sums may occur on the right side.) If this assumption is satisfied for all r in $A\langle\langle M_1 \rangle\rangle$, the extension indeed gives a semiring homomorphism. This follows by the equations

$$h(r + r') = h(r) + h(r') \quad \text{and} \quad h(rr') = h(r)h(r'),$$

of which the first one is immediate and the second one a consequence of the equations

$$h(rr') = \sum_{w \in M} (rr', w)h(w),$$

$$(rr', w) = \sum_{w = w_1 w_2} (r, w_1)(r', w_2),$$

$$h(r)h(r') = \left(\sum_{w_1 \in M} (r, w_1)h(w_1) \right) \left(\sum_{w_2 \in M} (r', w_2)h(w_2) \right).$$

13

Homomorphisms which are often met in the sequel are letter-to-letter homomorphisms (also called codings) of X^* into Y^* and, more generally, nonerasing homomorphisms of X^* into Y^* (i.e., $h(x) \neq \lambda$ for all $x \in X$). For such homomorphisms $h(r)$ will always be defined.

Exactly as for homomorphisms, the definition of a *substitution* on X can be extended to $A\langle\langle X^*\rangle\rangle$ with similar caveats concerning the existence of the image.

In the remainder of this section we assume that M is a direct product of the form $X_1^* \otimes \cdots \otimes X_n^*$, where $X_1, \ldots, X_n$ are alphabets. (Then the condition mentioned above concerning factorizations will be satisfied.)

If r is quasiregular then

$$\lim_{m \to \infty} \sum_{k=1}^{m} r^k$$

exists. It is called the *quasi-inverse* of r and denoted by r^+. The series $r^+ = s$ is the only series satisfying the equations

$$r + rs = r + sr = s.$$

Note also that a nonerasing homomorphism h satisfies the equation $(hr)^+ = h(r^+)$.

A subsemiring of $A\langle\langle M\rangle\rangle$ is *rationally closed* iff it contains the quasi-inverse of every quasiregular element. The family of A-rational series over M, in symbols $A^{\text{rat}}\langle\langle M\rangle\rangle$, is the smallest rationally closed subset of $A\langle\langle M\rangle\rangle$ which contains all polynomials. Thus, every A-rational series can be constructed from polynomials by a finite number of applications of the operations of sum, (Cauchy) product and quasi-inversion.

A series r of $A\langle\langle M\rangle\rangle$ is termed *A-recognizable* (in symbols $r \in A^{\text{rec}}\langle\langle M\rangle\rangle$) iff

$$r = (r, \lambda)\lambda + \sum_{w \neq \lambda} p(\mu w)w,$$

where $\mu: M \to A^{m \times m}$, $m \geq 1$, is a representation and $p: A^{m \times m} \to A$ is a mapping such that, for an $m \times m$ matrix (a_{ij}), the value $p(a_{ij})$ can be expressed as a linear combination of the entries a_{ij} with coefficients in A:

$$p(a_{ij}) = \sum_{i,j} a_{ij}p_{ij} \qquad (p_{ij} \in A).$$

We conclude this section with some examples. We consider series in $\mathbb{N}\langle\langle X^*\rangle\rangle$ with $X = \{x, \bar{x}\}$.

The series

$$r = \sum_{n=1}^{\infty} 2^n(x\bar{x})^n x + 3x = (2x\bar{x})^+ x + 3x$$

is $\mathbb{N}$-rational. Clearly, $\text{supp}(r)$ is denoted by the regular expression

$$(x\bar{x})^+ x \cup x.$$

Consider next the representation μ defined by

$$\mu(x) = \begin{pmatrix} 0 & 1 \\ 1 & 1 \end{pmatrix}, \qquad \mu(\bar{x}) = \begin{pmatrix} 0 & 0 \\ 0 & 0 \end{pmatrix},$$

and let p be the mapping defined by

$$p(a_{ij}) = a_{11} + a_{12}.$$

Then the $\mathbb{N}$-recognizable series

$$r' = \sum_{w \in X^*} p(\mu w) w$$

can be written in the form

$$r' = \sum_{n=0}^{\infty} a_n x^n,$$

where the sequence $a_0, a_1, a_2, \ldots$ constitutes the Fibonacci sequence.

As a final example, consider two sequences of polynomials $r_1^{(i)}$ and $r_2^{(i)}$, $i = 0, 1, 2, \ldots$, defined as follows:

$$r_1^{(0)} = r_2^{(0)} = 0,$$
$$r_1^{(i+1)} = r_2^{(i)} + r_1^{(i)} r_2^{(i)},$$
$$r_2^{(i+1)} = x r_1^{(i)} \bar{x} + \lambda,$$

for all $i \geq 0$. Then both of the sequences $r_1^{(i)}$ and $r_2^{(i)}$ converge and, moreover, the limit of the former sequence is the characteristic series of the Dyck language over X. These facts can be established directly. However, they become more apparent within the framework of the general theory developed in Chapter IV.

II
Rational series

This chapter develops the fundamental theory of rational formal power series. The corresponding theory for algebraic formal power series will be developed in Chapter IV. However, at least at the present state of knowledge, the former theory is stronger and much more comprehensive than the latter. Therefore, the present chapter can be viewed as the basic and the most important one in this book.

The automata-theoretic applications emanating from the theory of rational series concern basically finite automata and regular languages but extend to generalizations of quite a diverse nature, such as probabilistic automata and L systems. Chapter III is devoted to the applications, although some of the basic ones are occasionally dealt with in this chapter. The applications of the theory of algebraic series, dealing essentially with context-free languages, will be considered in Chapter IV.

Before going into details, we want to discuss the formalism chosen for our presentation. When dealing with rational series in $A\langle\langle M \rangle\rangle$, we mostly assume that A is a semiring (not necessarily commutative) and M is a direct product of the form $X_1^* \otimes \cdots \otimes X_n^*$, where $X_1, \ldots, X_n$ are alphabets. Additional assumptions needed for some results, such as A being commutative or M being the free monoid X^* where X is an alphabet, are always explicitly stated. Although from the point of view of most applications this approach is "unnecessarily" general (as in most cases it suffices to assume that $M = X^*$ and A equals one of the familiar semirings of numbers), it still has the advantage of providing a uniform framework. Moreover, the proofs are essentially the same for our general assumptions as in more special cases. On the other hand, we have not tried to push the results to a still further generality. We just want to point out that, for most of the results in this chapter, it is not essential that M is a direct product of the kind mentioned. It suffices that a length function satisfying

$$\lg w_1 w_2 = \lg w_1 + \lg w_2,$$

for all words w_1 and w_2, can be defined in M.

A brief description of the contents of this chapter follows. The chief aim in the first two sections is the Representation Theorem of Schützenberger, Theorem 2.3, showing that the families of rational and recognizable series in $A\langle\langle X^* \rangle\rangle$ coincide. The theorem is established by using the equational characterization of rational series developed in Section II.1. Interconnections between rational series and Hankel matrices considered in Section II.3 are very useful in proofs later on and also of direct interest, for instance, in providing minimal representations. After discussing closure properties of rational series under various operations, we are ready to present the fundamental interconnections between rational series and regular languages in Section II.5. The next section investigates the problem of whether a subsemiring A of a semiring B satisfies the following condition: whenever the coefficients of a B-rational series over X^* lie in A, then the series is A-rational. The behavior of the coefficients of a series in $\mathbb{R}^{\text{rat}}\langle\langle X^* \rangle\rangle$ constitutes the subject matter of Section II.7. After discussing positive rational series, a natural generalization of $\mathbb{N}$-rational series, we investigate in Sections II.9 and II.10 rational sequences, i.e., rational series over a one-letter alphabet. The results are of fundamental importance, for instance, in the theory of length sequences generated by L systems. The same holds true as regards the decidability results established in Section II.12. The intermediate section. II.11, develops the basic tools needed in the study of rational transductions.

II.1 Rational series and linear systems

We now start to investigate systems of equations (for power series) having a right-linear form. The reader familiar with systems of equations characterizing regular expressions will notice definite similarities. The systems of equations we are dealing with are proper which implies that, for instance, the equations $z = z$ and $z = 1 + z$ are excluded. Proper systems always have a unique solution. The solution is found by a method of successive approximations, a point which will be exploited further in Chapter IV, but in the simple case of right-linear systems the successive approximations amount to applying the operation of quasi-inversion, as seen in Theorem 1.1.

It will be seen in Theorem 1.2 that proper linear systems (for convenience we use this shorter term instead of calling the systems "right-linear") preserve the rationality of the series in the sense that the components of the solution vector are rational if the coefficients in the system are rational. The proof is identical with the proof of the corresponding result for regular expressions. The converse is given in Theorem 1.4: every rational series possesses an equational characterization, i.e., can be expressed as the first component of the solution of a proper linear system of a special kind.

Throughout this section A stands for a semiring (not necessarily commutative) and M denotes a monoid of the form $X_1^* \otimes \cdots \otimes X_n^*$ where $X_1, \ldots, X_n$ are alphabets.

Definition. A proper linear system is a system which has the form

$$(1) \qquad\qquad Z = P + QZ$$

where $P \in A\langle\langle M \rangle\rangle^{m \times 1}$ and Q is a quasiregular matrix in $A\langle\langle M \rangle\rangle^{m \times m}$. The number m is called the dimension of the system. A vector Y of $A\langle\langle M \rangle\rangle^{m \times 1}$ is called a solution of (1) if $Y = P + QY$.

Theorem 1.1. *System* (1) *has the unique solution* $Y = (I + Q^+)P$.

PROOF. Because $P + QY = P + (Q + QQ^+)P = P + Q^+P = Y$ this vector Y is a solution. Next let $X = \sum (X, w)w$ be any solution of (1). The quasi-regularity of Q implies that $(X, \lambda) = (P, \lambda)$ and (X, w) is fully determined by (P, w), the matrices (Q, v) and the vectors (X, v) where $\lg v < \lg w$ ($w \neq \lambda$). Hence the system cannot have but one solution. ☐

Theorem 1.2. *If in system* (1) P *and* Q *are rational then the solution is rational.*

PROOF. If the dimension of the system is 1 then the solution $y = (1 + q^+)p$ is surely rational. Hence we may consider a system with dimension m assuming that the theorem holds true always when the dimension is smaller than m.

Let $(y_1, \ldots, y_m)^T$ be the solution vector. The last equation

$$y_m = p_m + q_{m1}y_1 + \cdots + q_{mm}y_m$$

of the system implies that

$$(2) \qquad y_m = (1 + q_{mm}^+)(p_m + q_{m1}y_1 + \cdots + q_{m,m-1}y_{m-1}).$$

Substituting (2) in the first $m - 1$ equations we obtain the system

$$y_i = p_i + q_{im}(1 + q_{mm}^+)p_m + (q_{i1} + q_{im}(1 + q_{mm}^+)q_{m1})y_1 + \cdots$$
$$+ (q_{i,m-1} + q_{im}(1 + q_{mm}^+)q_{m,m-1})y_{m-1} \qquad (i = 1, \ldots, m - 1)$$

whose solution vector $(y_1, \ldots, y_{m-1})^T$ is rational by the induction hypothesis. Using (2) we see that y_m is rational, too. ☐

Corollary 1.3. *If* Q *is a quasiregular rational square matrix then the matrix* Q^+ *is rational.*

PROOF. Since $Q^+ = Q + QQ^+$ the columns of Q^+ are solutions of proper linear systems satisfying the condition of Theorem 1.2. ☐

Theorem 1.4. *Let r belong to $A^{\text{rat}}\langle\langle M \rangle\rangle$. Then there is a proper linear system $Z = P + QZ$ such that*

$$P = (P, \lambda)\lambda, \qquad Q = \sum_{\lg w = 1} (Q, w)w$$

and r is the first component of its solution vector.

PROOF. Let L denote the family of all series which are obtained in the manner described. It suffices to prove that L is rationally closed and contains all monomials a and w ($a \in A$, $\lg w = 1$).

The solutions of the systems

$$z = a + 0 \cdot z$$

and

$$\begin{pmatrix} z_1 \\ z_2 \end{pmatrix} = \begin{pmatrix} 0 \\ 1 \end{pmatrix} + \begin{pmatrix} 0 & w \\ 0 & 0 \end{pmatrix} \begin{pmatrix} z_1 \\ z_2 \end{pmatrix}$$

are a and $(w, 1)^{\text{T}}$. Hence a and w belong to L.

Now let s_1 and s_2 be series of L and assume that s_i is the first component of S_i which is the solution vector of the system $Z = P_i + Q_i Z$ ($i = 1, 2$). Consider the systems

$$\begin{pmatrix} z \\ Z_1 \\ Z_2 \end{pmatrix} = \begin{pmatrix} \bar{P}_1 + \bar{P}_2 \\ P_1 \\ P_2 \end{pmatrix} + \begin{pmatrix} 0 & \bar{Q}_1 & \bar{Q}_2 \\ 0 & Q_1 & 0 \\ 0 & 0 & Q_2 \end{pmatrix} \begin{pmatrix} z \\ Z_1 \\ Z_2 \end{pmatrix}$$

and

$$\begin{pmatrix} Z_1 \\ Z_2 \end{pmatrix} = \begin{pmatrix} P_1 \bar{P}_2 \\ P_2 \end{pmatrix} + \begin{pmatrix} Q_1 & P_1 \bar{Q}_2 \\ 0 & Q_2 \end{pmatrix} \begin{pmatrix} Z_1 \\ Z_2 \end{pmatrix}$$

where the bar denotes the first row. Obviously the first system has the solution $(s_1 + s_2, S_1, S_2)^{\text{T}}$. The second system has the solution $(S_1 s_2, S_2)^{\text{T}}$ since

$$P_1 \bar{P}_2 + Q_1(S_1 s_2) + (P_1 \bar{Q}_2)S_2$$
$$= P_1(\bar{P}_2 + \bar{Q}_2 S_2) + Q_1(S_1 s_2) = P_1 s_2 + (Q_1 S_1)s_2$$
$$= (P_1 + Q_1 S_1)s_2 = S_1 s_2.$$

Thus we see that $s_1 + s_2$ and $s_1 s_2$ belong to L.

Next let s be a quasiregular series of L and assume that s is the first component of the vector S which satisfies the equation $S = P + QS$. Because

$$P + (Q + P\bar{Q})(S(1 + s^+)) = P + QS(1 + s^+) + Ps(1 + s^+)$$
$$= P + QS + QSs^+ + Ps^+ = (P + QS)(1 + s^+) = S(1 + s^+)$$

(note that $\bar{P} = 0$ and $s = \bar{Q}S$) the solution of the system

$$Z = P + (Q + P\bar{Q})Z$$

is $S(1 + s^+)$. Thus s^+ belongs to L. $\qquad\square$

Combining Theorems 1.1 and 1.4 we obtain

Corollary 1.5. *Given a series r of $A^{\mathrm{rat}}\langle\langle M\rangle\rangle$ there are a natural number m, a vector P of $A^{m \times 1}$ and matrices μw ($\lg w = 1$) of $A^{m \times m}$ such that r is the first component of the vector*

$$\left(I + \Big(\sum_{\lg w = 1} (\mu w)w\Big)^+\right)P.$$

EXERCISES

1. Consider a linear system $Z = P + QZ$ where $P \in A^{m \times n}\langle\langle M\rangle\rangle$ and Q is a quasiregular matrix in $A^{m \times m}\langle\langle M\rangle\rangle$. Show that Theorems 1.1 and 1.2 remain true. Consider also systems which have the form $Z = P + ZQ$.

2. Write a quasiregular square matrix Q in the form

$$\begin{pmatrix} a & b \\ c & d \end{pmatrix}$$

where a and d are square matrices. Show that

$$Q^+ = \begin{pmatrix} A & B \\ C & D \end{pmatrix}$$

where $A = (a + bc + bd^+c)^+$.

3. Let Q_1 and Q_2 be quasiregular square matrices. Prove that

$$(Q_1 + Q_2)^+ = (I + Q_1^+)(Q_1 + Q_2 + Q_2(Q_1 + Q_2)^+).$$

4. Let A be a number field. Consider a nonproper system $Z = P + (Q_0 + Q)Z$ where $Q_0 \in A^{m \times m}$ and Q is quasiregular. Show that if 1 is not an eigenvalue of Q_0 then this system has a unique solution which is rational if P and Q are.

5. Let A be a commutative ring and let Q be a matrix of $A\langle\langle M\rangle\rangle^{m \times m}$ such that (Q, λ) is invertible. Show that Q has a unique inverse which is rational if Q is.

6. If S is the solution of $Z = P + QZ$ then the solution of $Z = Pr + QZ$ is Sr. Investigate the systems used in the proof of Theorem 1.4 keeping this fact in mind.

7. Show that if $r \in A^{\mathrm{rat}}\langle\langle M\rangle\rangle$ then

$$(r, w) = \left(\sum_{\substack{v_1 \cdots v_n = w \\ \lg v_i = 1}} \mu v_1 \cdots \mu v_n P\right)_1$$

where the μv_i's are square matrices and P is a column vector. If $M = X_1^* \otimes X_2^*$ and $w = w_1 \otimes w_2$ then the number of summands is $\binom{\lg w}{\lg w_1}$.

II.2 Recognizable series

Using the equational characterization for rational series, we are now ready to establish the Representation Theorem of Schützenberger, Theorem 2.3, which is fundamental in almost all considerations concerning rational series.

It should be emphasized that the theorem is valid for free monoids only, cf. exercise 2.2. The reader should also pay special attention to the following details in this section.

In the definition of recognizable series, the mapping p could equally well be defined by

$$p(a_{ij}) = \sum_{i,j} p'_{ij} a_{ij} p''_{ij} \qquad (p'_{ij}, p''_{ij} \in A).$$

Theorems 2.1 and 2.2 can be viewed as normal form results for recognizable series. In Theorem 2.1, it is necessary to take the first term separately because the $(1, m)$th entry in the identity matrix $(m \geq 2)$ equals zero. Corollary 2.4 is a useful lemma for bridging the gap between direct products and free monoids. Exercises 2.4–2.6 deal with the problem of when it is possible to represent a recognizable series using some diagonal entry in the matrices.

In this section, as in the preceding one, A is a semiring and M is a product monoid $X_1^* \otimes \cdots \otimes X_n^*$.

We recall that a series r of $A\langle\langle M \rangle\rangle$ is called recognizable (denoted $r \in A^{\mathrm{rec}}\langle\langle M \rangle\rangle$) iff

(1)
$$r = (r, \lambda)\lambda + \sum_{w \neq \lambda} p(\mu w)w$$

where $\mu: M \to A^{m \times m}$ is a representation and $p: A^{m \times m} \to A$ is a functional such that

$$p(a_{ij}) = \sum_{i,j} a_{ij} p_{ij} \qquad (p_{ij} \in A).$$

Theorem 2.1. *If $r \in A^{\mathrm{rec}}\langle\langle M \rangle\rangle$ then there is a representation $\mu: M \to A^{m \times m}$ such that*

$$r = (r, \lambda)\lambda + \sum_{w \neq \lambda} (\mu w)_{1,m} w.$$

PROOF. Assuming that r is given in the form

$$(r, \lambda)\lambda + \sum_{w \neq \lambda} \bar{p}(\bar{\mu}w)w \qquad (\bar{\mu}w \in A^{\bar{m} \times \bar{m}})$$

we define

$$\chi w = \begin{pmatrix} \bar{\mu}w & 0 & \cdots & 0 \\ 0 & \bar{\mu}w & & \vdots \\ \vdots & & \ddots & \vdots \\ 0 & & \cdots & \bar{\mu}w \end{pmatrix} \in A^{\bar{m}^2 \times \bar{m}^2}$$

$$\alpha = (1\,0\cdots 0;\, 01\cdots 0;\, \cdots;\, 0\cdots 01),$$

$$\beta = (\bar{p}_{11} \cdots \bar{p}_{1\bar{m}};\, \bar{p}_{21} \cdots \bar{p}_{2\bar{m}};\, \cdots;\, \bar{p}_{\bar{m}1} \cdots \bar{p}_{\bar{m}\bar{m}})^{\mathrm{T}}.$$

21

Then obviously $(r, w) = \alpha\chi w\beta$ for any nonempty word w. Define next

$$\mu w = \begin{pmatrix} 0 & \alpha\chi w & (r, w) \\ 0 & \chi w & \chi w\beta \\ 0 & 0 & 0 \end{pmatrix} \quad (w \neq \lambda).$$

Since $\mu w_1 \mu w_2 = \mu w_1 w_2$, μ is a representation. Thus we have proved the theorem. $\qquad\square$

Theorem 2.2. *If $r \in A^{\mathrm{rec}}\langle\langle M \rangle\rangle$ then there are a row vector α, a representation μ and a column vector β such that*

$$r = \sum \alpha\mu w\beta w.$$

Conversely, any series $\sum \alpha\mu w\beta w$ where α, μ, and β are as above belongs to $A^{\mathrm{rec}}\langle\langle M \rangle\rangle$.

PROOF. According to Theorem 2.1 we may write r in the form

$$(r, \lambda)\lambda + \sum_{w \neq \lambda} (1\ 0 \cdots 0)\bar{\mu}w(0 \cdots 01)^{\mathrm{T}}w.$$

Denote

$$\alpha = (1\ 0 \cdots 0, 0), \qquad \beta = ((r, \lambda), 0 \cdots 01)^{\mathrm{T}},$$

$$\mu w = \begin{pmatrix} 0 & (1\ 0 \cdots 0)\bar{\mu}w \\ 0 & \bar{\mu}w \end{pmatrix} \quad (w \neq \lambda).$$

It is immediately seen that μ is a representation and $r = \sum \alpha\mu w\beta w$.

The end of the proof of Theorem 2.1 shows that all series $\sum \alpha\mu w\beta w$ belong to $A^{\mathrm{rec}}\langle\langle M \rangle\rangle$. $\qquad\square$

Theorem 2.3. *The families $A^{\mathrm{rec}}\langle\langle X^* \rangle\rangle$ and $A^{\mathrm{rat}}\langle\langle X^* \rangle\rangle$ coincide.*

PROOF. Let $r = (r, \lambda)\lambda + \sum_{w \neq \lambda} (\mu w)_{1,m}w$ be an A-recognizable series. If

$$Q = \sum_{x \in X} (\mu x)x$$

then

$$Q^+ = \sum_{w \neq \lambda} (\mu w)w$$

by the definition of the quasi-inverse. Hence

$$r = (r, \lambda)\lambda + Q^+_{1,m}$$

and the rationality of r is implied by Corollary 1.3.

On the other hand, if r is an A-rational series then Corollary 1.5 gives us a representation μ and a vector P such that

$$r = (1\ 0 \cdots 0)\left(I + \sum_{w \neq \lambda} \mu ww\right)P = \sum_{w} (1\ 0 \cdots 0)\mu wPw. \qquad\square$$

Corollary 2.4. *Let r be a series of $A^{rat}\langle\langle M\rangle\rangle$. Then there are an alphabet X, a series s of $A^{rec}\langle\langle X^*\rangle\rangle$ and a coding homomorphism $h\colon X^* \to M$ such that $r = hs$.*

PROOF. Take an alphabet X such that there is a surjective coding homomorphism $h\colon X^* \to M$. Suppose that $P_1, \ldots, P_n$ are the polynomials of $A\langle M\rangle$ used in the generation of r. Choose polynomials $p_1, \ldots, p_n$ of $A\langle X^*\rangle$ such that $hp_i = P_i$. If s is the rational series which is obtained by using p_i instead of P_i in the generation of r then $hs = r$ and s is recognizable by Theorem 2.3. □

EXERCISES

1. Show that $A^{rec}\langle\langle M\rangle\rangle$ forms an A-semimodule.

2. Examine the proof of Theorem 2.3 and make it clear for yourself why the monoid must be free.

3. Let $r_i = \sum (\mu_i w)_{1,m_i} w = \sum \alpha_i \mu_i w \beta_i w$ $(i = 1, 2; m_i > 1)$ belong to $A^{rat}\langle\langle X^*\rangle\rangle$. Show that $r_1 r_2 = \sum (\mu w)_{1,m_1+m_2} w$ where

$$\mu x = \begin{pmatrix} \mu_1 x & \beta_1 \alpha_2 \mu_2 x \\ 0 & \mu_2 x \end{pmatrix}$$

and $r_1^+ = \sum (\chi w)_{1,m_1} w$ where

$$\chi x = \mu_1 x + \beta_1 \alpha_1 \mu_1 x.$$

Hint: Examine the proof of Theorem 1.4.

4. Let r be a series of $A^{rat}\langle\langle X^*\rangle\rangle$ which can be written in the form

$$\sum_{w \neq \lambda} (\mu w)_{1,1} w.$$

Show, using exercise 2 of II.1, that r is the quasi-inverse of an A-rational series.

5. If $r = s^+$ where $s \in A^{rat}\langle\langle X^*\rangle\rangle$ then there is a representation μ such that $r = \sum_{w \neq \lambda} (\mu w)_{1,1} w$.

Here is a sketch of the solution. The proof of Theorem 2.1 gives us a representation χ such that

$$s = \sum_{w \neq \lambda} (\chi w)_{1,m} w$$

and $(\chi w)_{1,1} = 0$. If

$$\mu x = \chi x + \chi x \begin{pmatrix} 0 & 0 & \cdots & 0 \\ \vdots & \vdots & & \vdots \\ 0 & 0 & \cdots & 0 \\ 1 & 0 & \cdots & 0 \end{pmatrix} = \chi x + \chi x M \qquad (x \in X)$$

then

$$\left(\sum \mu x x\right)^+ = \left(\sum \chi x x\right)^+ + \left(\sum \chi x x\right)^+ M + \left(\sum \chi x x\right)^+ M \left(\sum \mu x x\right)^+$$

by exercise 3 of II.1. Hence

$$\left(\sum \mu x x\right)^+_{1,1} = s + s\left(\sum \mu x x\right)^+_{1,1}.$$

23

6. Show that if r is a nonzero quasiregular element of $\mathbb{N}\langle X^* \rangle$ then r cannot be written in the form

$$\sum_{w \neq \lambda} (\mu w)_{1,1} w \qquad (\mu w \in \mathbb{N}^{m \times m}).$$

Let next r be a quasiregular series in $A^{\mathrm{rat}}\langle\langle X^* \rangle\rangle$ where A is a ring. Show that the equation $r = z + zr$ has a rational solution and deduce that it is possible to write r in the form

$$\sum_{w \neq \lambda} (\mu w)_{1,1} w.$$

7. Let A be a commutative semiring and let $r = \sum \alpha \mu w \beta w$ belong to $A^{\mathrm{rat}}\langle\langle X^* \rangle\rangle$. Show that

$$r = \sum \mathrm{Tr}\, \pi \mu w w$$

where Tr denotes trace and π is a square matrix.

8. Let $r = \sum \alpha \mu w \beta w$ be a series of $\mathbb{R}_+^{\mathrm{rat}}\langle\langle X^* \rangle\rangle$ such that all entries of β are positive. Show that r can be written in the form $\sum \bar{\alpha} \bar{\mu} w \bar{\beta} w$ where all entries of $\bar{\beta}$ are equal to one (and the entries of $\bar{\alpha}$ and $\bar{\mu} w$ belong to $\mathbb{R}_+$). Show also that if $(r, v) = 0$ then $(r, vw) = 0$ for all words w.

9. Let mi w denote the mirror image of the word w. Show that if $r \in A^{\mathrm{rat}}\langle\langle X^* \rangle\rangle$ and A is commutative then

$$\sum (r, \text{mi } w)w \in A^{\mathrm{rat}}\langle\langle X^* \rangle\rangle.$$

II.3 Hankel matrices

Hankel matrices were originally introduced as an aid to the theory of sequences of complex numbers but have later turned out to be useful in a number of other topics. This section gives various characterizations of rational series in terms of Hankel matrices. Apart from being of interest in their own right, these characterization results are also essential tools in many important proofs later on, for instance, in some of the proofs showing the interconnection between rational series and regular languages in Section II.5, as well as in proofs concerning Fatou properties in Section II.6.

In this section, it is useful to view the collection $A\langle\langle X^* \rangle\rangle$ of series (according to the original definition) as the set of functions $F: X^* \to A$, possessing the structure of a semimodule. As the reader may readily notice, the assumption of A being commutative is important.

A theory similar to the one developed in this section for $A^{\mathrm{rat}}\langle\langle X^* \rangle\rangle$ could be developed for $A^{\mathrm{rec}}\langle\langle M \rangle\rangle$. Important results are valid in the special case where A is a field K. For instance, Theorem 3.5 shows that all minimal representations of a series in $K^{\mathrm{rat}}\langle\langle X^* \rangle\rangle$ are similar. In this respect it is also illustrative to compare the situations in Theorem 3.3 and exercise 3.1.

After these preliminary remarks, we now give the basic definition.

Definition. Let r be a series of $A\langle\langle X^* \rangle\rangle$ where the semiring A is commutative.

By the *Hankel matrix* of r we mean the infinite matrix $H(r)$ whose rows and columns are indexed by the words of X^* and whose element with indexes u and v is equal to (r, uv).

Let us consider the semimodule A^{X^*} of all functions $F: X^* \to A$. For any word w of X^* and any function F of A^{X^*} we define a new function wF by the equation

$$(wF)(v) = F(vw).$$

Since

$$\left(w\left(\sum a_i F_i\right)\right)(v) = \left(\sum a_i F_i\right)(vw) = \sum a_i F_i(vw)$$
$$= \sum a_i(wF_i)(v) = \left(\sum a_i(wF_i)\right)(v)$$

the operator transforming F into wF is linear.

A subsemimodule B of A^{X^*} is called *stable* if the conditions $w \in X^*$ and $F \in B$ imply that $wF \in B$.

Of course A^{X^*} and $A\langle\langle X^*\rangle\rangle$ are the same regarded as sets. We use this identification in the following theorem. Further, by the vth column of $H(r)$ we mean the function which maps u into (r, uv).

Theorem 3.1. *Suppose that A is a commutative semiring and r belongs to $A\langle\langle X^*\rangle\rangle$. Then the following three conditions are equivalent:*

(i) *r belongs to $A^{\mathrm{rat}}\langle\langle X^*\rangle\rangle$;*
(ii) *the subsemimodule of A^{X^*} generated by the columns of $H(r)$ is contained in a finitely generated stable subsemimodule of A^{X^*};*
(iii) *r belongs to a finitely generated stable subsemimodule of A^{X^*}.*

PROOF. Suppose that (i) holds. By Theorems 2.2 and 2.3 we may write

$$r = \sum \alpha\mu w\beta w = \sum \left(\sum_{i=1}^{m}(\alpha\mu w)_i \beta_i\right)w.$$

Define $F_i(v) = (\alpha\mu v)_i$ $(i = 1, \ldots, m)$. Then

$$r = \sum_{i=1}^{m}\beta_i F_i.$$

The semimodule generated by these functions F_i is stable because

$$(wF_i)(v) = (\alpha\mu vw)_i = (\alpha\mu v\mu w)_i = \sum_{j=1}^{m}(\alpha\mu v)_j(\mu w)_{ji}$$
$$= \sum_{j=1}^{m}(\mu w)_{ji}F_j(v) = \left(\sum_{j=1}^{m}(\mu w)_{ji}F_j\right)(v).$$

Hence condition (iii) is valid.

Suppose next that (iii) holds. The stability of the subsemimodule B in question immediately implies that all the columns of $H(r)$ lie in B, too. Thus

25

the semimodule generated by the columns is contained in B and we see that condition (ii) is valid.

Suppose then that (ii) holds. Let $F_1, \ldots, F_m$ be the generators. The stability implies the existence of matrices μx such that

$$x F_i = \sum_{j=1}^{m} (\mu x)_{ji} F_j \qquad (x \in X).$$

These matrices induce a representation $\mu: X^* \to A^{m \times m}$. We want to show that

$$w F_i = \sum_{j=1}^{m} (\mu w)_{ji} F_j \qquad (w \in X^*).$$

Assuming that this equation holds when $w = w_1$ and $w = w_2$ we obtain

$$(w_1 w_2) F_i(v) = F_i(v w_1 w_2) = \sum_j (\mu w_2)_{ji} F_j(v w_1)$$

$$= \sum_j (\mu w_2)_{ji} \sum_k (\mu w_1)_{kj} F_k(v) = \sum_k (\mu w_1 \mu w_2)_{ki} F_k(v).$$

Thus the equation is valid when $w = w_1 w_2$ which implies that the equation is identically true.

If now $\beta_1, \ldots, \beta_m$ are elements of A such that

$$r = \sum_i \beta_i F_i$$

then

$$(r, w) = \sum_i \beta_i F_i(w) = \sum_i \beta_i (w F_i)(\lambda)$$

$$= \sum_i \beta_i \sum_j (\mu w)_{ji} F_j(\lambda) = (F_1(\lambda), \ldots, F_m(\lambda)) \mu w (\beta_1, \ldots, \beta_m)^{\mathrm{T}}$$

and we see that condition (i) holds. □

Corollary 3.2. *Let A be a finite commutative semiring. Then $r \in A^{\mathrm{rat}}\langle\langle X^* \rangle\rangle$ iff there are only finitely many different columns in $H(r)$.*

PROOF. Since A is finite any finitely generated subsemimodule of A^{X^*} is finite. Hence, if $r \in A^{\mathrm{rat}}\langle\langle X^* \rangle\rangle$ condition (ii) of Theorem 3.1 shows that $H(r)$ has only finitely many different columns.

On the other hand, the subsemimodule of A^{X^*} generated by the columns of a Hankel matrix is in any case stable. Therefore the finiteness of the number of different columns of $H(r)$ implies that condition (ii) of Theorem 3.1 is valid. □

Next we assume that the semiring is a field K. Then K^{X^*} is a vector space. Given a series r of $K\langle\langle X^* \rangle\rangle$ the dimension of the subspace of K^{X^*} generated by the columns of $H(r)$ is called the *rank* of r.

Theorem 3.3. *Let K be a field and let r be a series of $K\langle\langle X^*\rangle\rangle$. Then $r \in K^{\mathrm{rat}}\langle\langle X^*\rangle\rangle$ iff the rank of r is finite. If r has the finite rank N then there are a representation $\mu: X^* \to K^{N \times N}$ and vectors $\alpha \in K^{1 \times N}$, $\beta \in K^{N \times 1}$ such that $r = \sum \alpha\mu w\beta w$. Moreover, if $r = \sum \gamma\chi w\delta w$ where $\gamma \in K^{1 \times m}$, $\chi w \in K^{m \times m}$ and $\delta \in K^{m \times 1}$ then $m \geq N$.*

PROOF. Let $r = \sum \gamma\chi w\delta w$ ($\chi w \in K^{m \times m}$) be a series in $K^{\mathrm{rat}}\langle\langle X^*\rangle\rangle$. Define

$$F_i(v) = (\gamma\chi v)_i \quad (v \in X^*; i = 1, \ldots, m).$$

Because

$$(r, uv) = \gamma\chi u\chi v\delta = \sum_i (\gamma\chi u)_i(\chi v\delta)_i = \sum_i (\chi v\delta)_i F_i(u)$$

the vth column of $H(r)$ is a linear combination of the functions $F_1, \ldots, F_m$. Hence the subspace generated by the columns of $H(r)$ is contained in the subspace generated by the functions F_i. This implies that the rank of r is at most m.

Assume now that r is a series whose rank is finite and equal to N. Let the columns with indexes $v_1, \ldots, v_N$ form a basis of the vector space generated by all the columns of $H(r)$. Denote these columns by $F_1, \ldots, F_N$. For each letter x there is a matrix μx such that

$$xF_i = \sum_j (\mu x)_{ji}F_j.$$

(note that xF_i is the xv_ith column of $H(r)$). These matrices induce a representation $\mu: X^* \to K^{N \times N}$. It is easy to show (see the proof of Theorem 3.1) that we have

$$wF_i = \sum_j (\mu w)_{ji}F_j$$

for any word w. If now $r = \sum_i \beta_i F_i$ then

$$(r, w) = \sum_i \beta_i F_i(w) = \sum_i \beta_i \sum_j (\mu w)_{ji}F_j(\lambda)$$

$$= ((r, v_1), \ldots, (r, v_N))\mu w(\beta_1, \ldots, \beta_N)^{\mathrm{T}} = \alpha\mu w\beta. \qquad \square$$

Although the proof is now ready we continue by deriving some formulas which will be needed later.

Since the columns $F_1, \ldots, F_N$ form a basis there must be words $u_1, \ldots, u_N$ such that

$$\det \begin{pmatrix} (r, u_1v_1) & \cdots & (r, u_1v_N) \\ \vdots & \cdots & \vdots \\ (r, u_Nv_1) & \cdots & (r, u_Nv_N) \end{pmatrix} = \det U \neq 0.$$

Further, for any word w there are unique elements $\alpha_1(w), \ldots, \alpha_n(w)$ of K such that

$$(r, zw) = \sum_j \alpha_j(w)(r, zv_j) = \sum_j \alpha_j(w)F_j(z) \quad (z \in X^*).$$

Substituting here $u_1, \ldots, u_N$ for z we obtain the equation

$$\begin{pmatrix} (r, u_1w) \\ \vdots \\ (r, u_Nw) \end{pmatrix} = U \begin{pmatrix} \alpha_1(w) \\ \vdots \\ \alpha_N(w) \end{pmatrix}.$$

Because U is nonsingular this yields

(1)
$$\begin{pmatrix} \alpha_1(w) \\ \vdots \\ \alpha_N(w) \end{pmatrix} = U^{-1} \begin{pmatrix} (r, u_1w) \\ \vdots \\ (r, u_Nw) \end{pmatrix}.$$

Since the numbers $\alpha_j(w)$ are uniquely determined and

$$(r, zwv_i) = \sum_j (\mu w)_{ji}(r, zv_j) \qquad (z \in X^*)$$

we must have

$$(\mu w)_{ji} = \alpha_j(wv_i).$$

Using now formula (1) we see that

(2)
$$\mu w = U^{-1} \begin{pmatrix} (r, u_1wv_1) & \cdots & (r, u_1wv_N) \\ \vdots & & \vdots \\ (r, u_Nwv_1) & \cdots & (r, u_Nwv_N) \end{pmatrix}.$$

Corollary 3.4. *Assume that K is a field and r is a series of $K^{\text{rat}}\langle\langle X^* \rangle\rangle$ with rank N. Let $w_1, \ldots, w_{N+1}$ be distinct words. Then there are elements $c_1, \ldots, c_{N+1}$ of K, not all zero, such that*

$$c_1(r, ww_1) + \cdots + c_{N+1}(r, ww_{N+1}) = 0$$

for all words w.

PROOF. Since the dimension of the vector space generated by the columns of $H(r)$ is N the columns with indexes $w_1, \ldots, w_{N+1}$ must be linearly dependent. $\qquad\square$

Theorem 3.5. *Let K be a field and let r be a series of $K^{\text{rat}}\langle\langle X^* \rangle\rangle$ with rank N. If*

$$r = \sum \alpha_1 \mu_1 w \beta_1 w = \sum \alpha_2 \mu_2 w \beta_2 w$$

where $\mu_1 w$ and $\mu_2 w$ are $N \times N$ matrices then there is a nonsingular matrix U such that

$$\mu_1 w = U^{-1}\mu_2 w U, \qquad \alpha_1 = \alpha_2 U, \qquad \beta_1 = U^{-1}\beta_2.$$

PROOF. Suppose that r is written in the form $\sum \alpha\mu w\beta w$ where $\mu w \in K^{m \times m}$ and let V be the subspace of $K^{1 \times m}$ generated by the vectors $\alpha\mu w$ ($w \in X^*$).

Assertion 1. The dimension of V is at least N.

Let $\hat{\mu}w\colon K^{1 \times m} \to K^{1 \times m}$ be the linear operator defined by the matrix μw and let $\hat{\beta}\colon K^{1 \times m} \to K$ be the linear functional defined by the vector β. Then

$$(r, w) = \hat{\beta}(\hat{\mu}w(\alpha)) = \hat{\beta}\mid_V (\hat{\mu}w \mid_V (\alpha))$$

where $\mid_V$ denotes restriction onto V. If we now choose a basis for V then we obtain vectors $\alpha_0 \in K^{1 \times \dim V}$, $\beta_0 \in K^{\dim V \times 1}$ and matrices $\mu_0 w \in K^{\dim V \times \dim V}$ such that

$$(r, w) = \alpha_0 \mu_0 w \beta_0.$$

Hence our assertion is implied by Theorem 3.3.

Assertion 2. Define

$$V_0 = \{v \in V \mid \hat{\beta}(\hat{\mu}w(v)) = 0 \text{ for every } w\}.$$

If $m = N$ then $V_0 = \{0\}$.

We see immediately that V_0 is a subspace of V. Hence we may form the quotient space V/V_0. We also see that if $v_1 - v_2 \in V_0$ and $w \in X^*$ then $\hat{\mu}w(v_1) - \hat{\mu}w(v_2) \in V_0$. Therefore it makes sense to define

$$\hat{\chi}w(v + V_0) = \hat{\mu}w(v) + V_0.$$

Further, since $v_1 - v_2 \in V_0$ implies $\hat{\beta}(v_1) - \hat{\beta}(v_2) = 0$ we may define

$$\hat{\delta}(v + V_0) = \hat{\beta}(v).$$

We know that the dimension of V/V_0 equals $\dim V - \dim V_0 = M$. Because

$$\hat{\delta}(\hat{\chi}w(\alpha + V_0)) = (r, w)$$

there are vectors $\gamma \in K^{1 \times M}$, $\delta \in K^{M \times 1}$ and matrices $\chi w \in K^{M \times M}$ such that $(r, w) = \gamma \chi w \delta$. Assertion 1 implies that if $m = N$ then $\dim V = N$. Since $M \geq N$ by Theorem 3.3 we must have $\dim V_0 = 0$.

Let now V_i denote the vector space generated by the vectors $\alpha_i \mu_i w$ $(i = 1, 2)$ By assertion 1 these spaces are N-dimensional. Assuming that $\alpha_2 \mu_2 w_1, \ldots,$ $\alpha_2 \mu_2 w_N$ form a basis of V_2 we define a linear mapping $\hat{U}\colon V_2 \to V_1$ by setting

$$\hat{U}\alpha_2 \mu_2 w_i = \alpha_1 \mu_1 w_i.$$

Assertion 3. We have $\hat{U}\alpha_2 \mu_2 w = \alpha_1 \mu_1 w$ for all words w.

Let $k_1, \ldots, k_N$ be elements of K such that

$$\alpha_2 \mu_2 w = k_1 \alpha_2 \mu_2 w_1 + \cdots + k_N \alpha_2 \mu_2 w_N.$$

Then

$$\begin{aligned}
\hat{\beta}_1(\hat{\mu}_1 z(\hat{U}\alpha_2 \mu_2 w)) &= \hat{\beta}_1(\hat{\mu}_1 z(k_1 \alpha_1 \mu_1 w_1 + \cdots + k_N \alpha_1 \mu_1 w_N)) \\
&= (k_1 \alpha_1 \mu_1 w_1)\mu_1 z \beta_1 + \cdots + (k_N \alpha_1 \mu_1 w_N)\mu_1 z \beta_1 \\
&= k_1(r, w_1 z) + \cdots + k_N(r, w_N z) \\
&= (k_1 \alpha_2 \mu_2 w_1)\mu_2 z \beta_2 + \cdots + (k_N \alpha_2 \mu_2 w_N)\mu_2 z \beta_2 \\
&= \hat{\beta}_2(\hat{\mu}_2 z(k_1 \alpha_2 \mu_2 w_1 + \cdots + k_N \alpha_2 \mu_2 w_N)) \\
&= \hat{\beta}_2(\hat{\mu}_2 z(\alpha_2 \mu_2 w)) = (r, wz) = \hat{\beta}_1(\hat{\mu}_1 z(\alpha_1 \mu_1 w))
\end{aligned}$$

for all words z. Therefore we obtain assertion 3 by using assertion 2.

Assertion 4. The mapping $\hat{U}$ is an isomorphism.

Since V_1 and V_2 have the same dimension $\hat{U}$ is an isomorphism iff it is surjective. Hence assertion 4 is a consequence of assertion 3.

Let now U be the matrix of $\hat{U}$, i.e. the matrix for which $\alpha_2\mu_2wU = \alpha_1\mu_1w$ $(w \in X^*)$. Since

$$(\alpha_2\mu_2w_i)(U\mu_1wU^{-1}) = \alpha_1\mu_1w_iU^{-1}U\mu_1wU^{-1} = \alpha_1\mu_1w_i\mu_1wU^{-1} = (\alpha_2\mu_2w_i)\mu_2w$$

$(i = 1, \ldots, N)$ we must have $U\mu_1wU^{-1} = \mu_2w$. Further, since $(\alpha_2\mu_2w_i)(U\beta_1) = \alpha_1\mu_1w_iU^{-1}U\beta_1 = \alpha_1\mu_1w_i\beta_1 = \alpha_2\mu_2w_i\beta_2$ $(i = 1, \ldots, N)$ the equality $U\beta_1 = \beta_2$ holds. $\qquad\square$

The above theorem may be stated by saying that all minimal representations of a series of $K^{\mathrm{rat}}\langle\langle X^*\rangle\rangle$ are similar. Note that formula (2) gives us a minimal representation.

Theorem 3.6. *Assume that A is a principal ideal domain, K is its quotient field and r is a series in $A\langle\langle X^*\rangle\rangle$. Then r is A-rational iff it is K-rational. More exactly, if r has the finite rank N then there are a representation $\mu: X^* \to A^{N \times N}$ and vectors $\alpha \in A^{1 \times N}$ and $\beta \in A^{N \times 1}$ such that*

$$r = \sum \alpha\mu w\beta w.$$

PROOF. Trivially every A-rational series is K-rational. Hence it is sufficient to find α, β, and μ given that r has finite rank N.

Consider the A-module $A(r)$ generated by the columns of $H(r)$. If $F_1, \ldots, F_N$ are linearly independent columns in $H(r)$ then the wth column can be written as a linear combination $\alpha_1(w)F_1 + \cdots + \alpha_N(w)F_N$ where $\alpha_i(w) \in K$. But the coefficients are given by formula (1) of this section. Hence $\alpha_i(w) = a_i(w)/a$ where $a_i(w) \in A$ and a is an element of A depending only upon the matrix U.

Now we see that $A(r)$ is contained in the A-module generated by the functions $(1/a)F_1, \ldots, (1/a)F_N$. Because A is a principal ideal domain this implies that $A(r)$ is finitely generated and has, in fact, a basis $G_1, \ldots, G_m$ where $m \leq N$. Since all the columns of $H(r)$ are contained in the vector space generated by $G_1, \ldots, G_m$ we must have $m = N$. The semimodule $A(r)$ being stable by its definition we can construct μ, α and β as in the last part of the proof of Theorem 3.1. $\qquad\square$

EXERCISES

1. Consider the Hankel matrix

$$\begin{pmatrix} 0 & 1 & 2 & \cdot \\ 1 & 2 & 3 & \cdot \\ 2 & 3 & 4 & \cdot \\ \vdots & \vdots & \vdots & \vdots \end{pmatrix}$$

of the series $r = \sum n x^n$. Show that the columns of $H(r)$ belong to the stable $\mathbb{N}$-semimodule generated by $(0\ 1\ 2 \cdots)^T$ and $(1\ 1\ 1 \cdots)^T$. Show also that the $\mathbb{N}$-semimodule generated by the columns of $H(r)$ has no finite set of generators.

2. Examine what happens when columns of $H(r)$ are replaced with rows of $H(r)$ in this chapter.

3. Assume that K is a field and $r \in K\langle X^* \rangle$. Then we can express r in the form $\sum \alpha \mu w \beta w$ where $\mu w = 0$ for every long word w.

4. Let r be a series of $\mathbb{R}^{\text{rat}}\langle\langle X^* \rangle\rangle$ and let μ be a minimal representation of r. Prove the existence of constants B and M such that

$$\max_{i,j} |(\mu w)_{ij}| \leqslant B \max_{\lg v \leqslant \lg w + M} |(r, v)|.$$

5. Let $r = \sum \alpha \mu w \beta w$ belong to $K^{\text{rat}}\langle\langle X^* \rangle\rangle$ (K a field, $\alpha \in K^{1 \times m}$, $\alpha \neq 0$) and let γ be a nonzero vector in $K^{1 \times m}$. Then we can express r in the form $\sum \gamma \chi w \delta w$.

6. Show that the ranks of $r_1 + r_2$ and $r_1 r_2$ do not exceed the sum of the ranks of r_1 and r_2.

7. Assume that $r \in K^{\text{rat}}\langle\langle X^* \rangle\rangle$ (K a field) and N is the rank of r. Show that if $\lg w_0 = N$ then there are words $w_1, \ldots, w_N$ and elements $c_1, \ldots, c_N$ of K such that $\lg w_i < N$ ($i = 1, \ldots, N$) and

$$(r, w w_0) = c_1 (r, w w_1) + \cdots + c_N (r, w w_N)$$

for all words w.

Hint: If $r = \sum \alpha \mu w \beta w$ ($\mu w \in K^{N \times N}$) and $v_{N+1} = w_0 = x_1 \cdots x_N$, $v_1 = \lambda$, $v_2 = x_N, \ldots, v_N = x_2 \cdots x_N$ then there is an index m such that

$$\mu v_m \beta = c_{m-1} \mu v_{m-1} \beta + \cdots + c_1 \mu v_1 \beta.$$

8. Let A be a Noetherian integral domain and let K be its quotient field. Show that if r is a series of $A\langle\langle X^* \rangle\rangle$ with finite rank then the A-module generated by the columns of $H(r)$ is finitely generated and $r \in A^{\text{rat}}\langle\langle X^* \rangle\rangle$.
Hint. Follow the proof of Theorem 3.6.

II.4 Operations preserving rationality

Closure properties of rational and recognizable series under various operations constitute the subject matter of this section. We consider homomorphisms, defined both for coefficient semirings and for monoids, inverse homomorphisms and Hadamard products. The essential tool in the proofs is the equational characterization of rational series.

The following points are worth noticing. Theorem 4.3 is valid for recognizable series only. Similar differences between recognizable and rational series can be seen in Theorems 4.4 and 4.5. If we want to extend projections $p: M_1 \to M_2$ into semirings of power series, difficulties are caused by the fact that the families $\{w \mid p w = v\}$ are infinite. Therefore, the summability assumptions made in the latter part of this section are needed. Note also that every homomorphism $h: M_1 \to M_2$ can be expressed as the product of a projection and a nonerasing homomorphism. Thus, the "harmful" effects of homomorphisms reduce to those of projections, a point further exploited in connection with rational transductions in Section III.1.

Theorem 4.1. *Let $h: A \to B$ be a semiring homomorphism. If $r \in A^{\text{rat}}\langle\langle M \rangle\rangle$ then $hr \in B^{\text{rat}}\langle\langle M \rangle\rangle$.*

PROOF. Let $Z = P + QZ$ be the linear system given by Theorem 1.4 and let S be its solution vector. Then hS is the solution vector of the system $Z = hP + hQZ$. Thus the B-rationality of hr is implied by Theorem 1.2. $\quad\square$

Theorem 4.2. *Suppose that $H: A\langle\langle M_1 \rangle\rangle \to A\langle\langle M_2 \rangle\rangle$ is a substitution homomorphism such that Hw is a quasiregular rational series for every nonempty word w. If $r \in A^{\text{rat}}\langle\langle M_1 \rangle\rangle$ then $Hr \in A^{\text{rat}}\langle\langle M_2 \rangle\rangle$.*

The proof is analogous to the above one.

Theorem 4.3. *Let $H: M_1 \to M_2$ be a monoid morphism. If $r \in A^{\text{rec}}\langle\langle M_2 \rangle\rangle$ then the series*

$$H^{-1}r = \sum (r, Hw)w$$

belongs to $A^{\text{rec}}\langle\langle M_1 \rangle\rangle$.

PROOF. Write r in the form $\sum \alpha \mu w \beta w$ and define $\chi w = \mu Hw$. It is immediately seen that χ is a matrix representation and

$$H^{-1}r = \sum \alpha \chi w \beta w. \qquad\qquad \square$$

Theorem 4.4. *Let A be a commutative semiring. Then the Hadamard product of two A-recognizable series is A-recognizable. In the case of a free monoid the Hadamard product of two A-rational series is A-rational.*

PROOF. By Theorem 2.1 we may write

$$r_i = (r_i, \lambda)\lambda + \sum (\mu_i w)_{1, m_i} w \qquad (i = 1, 2).$$

Let μw be the Kronecker product of $\mu_1 w$ and $\mu_2 w$. The commutativity of A implies that μ is a representation. Therefore

$$r_1 \odot r_2 = (r_1, \lambda)(r_2, \lambda)\lambda + \sum (\mu w)_{1, m_1 m_2} w$$

is A-recognizable. $\quad\square$

Theorem 4.5. *Let A_1 and A_2 be subsemirings of A such that the elements of A_1 commute with those of A_2. If $r \in A_1^{\text{rec}}\langle\langle M \rangle\rangle$ and if $s \in A_2^{\text{rat}}\langle\langle M \rangle\rangle$ then $r \odot s \in A^{\text{rat}}\langle\langle M \rangle\rangle$.*

PROOF. By Corollary 2.4 we may express s in the form $h\bar{s}$ where $\bar{s} \in A_2^{\text{rec}}\langle\langle X^* \rangle\rangle$ and $h: X^* \to M$ is a coding homomorphism. By Theorem 4.3 the series $h^{-1}r$ belongs to $A_1^{\text{rec}}\langle\langle X^* \rangle\rangle$. Obviously

$$r \odot s = h(h^{-1}r \odot \bar{s}).$$

Since the elements of A_1 commute with the elements of A_2 the series $h^{-1}r \odot s$ is A-rational (the proof of Theorem 4.4 works also in this case). Therefore we may apply Theorem 4.2. $\qquad\square$

Let $p: M_1 \to M_2$ be a monoid homomorphism such that $\lg w = 1$ implies $\lg pw \le 1$. If p is not length preserving then it is called a *projection*.

Assume now that $p: M_1 \to M_2$ is a projection. It is clear that if A is a semiring then we can extend p into a homomorphism of $A\langle M_1 \rangle$ into $A\langle M_2 \rangle$. However, if we want to extend p outside $A\langle M_1 \rangle$ then we have to assume that A is a topological semiring. This is due to the fact that the families $\{w \mid pw = v\}$ are infinite.

Suppose that A is a complete valued field and r belongs to $A\langle\langle M_1 \rangle\rangle$. If $p: M_1 \to M_2$ is a projection and if all the families

$$\{|(r, w)| \mid pw = v\} \qquad (v \in M_2)$$

are summable then we define

$$pr = \sum_v \left(\sum_{pw = v} (r, w) \right) v.$$

Theorem 4.6. *Let A be a complete valued field and let $p: X^* \to Y^*$ be a projection. If r is a series of $A^{\text{rat}}\langle\langle X^* \rangle\rangle$ such that pr exists then pr belongs to $A^{\text{rat}}\langle\langle Y^* \rangle\rangle$.*

PROOF. Write $r = \sum \alpha \mu w \beta w$ where μ is the minimal representation appearing in formula (2) of II.3. This formula immediately implies that the matrix family

$$\{\mu w \mid pw = \lambda\}$$

is (componentwise) absolutely summable (note that $\{(r, u_i w v_j) \mid pw = \lambda\}$ is a subfamily of $\{(r, w) \mid pw = pu_i v_j\}$). Let σ denote the sum of this matrix family.

Define now

$$\chi y = \left(\sum_{px = y} \mu x \right) \sigma, \qquad \gamma = \alpha \sigma, \qquad \delta = \beta.$$

If $v = y_1 \cdots y_n$ $(y_i \in Y)$ then

$$(pr, v) = \sum_{pw = v} \alpha \mu w \beta$$

$$= \sum_{\substack{pw_i = \lambda \\ px_i = y_i}} \alpha \mu w_0 \mu x_1 \mu w_1 \cdots \mu x_n \mu w_n \beta = \gamma \chi v \delta$$

which shows that $pr \in A^{\text{rat}}\langle\langle Y^* \rangle\rangle$. $\qquad\square$

We say that a topological semiring A is *complete* if every denumerable family of elements of A is summable and if

$$\sum a_i \sum b_j = \sum a_i b_j.$$

It is clear that in the case of a complete semiring A we can extend p onto $A\langle\langle M_1 \rangle\rangle$ by setting

$$pr = \sum_v \left(\sum_{pw = v} (r, w) \right) v.$$

Theorem 4.7. *Let A be a complete semiring and let $p: X^* \to Y^*$ be a projection. If r is a series of $A^{\mathrm{rat}}\langle\langle X^* \rangle\rangle$ then pr belongs to $A^{\mathrm{rat}}\langle\langle Y^* \rangle\rangle$.*

PROOF. We need only write r in the form $\sum \alpha\mu w\beta w$ and define χ, γ and δ exactly as in the preceding proof. □

Corollary 4.8. *Let A be a complete semiring and let $p: M_1 \to M_2$ be a projection. If r is a series of $A^{\mathrm{rat}}\langle\langle M_1 \rangle\rangle$ then pr belongs to $A^{\mathrm{rat}}\langle\langle M_2 \rangle\rangle$.*

PROOF. By Corollary 2.4 we may express r in the form $h\bar{r}$ where $\bar{r} \in A^{\mathrm{rat}}\langle\langle X^* \rangle\rangle$ and $h: X^* \to M_1$ is length preserving. Let now $k: Y^* \to M_2$ be a surjective length preserving homomorphism and define $\bar{p}: X^* \to Y^*$ as follows:

if $phx = \lambda$ then $\bar{p}x = \lambda$;
if $phx = y \neq \lambda$ then $\bar{p}x = \bar{y}$ where $\bar{y}$ is a letter which satisfies the equation $k\bar{y} = y$.

Then $ph = k\bar{p}$ and using the completeness of A it is easy to see that $pr = p(h\bar{r}) = k(\bar{p}\bar{r})$. Hence the corollary is implied by Theorems 4.7 and 4.2. □

EXAMPLES. The Boolean semiring $\mathbb{B} = \{0, 1\}$ with the discrete topology is complete.

If A is a subring of $\mathbb{R}$ (the field of real numbers) we denote $A_+^{(\infty)} = \{a \in A \mid a \geq 0\} \cup \{\infty\}$ and define

$$a + \infty = \infty + a = \infty + \infty = \infty,$$

$$a\infty = \infty a = \infty\infty = \infty \qquad (a \neq 0),$$

$$0\infty = \infty 0 = 0.$$

It is easy to see that $A_+^{(\infty)}$ is a semiring. Next we introduce the metric

$$d(a, b) = \left| \frac{1}{1 + a} - \frac{1}{1 + b} \right|,$$

$$d(a, \infty) = d(\infty, a) = \frac{1}{a + 1}.$$

It is again easy to see that $\mathbb{Z}_+^{(\infty)}$ forms a complete topological semiring together with the topology induced by d. On the contrary, the semirings $\mathbb{R}_+^{(\infty)}$ and $\mathbb{Q}_+^{(\infty)}$ become not topological (e.g., $n \cdot 1/n \to 1 \neq \infty \cdot 0$).

However, $\mathbb{R}_+^{(\infty)}$ is a complete semitopological semiring (the product is separately continuous) where $\sum a_i \cdot \sum b_j = \sum a_i b_j$. Obviously Theorem 4.7 holds also for semirings with these properties.

EXERCISES

1. If $r \in A^{\mathrm{rat}}\langle\langle X^* \rangle\rangle$ then

$$\sum_{n} \left(\sum_{\lg w = n} (r, w) \right) t^n \quad \text{and} \quad \sum_{n} \left(\sum_{\lg w \leqslant n} (r, w) \right) t^n$$

belong to $A^{\mathrm{rat}}\langle\langle t^* \rangle\rangle$.

2. If $r \in A^{\mathrm{rat}}\langle\langle X^* \rangle\rangle$, $s \in A\langle\langle X^* \rangle\rangle$ and the values of r and s differ at finitely many words only then $s \in A^{\mathrm{rat}}\langle\langle X^* \rangle\rangle$.

Hint: For any natural number k we have

$$\sum_{\lg w \geqslant k} (r, w) w \in A^{\mathrm{rat}}\langle\langle X^* \rangle\rangle.$$

3. If $\sum_n r_n t^n \in A^{\mathrm{rat}}\langle\langle t^* \rangle\rangle$ then $\sum r_n t^{m+np}$ and $\sum r_{m+np} t^n$ (m and p fixed) belong to $A^{\mathrm{rat}}\langle\langle t^* \rangle\rangle$.

4. Suppose that $r \in A^{\mathrm{rat}}\langle\langle X^* \rangle\rangle$, A is commutative and $w_i \in X^*$ ($i = 1, 2, 3$). Then

$$\sum (r, w_1^n w_2 w_3^n) t^n \in A^{\mathrm{rat}}\langle\langle t^* \rangle\rangle.$$

5. Show that the relation defined in X^* by

$$w_1 \equiv w_2 \Leftrightarrow \exists v_1, v_2 \colon w_1 = v_1 v_2, \; w_2 = v_2 v_1$$

is an equivalence relation. Let $[w]$ denote the class of the word w ($[w]$ might be called the circular word determined by w). Prove that if A is commutative and $r \in A^{\mathrm{rat}}\langle\langle X^* \rangle\rangle$ then

$$s = \sum_{w} \left(\sum_{v \in [w]} (r, v) \right) w \in A^{\mathrm{rat}}\langle\langle X^* \rangle\rangle.$$

Hint: If $r = \sum \alpha \mu w \beta w$ then

$$(s, w) = \sum_{\substack{v_1 v_2 = w \\ v_1 \neq \lambda}} \sum_{i} (\mu v_1 \beta)_i (\alpha \mu v_2)_i.$$

6. Let r and s be series of $A^{\mathrm{rat}}\langle\langle X^* \rangle\rangle$. Define $Y = X \cup \bar{X}$ where $\bar{X}$ is a copy of X,

$$px = x, \qquad p\bar{x} = \lambda,$$
$$\bar{p}x = \lambda, \qquad \bar{p}\bar{x} = x$$

and

$$hx = h\bar{x} = x.$$

Show that

$$r \,\mathrm{I\!I\!I}\, s = h \left(\sum_{w \in Y^*} (r, pw)(s, \bar{p}w) w \right)$$

belongs to $A^{\mathrm{rat}}\langle\langle X^* \rangle\rangle$ if A is commutative.

The series $r \,\mathrm{I\!I\!I}\, s$ is called the *Hurwitz product* (or the *shuffle product*) of r and s.

7. Make use of the following ideas to obtain a new proof for Theorem 4.5.

Suppose that $r = \sum \alpha\mu w\beta w \in A^{\text{rec}}\langle\langle M\rangle\rangle$ $(\mu w \in A^{m \times m})$ and $s \in A^{\text{rat}}\langle\langle M\rangle\rangle$. By substituting $(\mu x)x$ for x in s (lg $x = 1$) we obtain an $A^{m \times m}$-rational series $t = \sum (s, w)\mu w w$. Corollary 1.3 implies that t is rational when considered as a matrix. Hence $r \odot s = \alpha t\beta$ is rational.

8. Prove Theorem 4.4 (in the case of a free monoid) by using Theorem 3.1. Prove also that if r, $s \in A^{\text{rat}}\langle\langle X^*\rangle\rangle$ and A is a field then the rank of $r \odot s$ is at most the product of the ranks of r and s.

9. If $r \in \mathbb{Z}^{\text{rat}}\langle\langle X^*\rangle\rangle$, $p: X^* \to Y^*$ is a projection and pr exists then $pr \in \mathbb{Z}^{\text{rat}}\langle\langle Y^*\rangle\rangle$.

10. If A is complete, $r \in A^{\text{rat}}\langle\langle X^*\rangle\rangle$ and $L \subseteq X^*$ then $\sum (\sum_{v \in L} (r, vw))w$ belongs to $A^{\text{rat}}\langle\langle X^*\rangle\rangle$.

II.5 Regular languages and rational series

We now establish the basic interconnections between rational series and regular languages. (Because of these results, regular languages are sometimes referred to as rational languages.) We first prove that the characteristic series of a regular language is A-rational, for any semiring A. Conversely, we show that languages of the form

$$L_a = \{w \mid (r, w) = a\}$$

are regular if $r \in A^{\text{rat}}\langle\langle X^*\rangle\rangle$ and A satisfies certain additional assumptions. The proofs reveal clearly how finite automata and recognizable series are interrelated: the matrices defining a representation are generalizations of the transition matrices of a finite automaton.

It is a consequence of the second result mentioned above that if A is a positive semiring, for instance $A = \mathbb{N}$, then the support of any series in $A^{\text{rat}}\langle\langle X^*\rangle\rangle$ is regular. On the other hand, the support of a $\mathbb{Z}$-rational series over X^* need not even be context-free. We also prove (in Theorem 5.6) that the coefficients of an $\mathbb{N}$-rational series can in a certain way be expressed in terms of a regular language L.

The proof of our first theorem makes use only of the matrix representation.

Theorem 5.1. *Let L be a regular language and let A be a semiring. Then the characteristic series of L is A-rational.*

PROOF. Let $(s_1, \{s_1, \ldots, s_m\}, f, F)$ be a finite deterministic automaton accepting L. Define

$$(\mu x)_{ij} = \begin{cases} 1 & \text{if } f(s_i, x) = s_j, \\ 0 & \text{otherwise,} \end{cases}$$

$$\alpha = (1\ 0 \cdots 0),$$

$$\beta = (\beta_1, \ldots, \beta_m)^{\text{T}},$$

$$\beta_i = \begin{cases} 1 & \text{if } s_i \in F, \\ 0 & \text{otherwise.} \end{cases}$$

We observe that if $f(s_1, w) = s_k$ then

$$(\alpha \mu w)_i = \begin{cases} 1 & \text{if } i = k, \\ 0 & \text{otherwise.} \end{cases}$$

Hence $\sum \alpha \mu w \beta w$ is the characteristic series of L. $\qquad \square$

Theorem 5.2. *Assume that one of the following conditions holds:*

(i) *A is a finite commutative semiring and $r \in A^{\mathrm{rat}}\langle\langle X^* \rangle\rangle$;*
(ii) *A is an integral domain, $r \in A^{\mathrm{rat}}\langle\langle X^* \rangle\rangle$ and the range of r is finite.*

Then every language

$$L_a = \{w \mid (r, w) = a\}$$

is regular.

PROOF. We show at first that $H(r)$ has only finitely many different columns. If condition (i) is valid then Corollary 3.2 gives our assertion.

If condition (ii) is valid then $r \in K^{\mathrm{rat}}\langle\langle X^* \rangle\rangle$ where K is the quotient field of A. Applying now formula (1) of II.3 we see that the number of columns of $H(r)$ is at most M^N where N is the rank of r and M is the cardinality of its range.

Define

$$(r_a, w) = \begin{cases} 1 & \text{if } (r, w) = a, \\ 0 & \text{otherwise.} \end{cases}$$

We see that r_a is a series of $\mathbb{B}\langle\langle X^* \rangle\rangle$ and $H(r_a)$ has only finitely many different columns. Hence r_a is $\mathbb{B}$-rational by Corollary 3.2.

Let now $s = \sum \alpha \mu w \beta w$ be a series of $\mathbb{B}^{\mathrm{rat}}\langle\langle X^* \rangle\rangle$ where $\mu w \in \mathbb{B}^{m \times m}$. Introduce the finite deterministic automaton $(s_1, \{s_1, \ldots, s_{2^m}\}, f, F)$ where $s_1 = \alpha, s_2, \ldots, s_{2^m}$ are the vectors of $\mathbb{B}^{1 \times m}$,

$$f(s_i, x) = s_i \mu x$$

and

$$F = \{s_i \mid s_i \beta = 1\}.$$

Because $f(s_1, w) = \alpha \mu w$ we have $(s, w) = 1$ iff $f(s_1, w) \in F$. Therefore the support of s is regular.

Since the support of r_a is L_a we have proved the theorem. $\qquad \square$

We say that a semiring A is *positive* if the mapping $h: A \to \mathbb{B}$ defined by

$$h(0) = 0,$$
$$h(a) = 1 \quad (a \neq 0)$$

is a homomorphism.

Corollary 5.3. *Let A be a positive semiring. Then the support of any series of $A^{\mathrm{rat}}\langle\langle X^* \rangle\rangle$ is regular.*

PROOF. If $r \in A^{\text{rat}}\langle\langle X^* \rangle\rangle$ and h is the morphism mapping A onto $\mathbb{B}$ then the series hr is $\mathbb{B}$-rational by Theorem 4.1 and, moreover, the supports of r and hr coincide. Thus we may apply Theorem 5.2 (or the last part of its proof).

$\square$

Using Theorem 5.1 and Corollary 5.3 we obtain

Corollary 5.4. *The following three conditions are equivalent:*

   (i) *L is a regular language over X;*
   (ii) *the series* char *L belongs to* $\mathbb{B}^{\text{rat}}\langle\langle X^* \rangle\rangle$;
   (iii) *the series* char *L belongs to* $\mathbb{N}^{\text{rat}}\langle\langle X^* \rangle\rangle$.

Corollary 5.5.

   (i) *If* $r \in \mathbb{Z}^{\text{rat}}\langle\langle X^* \rangle\rangle$, $m \in \mathbb{N}$, $m \neq 0$ *and* $j \in \mathbb{N}$ *then the language*

$$\{w \mid (r, w) \equiv j \,(\text{mod } m)\}$$

   is regular.
   (ii) *If* $r \in \mathbb{N}^{\text{rat}}\langle\langle X^* \rangle\rangle$ *and* $j \in \mathbb{N}$ *then the language*

$$\{w \mid (r, w) = j\}$$

   is regular.

PROOF. Both assertions are implied by Theorem 5.2. In the first case we apply the canonical homomorphism of $\mathbb{Z}$ onto the residue class ring $\mathbb{Z}/(m\mathbb{Z})$. In the second case we apply the canonical homomorphism of $\mathbb{N}$ onto

$$\mathbb{N}^{(j+1)} = \{0, 1, \ldots, j, \infty\}$$

which is obtained by identifying the elements $j + 1, j + 2, \ldots$ of $\mathbb{N}$. $\square$

Theorem 5.6. *Let r be a series in* $\mathbb{N}\langle\langle X^* \rangle\rangle$. *Then the following conditions are equivalent:*

   (i) *r belongs to* $\mathbb{N}^{\text{rat}}\langle\langle X^* \rangle\rangle$;
   (ii) *there are a regular language L and a coding homomorphism h such that*

$$(r, w) = \text{card}(h^{-1}w \cap L) \qquad (w \neq \lambda).$$

PROOF. Let R denote the subfamily of $\mathbb{N}\langle\langle X^* \rangle\rangle$ consisting of those series which satisfy (ii).

If $r \in R$ and s is the characteristic series of $L \cap X^+$ then

$$r = (r, \lambda)\lambda + hs.$$

Because s is $\mathbb{N}$-rational this formula implies that $R \subseteq \mathbb{N}^{\text{rat}}\langle\langle X^* \rangle\rangle$.

Suppose now that r_1 and r_2 are quasiregular elements of R and

$$(r_i, w) = \text{card}(h_i^{-1}w \cap L_i) \qquad (w \in X^*; i = 1, 2).$$

Obviously we may assume that L_1 and L_2 are over disjoint alphabets Y_1 and Y_2. Let h be the common extension of h_1 and h_2 onto $(Y_1 \cup Y_2)^*$ and let s_i be the characteristic series of L_i $(i = 1, 2)$. Then

$$r_i = h s_i \qquad (i = 1, 2),$$
$$r_1 + r_2 = h(s_1 + s_2)$$

and

$$r_1 r_2 = h(s_1 s_2).$$

Further, if we set $r_2 = r_1$ then we obtain

$$r_1^+ = r_1 + (r_1 r_1)^+ + r_1 (r_1 r_1)^+$$
$$= h(s_1 + (s_1 s_2)^+ + s_2 (s_1 s_2)^+).$$

These formulas show that

$$(r_1 + r_2, w) = \mathrm{card}(h^{-1} w \cap (L_1 + L_2)),$$
$$(r_1 r_2, w) = \mathrm{card}(h^{-1} w \cap (L_1 L_2))$$

and

$$(r_1^+, w) = \mathrm{card}(h^{-1} w \cap (L_1 + (L_1 L_2)^+ + L_2 (L_1 L_2)^+)).$$

It is clear that $\mathbb{N}\langle X^* \rangle \subseteq R$. Therefore, if we prove that R is rationally closed then we obtain the inclusion $\mathbb{N}^{\mathrm{rat}}\langle\langle X^* \rangle\rangle \subseteq R$ which together with the converse inclusion implies our theorem.

We have already seen that R is closed with respect to quasi-inversion. Thus we have only to show that R is a semiring.

Let $r_i = (r_i, \lambda)\lambda + \bar{r}_i$ $(i = 1, 2)$ be elements of R. Then

$$r_1 + r_2 = ((r_1, \lambda) + (r_2, \lambda))\lambda + \bar{r}_1 + \bar{r}_2$$

and

$$r_1 r_2 = (r_1, \lambda)(r_2, \lambda)\lambda + (r_1, \lambda)\bar{r}_2 + (r_2, \lambda)\bar{r}_1 + \bar{r}_1 \bar{r}_2.$$

By the formulas derived above $\bar{r}_1 + \bar{r}_2$ and $(r_1, \lambda)\bar{r}_2 + (r_2, \lambda)\bar{r}_1 + \bar{r}_1 \bar{r}_2$ belong to R (note that $(r_1, \lambda)\bar{r}_2$ and $(r_2, \lambda)\bar{r}_1$ are repeated sums) and hence also $r_1 + r_2$ and $r_1 r_2$ belong to R. $\qquad\square$

EXERCISES

1. Let $L_1, \ldots, L_k$ be regular languages forming a partition of X^* and let $r_1, \ldots, r_k$ belong to $A^{\mathrm{rat}}\langle\langle X^* \rangle\rangle$. Show that the series r defined by

$$(r, w) = (r_i, w) \qquad (w \in L_i)$$

belongs to $A^{\mathrm{rat}}\langle\langle X^* \rangle\rangle$.
Hint: Use Theorem 4.5 if A is not commutative.

2. Let L_1 and L_2 be regular languages over X and let r belong to $A^{\mathrm{rat}}\langle\langle X^*\rangle\rangle$. Define

$$(s, w) = \sum_{\substack{w_1 v w_2 = w \\ w_1 \in L_1 \\ w_2 \in L_2}} (r, v).$$

Show that $s \in A^{\mathrm{rat}}\langle\langle X^*\rangle\rangle$.

3. If $r \in \mathbb{N}^{\mathrm{rat}}\langle\langle X^*\rangle\rangle$ and $I = \{i + np \mid n \in \mathbb{N}\}$ (i and p fixed natural numbers) then the language

$$\{w \mid (r, w) \in I\}$$

is regular.

4. If $r \in \mathbb{Z}^{\mathrm{rat}}\langle\langle X^*\rangle\rangle$ and the range of r consists of finitely many natural numbers then $r \in \mathbb{N}^{\mathrm{rat}}\langle\langle X^*\rangle\rangle$.

5. Let r belong to $\mathbb{N}^{(\infty)\mathrm{rat}}\langle\langle X^*\rangle\rangle$ (see examples of II.4). Prove that the languages

$$\{w \mid (r, w) = j\} \qquad (j \in \mathbb{N})$$

and

$$\{w \mid (r, w) = \infty\}$$

are regular.
Hint: By identifying the elements of $\mathbb{N}\backslash\{0\}$ we obtain a semiring with three elements.

6. Define $h: \{x, y\}^* \to x^* \otimes y^*$ by $hx = x$, $hy = y$. Show that $r = \sum x^n \otimes y^n$ is $\mathbb{N}$-rational but $h^{-1}r$ is not. See then Theorem 4.3.

7. Prove that the series

$$r = \sum x^n y^m \otimes z^n \quad \text{and} \quad s = \sum x^m y^n \otimes z^n$$

are $\mathbb{N}$-rational but the series $r \odot s$ is not. See then Theorem 4.5.
Hint: Erase z and use exercise 4.

8. Prove that

$$\text{char supp}\left(\sum x^n y^m \otimes z^n + \sum x^m y^n \otimes z^n\right)$$

is $\mathbb{B}$-rational but not $\mathbb{N}$-rational. Compare this result with Corollary 5.4.

9. Let r be a series in $\mathbb{N}^{(\infty)}\langle\langle X^*\rangle\rangle$. Prove that $r \in \mathbb{N}^{(\infty)\mathrm{rat}}\langle\langle X^*\rangle\rangle$ iff there are a regular language L and a projection p such that

$$(r, w) = \text{card}(p^{-1}w \cap L) \qquad (w \neq \lambda).$$

Hint: Exercise 4 is useful.

II.6 Fatou properties

Consider a subsemiring A of a semiring B. B is referred to as a Fatou extension of A if, for all alphabets X, whenever the coefficients of a B-rational series over X^* lie in A then the series is A-rational. The notion of a Fatou extension can of course be defined in a much more general set-up but here we are interested only in the specific structures $A\langle\langle X^*\rangle\rangle$ and $B\langle\langle X^*\rangle\rangle$ and the property of being a rational series, associated to these structures. In the same way we will define in Chapter IV the notion of a Fatou extension associated with the property of being an algebraic series.

A field is always a Fatou extension of its subfield (Theorem 6.1), and the semiring $\mathbb{Q}_+$ is a Fatou extension of $\mathbb{N}$ (Theorem 6.3). These results rely heavily on the theory of Hankel matrices. A very important open problem is whether or not $\mathbb{R}_+$ is a Fatou extension of $\mathbb{Q}_+$.

We go now into the formal details, repeating first the basic definition.

Let A be a subsemiring of B. We say that B is a *Fatou extension* of A if

$$A\langle\langle X^*\rangle\rangle \cap B^{\mathrm{rat}}\langle\langle X^*\rangle\rangle = A^{\mathrm{rat}}\langle\langle X^*\rangle\rangle$$

for all alphabets X.

Theorem 6.1. *Let K be a subfield of the field L. Then L is a Fatou extension of K. More specifically, if r is a series of $L^{\mathrm{rat}}\langle\langle X^*\rangle\rangle \cap K\langle\langle X^*\rangle\rangle$ with rank N then r can be expressed in the form $\sum \alpha\mu w\beta w$ where $\alpha \in K^{1 \times N}$, $\mu w \in K^{N \times N}$ and $\beta \in K^{N \times 1}$.*

PROOF. Since the rank of a series r is the dimension of the vector space generated by the columns of $H(r)$ the rank of r equals N iff $H(r)$ has an $N \times N$ subdeterminant different from zero while all larger subdeterminants of $H(r)$ are equal to zero. This means that the rank of r in $L\langle\langle X^*\rangle\rangle$ is the same as its rank in $K\langle\langle X^*\rangle\rangle$. Hence the theorem is an immediate consequence of Theorem 3.3. $\quad\square$

Theorem 6.2. *Let A be a principal ideal domain which is a subring of the field L. Then L is a Fatou extension of A. More specifically if r is a series of $L^{\mathrm{rat}}\langle\langle X^*\rangle\rangle \cap A\langle\langle X^*\rangle\rangle$ with rank N then we can express r in the form $\sum \alpha\mu w\beta w$ where $\alpha \in A^{1 \times N}$, $\mu w \in A^{N \times N}$ and $\beta \in A^{N \times 1}$.*

PROOF. We need only Theorems 6.1 and 3.6. $\quad\square$

Theorem 6.3. *The semiring $\mathbb{Q}_+$ is a Fatou extension of $\mathbb{N}$.*

PROOF. Let r belong to $Q_+^{\mathrm{rat}}\langle\langle X^*\rangle\rangle \cap \mathbb{N}\langle\langle X^*\rangle\rangle$. By Theorems 6.2 and 3.1 r belongs to a finitely generated stable $\mathbb{Z}$-submodule of $\mathbb{Z}^{X^*}$. This $\mathbb{Z}$-module is also a finitely generated stable $\mathbb{N}$-semimodule (it is generated by the generators of the $\mathbb{Z}$-module together with their negatives). Denote it by S_1.

Theorem 3.1 gives also the existence of a finitely generated stable $\mathbb{Q}_+$-subsemimodule S_3 of $Q_+^{X^*}$ containing r. Let $\{G_1, \ldots, G_m\}$ be a generator set for this semimodule and define

$$S_2 = \{n_1 G_1 + \cdots + n_m G_m \mid n_i \in \mathbb{N}\}.$$

We know that $S_0 = S_1 \cap S_2$ is a finitely generated $\mathbb{N}$-subsemimodule of $\mathbb{N}^{X^*}$.

41

Denote

$$S = \{s \in S_1 \mid ns \in S_0 \text{ for a natural number } n\}.$$

It is known that S is a finitely generated $\mathbb{N}$-subsemimodule of $\mathbb{N}^{X^*}$. Because r belongs to S_1 and can be written in the form $q_1 G_1 + \cdots + q_m G_m$ where $q_i \in \mathbb{Q}_+$ the series r is an element of S.

Suppose now that $s \in S$ and $w \in X^*$. Since S_3 is stable we have elements q_{ij} of $\mathbb{Q}_+$ such that

$$wG_i = q_{i1} G_1 + \cdots + q_{im} G_m.$$

If $ns = n_1 G_1 + \cdots + n_m G_m$ and if lq_{ij} is an integer for every i and j then

$$nl(ws) = w(n_1 l G_1 + \cdots + n_m l G_m)$$

$$= (n_1 l q_{11} + \cdots + n_m l q_{m1})G_1 + \cdots + (n_1 l q_{1m} + \cdots + n_m l q_{mm})G_m.$$

This equation shows that S is also stable. The proof is now finished by using Theorem 3.1. ☐

Theorem 6.4. *Let A be a subring of $\mathbb{R}$. Then $A_+^{(\infty)}$ is a Fatou extension of A_+.*

PROOF. Let r_1 and r_2 be series of $A_+^{(\infty)}\langle\langle X^*\rangle\rangle$. The definition of $A_+^{(\infty)}$ immediately implies that the following claims are true:

if $r_1 + r_2 \in A_+\langle\langle X^*\rangle\rangle$ then $r_1, r_2 \in A_+\langle\langle X^*\rangle\rangle$;
if $r_1, r_2 \neq 0$ and $r_1 r_2 \in A_+\langle\langle X^*\rangle\rangle$ then $r_1, r_2 \in A_+\langle\langle X^*\rangle\rangle$;
if r_1 is quasiregular and $r_1^+ \in A_+\langle\langle X^*\rangle\rangle$ then $r_1 \in A_+\langle\langle X^*\rangle\rangle$.

Therefore, if $r \in A_+^{(\infty)\mathrm{rat}}\langle\langle X^*\rangle\rangle \cap A_+\langle\langle X^*\rangle\rangle$ then the initial polynomials of r must lie in $A_+\langle X\rangle$. ☐

Lemma 6.5. *Let A be an integral domain and K its quotient field. If $r \in K^{\mathrm{rat}}\langle\langle X^*\rangle\rangle$ then there is a nonzero element a of A such that*

$$\sum (r, w)a^{1 + \lg w}w \in A^{\mathrm{rat}}\langle\langle X^*\rangle\rangle.$$

PROOF. Write r in the form $(r, \lambda)\lambda + \sum (\mu w)_{1, m}w$ and choose a nonzero element a of A such that $a(r, \lambda) \in A$ and $a\mu x \in A^{m \times m}$ $(x \in X)$. Defining now $\chi x = a\mu x$ we obtain

$$\sum (r, w)a^{1 + \lg w}w = a(r, \lambda)\lambda + a \sum (\chi w)_{1, m}w. \qquad \square$$

Lemma 6.6. *Assume that A is a subring of the commutative ring B and B is a finitely generated A-module. If $r \in B^{\mathrm{rat}}\langle\langle X^*\rangle\rangle$ and $\{\theta_1, \ldots, \theta_k\}$ is a set of generators for B then we can express r in the form $\theta_1 r_1 + \cdots + \theta_k r_k$ where $r_i \in A^{\mathrm{rat}}\langle\langle X^*\rangle\rangle$.*

PROOF. Let $Z = P + QZ$ be the linear system given by Theorem 1.4 and write

$$P = \theta_1 P_1 + \cdots + \theta_k P_k,$$
$$Q = \theta_1 Q_1 + \cdots + \theta_k Q_k,$$
$$\theta_i \theta_j = \sum_l a_{ijl} \theta_l.$$

Consider now the linear system

$$\begin{pmatrix} Z_1 \\ \vdots \\ Z_k \end{pmatrix} = \begin{pmatrix} P_1 \\ \vdots \\ P_k \end{pmatrix} + \begin{pmatrix} Q'_{11} & \cdots & Q'_{1k} \\ \vdots & & \vdots \\ Q'_{k1} & \cdots & Q'_{kk} \end{pmatrix} \begin{pmatrix} Z_1 \\ \vdots \\ Z_k \end{pmatrix}$$

where $Q'_{ij} = \sum_i a_{ijl} Q_i$. If $(S_1, \ldots, S_k)^{\mathrm{T}}$ is the solution of this system then

$$\sum_l \theta_l S_l = \sum_l \theta_l P_l + \sum_i \theta_i \sum_j Q'_{ij} S_j$$

$$= \sum_l \theta_l P_l + \sum_{i,j} \left(\sum_l a_{ijl} \theta_l \right) Q_i S_j$$

$$= \sum_l \theta_l P_l + \sum_{i,j} (\theta_i Q_i)(\theta_j S_j) = P + Q \left(\sum_l \theta_l S_l \right).$$

Hence we have $r = \sum_l \theta_l r_l$ where r_l is the first component of S_l. $\qquad \square$

EXERCISES

1. Assume that $r \in \mathbb{N}^{\mathrm{rat}}\langle\langle X^* \rangle\rangle$, $s \in \mathbb{N}^{\mathrm{rat}}\langle\langle X^* \rangle\rangle$, s has positive coefficients and the rank of s in $\mathbb{Q}^{\mathrm{rat}}\langle\langle X^* \rangle\rangle$ is equal to one. Show that if the series

$$\sum \frac{(r, w)}{(s, w)} w$$

has integer coefficients then it belongs to $\mathbb{N}^{\mathrm{rat}}\langle\langle X^* \rangle\rangle$.

2. Let A be a Noetherian integral domain and let K be its quotient field. Show that K is a Fatou extension of A.
   Hint: See exercise 8 of II.3.

3. Make the assumptions of Lemma 6.6 and show that r can be expressed in the form $\sum \alpha \mu w \beta w$ where $\mu w \in A^{m \times m}$.

II.7 On rational series with real coefficients

We now consider rational series with real coefficients over a free monoid. Using the matrix representation, we first derive (Theorem 7.1) for the absolute values $|(r, w)|$ of the coefficients an upper bound exponential with respect to the length of w. In case of $\mathbb{Q}$-rational series, a positive lower bound exponential with respect to the length of w can be obtained for the absolute values of nonzero coefficients (Theorem 7.3). Corollary 7.5 (which remains valid for

$\mathbb{C}$ instead of $\mathbb{R}$) can be viewed to express a Fatou property. Lemma 7.7 is a "pumping lemma" for $\mathbb{R}$-rational series.

We would like to point out that very little is known about the distribution of coefficients in a $\mathbb{Z}$-rational (or even in an $\mathbb{N}$-rational) series. Strange phenomena like those exemplified in exercise 7.7 may occur.

Theorem 7.1. *If $r \in \mathbb{R}^{\text{rat}}\langle\langle X^*\rangle\rangle$ then there is a positive constant M such that*

$$|(r, w)| \le M^{1 + \lg w}.$$

PROOF. Write r in the form

$$(r, \lambda)\lambda + \sum (\mu w)_{1, m} w$$

and denote

$$M_\mu = \max_{\substack{x \in X \\ 1 \le i, j \le m}} |(\mu x)_{ij}|.$$

Because

$$\max_{i, j} |(\mu w)_{ij}| \le m^{\lg w - 1} M^{\lg w} \qquad (w \ne \lambda)$$

we have $|(r, w)| \le (m M_\mu)^{\lg w}$ for every nonempty word w. Hence we may choose

$$M = \max\{|(r, \lambda)|, m M_\mu, 1\}. \qquad \square$$

Corollary 7.2. *If $r \in \mathbb{R}^{\text{rat}}\langle\langle X^*\rangle\rangle$ then there is a positive number A such that the family*

$$\{(r, w)/A^{1 + \lg w}\}$$

is absolutely summable.

PROOF. If $|(r, w)| \le M^{1 + \lg w}$ and if C is the cardinality of X then we may choose $A = 2CM$. $\qquad \square$

Theorem 7.3. *If $r \in \mathbb{Q}^{\text{rat}}\langle\langle X^*\rangle\rangle$ then there is a positive number q such that for any word w we have either $(r, w) = 0$ or $|(r, w)| > q^{1 + \lg w}$.*

PROOF. Lemma 6.5 gives us a natural number a $(a \ne 0)$ such that

$$\sum (r, w)a^{1 + \lg w}w \in \mathbb{Z}^{\text{rat}}\langle\langle X^*\rangle\rangle.$$

Therefore we have always either $(r, w) = 0$ or $|(r, w)| > \frac{1}{2}a^{-1 - \lg w} \ge (2a)^{-1 - \lg w}$.

Lemma 7.4. *Assume that K and L are subfields of $\mathbb{R}$, $K \subseteq L$ and all elements of L are algebraic over K. If $r \in L^{\text{rat}}\langle\langle X^*\rangle\rangle$ then we can write $r = r_0 + \theta r_1 + \cdots + \theta^{k-1} r_{k-1}$ where $r_i \in K^{\text{rat}}\langle\langle X^*\rangle\rangle$ and θ is an element of L with degree k.*

PROOF. Write $r = \sum \alpha \mu w \beta w$ and let K_r be the extension of K generated by the entries of α, β and the matrices μx $(x \in X)$. We know that K_r is defined by a single element which is algebraic over K. If k is the degree of θ then the numbers $1, \theta, \ldots, \theta^{k-1}$ form a basis of K_r considered as a vector space over K. Because $r \in K_r^{\text{rat}}\langle\langle X^* \rangle\rangle$ Lemma 7.4 is a direct consequence of Lemma 6.6. $\square$

Corollary 7.5. *Let L be a subfield of $\mathbb{R}$ whose elements are algebraic (over $\mathbb{Q}$). If $r \in L^{\text{rat}}\langle\langle X^* \rangle\rangle$ then there is a series s of $L^{\text{rat}}\langle\langle X^* \rangle\rangle$ such that $r \odot s \in \mathbb{Q}^{\text{rat}}\langle\langle X^* \rangle\rangle$ and $(r, w) = 0$ iff $(s, w) = 0$. Further, there is a positive number q such that we have always either $(r, w) = 0$ or $|(r, w)| > q^{1 + \lg w}$.*

PROOF. Write $r = r_0 + \theta r_1 + \cdots + \theta^{k-1} r_{k-1}$ and define

$$s = \bigodot_{i=2}^{k} (r_0 + \theta_i r_1 + \cdots + \theta_i^{k-1} r_{k-1})$$

where $\theta_1 = \theta$, $\theta_2, \ldots, \theta_k$ are the conjugates of θ. This definition of s immediately implies that $(r, w) = 0$ iff $(s, w) = 0$. The series s and $r \odot s$ are $\mathbb{R}$-rational by Theorem 4.4. But the coefficients of $r \odot s$ belong to $\mathbb{Q}$ because they are symmetric in $\theta_1, \ldots, \theta_k$. Therefore we may use Theorem 6.1 and conclude that $r \odot s$ is $\mathbb{Q}$-rational.

If w is a word such that $(r, w) \neq 0$ then $(s, w) = (r \odot s, w)/(r, w)$ and $(r, w) = (r \odot s, w)/(s, w)$. The first of these equations shows that s belongs to $L\langle\langle X^* \rangle\rangle$. Hence we may again apply Theorem 6.1 and conclude that s belongs to $L^{\text{rat}}\langle\langle X^* \rangle\rangle$. The second equation together with Theorems 7.3 and 7.1 gives us a number q with the desired properties. $\square$

Lemma 7.6. *If $r = \sum \alpha \mu w \beta w \in K^{\text{rat}}\langle\langle X^* \rangle\rangle$ where K is a field, $v \in X^*$ and if*

$$t^m - c_{m-1} t^{m-1} - \cdots - c_0 \text{ is the minimal polynomial of } \mu v \text{ then}$$

$$(r, w_1 v^m w_2) = c_{m-1}(r, w_1 v^{m-1} w_2) + \cdots + c_0(r, w_1 w_2)$$

for all words w_1 and w_2.

This lemma is an immediate consequence of the definition of a minimal polynomial.

Lemma 7.7. *Let r be a series of $\mathbb{R}^{\text{rat}}\langle\langle X^* \rangle\rangle$. Then there is a natural number k with the following property: if $(r, w) \neq 0$ and $\lg w \geq k$ then w has a factorization $w_1 v w_2$ where $v \neq \lambda$ and $(r, w_1 v^n w_2) \neq 0$ infinitely many times.*

PROOF. Let r be written in the form $\sum \alpha \mu w \beta w$. According to a theorem of Jacob [Ja1] we have a natural number k with the following property: if $\lg w \geq k$ and $\mu w \neq 0$ then $w = w_1 v w_2$ where $v \neq \lambda$ and μv is pseudo-regular.

Next we utilize Lemma 7.6. Because μv is pseudo-regular the number c_0 cannot be zero (if $\mu v = M^{-1}(\begin{smallmatrix} 0 & 0 \\ 0 & 0 \end{smallmatrix})M$ then the minimal polynomial of μv is a factor of the characteristic polynomial of χ). This implies the existence of a recursion formula

$$(r, w_1v^n w_2) = d_1(r, w_1v^n vw_1) + \cdots + d_m(r, w_1v^n v^m w_2)$$

which is valid for all natural numbers n.

Suppose now that $\lg w \geq k$ and $(r, w) \neq 0$. Then $\mu w \neq 0$. If v is the word given by Jacob's theorem then the above recursion formula implies that if $(r, w_1v^n w_2) = 0$ for every large n then $(r, w_1v^n w_2) = 0$ for every n. Hence v has the desired property. $\qquad\square$

EXERCISES

1. If $r \in \mathbb{Q}^{\text{rat}}\langle\langle X^* \rangle\rangle$ then there is a positive number q such that we have always either $(r, w_1) = (r, w_2)$ or $|(r, w_1) - (r, w_2)| > q^{1 + \max\{\lg w_1, \lg w_2\}}$.

2. Given a sequence $(\varepsilon(n))$ of positive numbers there is an $\mathbb{R}$-rational series $\sum r_n t^n$ such that $0 < r_n < \varepsilon(n)$ infinitely often.
   Hint: Define $R_n = \sin 2\pi n\alpha = (1/2i)(e^{2\pi in\alpha} - e^{-2\pi in\alpha})$ where $\alpha = a_1/2 + a_2/2^2 + \cdots$ ($a_i = 0, 1$) and the sequence (a_i) has long subsequences consisting of zeroes.

3. If $\sum r_n t^n \in \mathbb{Q}^{\text{rat}}\langle\langle t^* \rangle\rangle$, $\sum s_n t^n \in \mathbb{Z}\langle\langle t^* \rangle\rangle$ and $\lim(r_n - s_n) = 0$ then $\sum s_n t^n \in \mathbb{Z}^{\text{rat}}\langle\langle t^* \rangle\rangle$.
   Hint: The numbers r_n satisfy a recursion formula with rational coefficients and the numbers s_n satisfy this same formula from a point on.

4. Let r be a series of $\mathbb{R}^{\text{rat}}\langle\langle X^* \rangle\rangle$ with rank N and let s be a series of $\mathbb{R}^{\text{rat}}\langle\langle t^* \rangle\rangle$ with rank M. Show that if u_1, u_2 and v are words of X^* and if $(r, u_1v^n u_2) = (s, t^n)$ when $n = 0, \ldots, N + M - 1$ then $(r, u_1v^n u_2) = (s, t^n)$ identically.
   Hint: Lemma 7.6.

5. Show that $\sum nx^n y^m$ and $\sum mx^n y^m$ are $\mathbb{N}$-rational but $\sum \max\{n, m\}x^n y^m$ and $\sum |n - m|x^n y^m$ are not even $\mathbb{Z}$-rational.

6. Show that $L = \{x^n y^{nm}\}$ is neither the support nor the complement of the support of an $\mathbb{R}$-rational series.
   Hint: Only Lemma 7.6 is needed.

7. The behavior of the coefficients of a series $r \in \mathbb{Z}^{\text{rat}}\langle\langle X^* \rangle\rangle$ may be very odd as one may see by considering the series

$$\sum_{\substack{n+m+l+k \equiv 0 \\ (\text{mod } 4)}} \left((n + m + l + k)\left((n^2 - n - m)^2 \right.\right.$$

$$\left.\left. + \left(n + m - \frac{n + m + l + k}{4} - l\right)^2\right) + n\right)x^n y^m z^l w^k$$

and

$$\sum ((n + m)(2^n - n - m)^2 + n)x^n y^m.$$

Construct further examples.

II.8 On positive series

For a subring A of $\mathbb{R}$, we denote by A_+ the semiring consisting of all non-negative numbers in A. It may happen that a series in $A^{\mathrm{rat}}\langle\langle X^*\rangle\rangle$ has coefficients in A_+ but does not belong to $A_+^{\mathrm{rat}}\langle\langle X^*\rangle\rangle$. Those series of $A^{\mathrm{rat}}\langle\langle X^*\rangle\rangle$ which belong to $A_+^{\mathrm{rat}}\langle\langle X^*\rangle\rangle$ are called *positive*. Thus, the family $\mathbb{N}^{\mathrm{rat}}\langle\langle X^*\rangle\rangle$ is the family of positive series in $\mathbb{Z}^{\mathrm{rat}}\langle\langle X^*\rangle\rangle$. The results in this section are generalizations of the basic situation involving $\mathbb{Z}$ and $\mathbb{N}$.

Every A-rational series can be expressed as the difference of two A_+-rational series (Corollary 8.2). If the absolute values of the coefficients of an A-rational series can be majorized in a certain strict sense by the coefficients of a positive series, then the sum of the two series is positive (Theorem 8.4). A corollary of this result is that if the coefficients of a $\mathbb{Z}$-rational series s satisfy

$$|(s, w)| \le k^{\lg w} < K^{\lg w},$$

where K is a natural number, then the series

$$\sum (K^{\lg w} + (s, w))w$$

is $\mathbb{N}$-rational. Results of this nature, showing how a $\mathbb{Z}$-rational series can be transformed into an $\mathbb{N}$-rational one by adding a suitable dominating term to the coefficients, are very useful in certain applications, for instance, in constructions involving length sequences generated by L systems.

We also prove (Theorem 8.6) that if the number 1 is subtracted from the coefficients of an $\mathbb{N}$-rational series, the resulting series is still $\mathbb{N}$-rational (providing of course that all coefficients in the original series are positive). Corollary 8.7 could be extended to concern $\mathbb{R}_+$-rational series, by applying the method of Theorem 8.6 to the difference

$$r - \sum q^{-1-\lg w}.$$

If A is a subring of $\mathbb{R}$ then $A_+ = A \cap [0, \infty)$ is a semiring. Those series of $A^{\mathrm{rat}}\langle\langle X^*\rangle\rangle$ which belong to $A_+^{\mathrm{rat}}\langle\langle X^*\rangle\rangle$ are called *positive*.

Lemma 8.1. *Let A be a subring of $\mathbb{R}$ and let $r = \sum \alpha\mu w(1\,0\cdots 0)^{\mathrm{T}}w$ be a series of $A^{\mathrm{rat}}\langle\langle X^*\rangle\rangle$. Write $\alpha = \alpha_1 - \alpha_2$ and $\mu x = \mu_1 x - \mu_2 x \ (x \in X)$ where the entries of $\alpha_1, \alpha_2, \mu_1 x$ and $\mu_2 x$ belong to A_+. If now*

$$\gamma = (\alpha_1, \alpha_2)$$

and

$$\chi x = \begin{pmatrix} \mu_1 x & \mu_2 x \\ \mu_2 x & \mu_1 x \end{pmatrix}$$

then

$$r = \sum \gamma\chi w(1\,0\cdots 0; 0\cdots 0)^{\mathrm{T}}w - \sum \gamma\chi w(0\cdots 0; 1\,0\cdots 0)^{\mathrm{T}}w.$$

PROOF. We show that if

$$\gamma \chi w = (\gamma_1(w), \gamma_2(w))$$

then $\gamma_1(w) - \gamma_2(w) = \alpha \mu w$.

Assume that this assertion holds true for a word w and let x be a letter of X. Then

$$\gamma_1(wx) - \gamma_2(wx) = \gamma_1(w)\mu_1 x + \gamma_2(w)\mu_2(x) - \gamma_1(w)\mu_2 x - \gamma_2(w)\mu_1 x$$

$$= (\gamma_1(w) - \gamma_2(w))(\mu_1 x - \mu_2 x) = \alpha \mu w \mu x = \alpha \mu w x.$$

Because the assertion is true when $w = \lambda$ the equation just obtained implies that it is identically true. □

Corollary 8.2. *If A is a subring of $\mathbb{R}$ then every series of $A^{\mathrm{rat}}\langle\langle X^*\rangle\rangle$ is the difference of two series of $A_+^{\mathrm{rat}}\langle\langle X^*\rangle\rangle$.*

PROOF. If $r = \sum \alpha \mu w \beta w$ is a series of $A^{\mathrm{rat}}\langle\langle X^*\rangle\rangle$ and if we denote

$$\bar{\alpha} = ((r, \lambda), \alpha)$$

and

$$\bar{\mu}w = \begin{pmatrix} 0 & 0 \\ \mu w \beta & \mu w \end{pmatrix}$$

then $r = \sum \bar{\alpha}\bar{\mu}w(1\ 0 \cdots 0)^{\mathrm{T}}w$. Thus we may use Lemma 8.1. □

Lemma 8.3. *Let $r_1 = \sum \alpha_1 \mu_1 w \beta_1 w$ and $r_2 = \sum \alpha_2 \mu_2 w \beta_2 w$ be A_+-rational series ($\mu_i w \in A_+^{m_i \times m_i}$). Define*

$$g = \frac{2}{(\beta_1)_1 + \cdots + (\beta_1)_{m_1}},$$

$$\alpha = (\alpha_1 - g\alpha_2\beta_2(1 \cdots 1); \alpha_2),$$

$$\mu x = \begin{pmatrix} \mu_1 x & 0 \\ \chi x & \mu_2 x \end{pmatrix}$$

where

$$(\chi x)_{ij} = ((\mu_1 x)_{1j} + \cdots + (\mu_1 x)_{m_1 j})g(\beta_2)_i$$

$$- g(\beta_2)_1(\mu_2 x)_{i1} - \cdots - g(\beta_2)_{m_2}(\mu_2 x)_{im_2}$$

and

$$\beta = (\beta_1, \beta_2)^{\mathrm{T}}.$$

Then we have $\alpha \mu w \beta = (r_1, w) - (r_2, w)$.

PROOF. We claim that

$$\alpha \mu w = (\alpha_1 \mu_1 w - g\alpha_2 \mu_2 w \beta_2(1 \cdots 1); \alpha_2 \mu_2 w).$$

Assume that the equation mentioned is valid for a word w. If now $x \in X$ then

$$\alpha\mu wx = (\alpha_1\mu_1 w\mu_1 x - g\alpha_2\mu_2 w\beta_2(1 \cdots 1)\mu_1 x + \alpha_2\mu_2 w\chi x; \alpha_2\mu_2 w\mu_2 x).$$

Because the jth component of $-g\alpha_2\mu_2 w\beta_2(1 \cdots 1)\mu_1 x + \alpha_2\mu_2 w\chi x$ equals

$$-g\alpha_2\mu_2 w\beta_2((\mu_1 x)_{1j} + \cdots + (\mu_1 x)_{m_1 j})$$
$$+ ((\mu_1 x)_{1j} + \cdots + (\mu_1 x)_{m_1 j})g\alpha_2\mu_2 w\beta_2$$
$$- g(\beta_2)_1(\alpha_2\mu_2 w\mu_2 x)_1 - \cdots - g(\beta_2)_{m_2}(\alpha_2\mu_2 w\mu_2 x)_{m_2} = g\alpha_2\mu_2 w x\beta_2$$

we have

$$\alpha\mu wx = (\alpha_1\mu_1 wx - g\alpha_2\mu_2 wx\beta_2(1 \cdots 1); \alpha_2\mu_2 wx).$$

The above immediately implies that the equation is identically true. Hence

$$\alpha\mu w\beta = \alpha_1\mu_1 w\beta_1 - g\alpha_2\mu_2 w\beta_2((\beta_1)_1 + \cdots + (\beta_1)_{m_1}) + \alpha_2\mu_2 w\beta_2$$
$$= \alpha_1\mu_1 w\beta_1 - \alpha_2\mu_2 w\beta_2. \qquad \square$$

Theorem 8.4. *Let A be a subfield of $\mathbb{R}$ and let $r = \sum \alpha\mu w\beta w$ be a series of $A_+^{\mathrm{rat}}\langle\langle X^* \rangle\rangle$ where the matrices μw have positive entries. If s is a series of $A^{\mathrm{rat}}\langle\langle X^* \rangle\rangle$ such that $r + s \in A_+\langle\langle X^* \rangle\rangle$ and*

$$|(s, w)| \le d_1^{\lg w} < d_2^{\lg w} \le (r, w)$$

for all long words w then $r + s \in A_+^{\mathrm{rat}}\langle\langle X^* \rangle\rangle$.

PROOF. Since the entries of the μw's are positive we can find a positive constant C_2 such that

$$\min(\mu w)_{ij} \ge C_2 d_2^{\lg w}$$

for all long words w.

If $s = \sum \gamma\chi w\delta w$ where χ is a minimal representation then Theorem 3.5 and formula (2) of II.3 imply the existence of a positive constant C_1 such that

$$\max|(\chi w)_{ij}| \le C_1 d_1^{\lg w}.$$

We may assume that $\delta = (1\ 0 \cdots 0)^{\mathrm{T}}$ (this situation is reached by replacing χw with $U\chi w U^{-1}$ where $U\delta = (1\ 0 \cdots 0)^{\mathrm{T}}$).

For any natural number n we define X_n to be the alphabet consisting of those words of X^* whose length is n. Next we introduce the series

$$\bar{r}_{n,v} = \sum (\alpha\mu v)\bar{\mu} w\beta w \in A_+^{\mathrm{rat}}\langle\langle X_n^* \rangle\rangle$$

and

$$\bar{s}_{n,v} = \sum (\gamma\chi v)\bar{\chi} w\delta w \in A^{\mathrm{rat}}\langle\langle X_n^* \rangle\rangle$$

where $v \in X^*$, $\bar{\mu}\bar{x} = \mu\bar{x}$ and $\bar{\chi}\bar{x} = \chi\bar{x}$ ($\bar{x} \in X_n$). If $h: X_n^* \to X^*$ is the natural homomorphism then

$$r + s = p_n + \sum_{n \le \lg v < 2n} vh(\bar{r}_{n,v} + \bar{s}_{n,v})$$

where $p_n \in A_+\langle X^* \rangle$. Thus we have only to prove that all the series $\bar{r}_{n,v} + \bar{s}_{n,v}$ where $n \leq \lg v < 2n$ are A_+-rational when n is very large.

The inequalities given in the beginning of this proof imply that

$$\min(\bar{\mu}\bar{x})_{ij} \geq C_2 d_2^n,$$

$$\min(\alpha\mu v)_i \geq C_3 d_2^{\lg v},$$

$$\max|(\bar{\chi}\bar{x})_{ij}| \leq C_1 d_1^n$$

and

$$\max|(\gamma\chi v)_i| \leq C_0 d_1^{\lg v}.$$

Applying Lemma 8.1 we obtain two A_+-rational series $\bar{s}_1 = \sum \gamma_0 \chi_0 w \delta_1 w$ and $\bar{s}_2 = \sum \gamma_0 \chi_0 w \delta_2 w$ such that $\bar{s}_{n,v} = \bar{s}_1 - \bar{s}_2$ and the inequalities

$$\max(\chi_0 \bar{x})_{ij} \leq C_1 d_1^n$$

and

$$\max(\gamma_0)_i \leq C_0 d_1^{\lg v}$$

hold. If we denote

$$\bar{s}_3 = \sum \gamma_0 \chi_0 w (1 \cdots 1)^T w$$

and

$$\bar{s}_4 = \sum \gamma_0 \chi_0 w (1 \cdots 1\ 0\ 1 \cdots 1)^T w$$

then

$$\bar{r}_{n,v} + \bar{s}_{n,v} = (\bar{s}_1 + \bar{s}_4) + (\bar{r}_{n,v} - \bar{s}_3).$$

Hence we have to consider $\bar{r}_{n,v} - \bar{s}_3$.

We write $\bar{r}_{n,v} = \sum \alpha_1 \mu_1 w \beta_1 w$ and $\bar{s}_3 = \sum \alpha_2 \mu_2 w \beta_2 w$ where

$$\alpha_1 = \alpha\mu v, \qquad \mu_1 = \bar{\mu}, \qquad \beta_1 = \beta,$$

$$\alpha_2 = \gamma_0, \qquad \mu_2 = \chi_0, \qquad \beta_2 = (1 \cdots 1)^T.$$

We have shown above that

$$\min(\mu_1 \bar{x})_{ij} \geq C_2 d_2^n,$$

$$\min(\alpha_1)_i \geq C_3 d_2^{\lg v},$$

$$\max(\mu_2 \bar{x})_{ij} \leq C_1 d_1^n$$

and

$$\max(\alpha_2)_i \leq C_0 d_1^{\lg v}.$$

It is now easy to see that if n is very large then the vector α and the matrices μx appearing in Lemma 8.3 have nonnegative entries. $\qquad \square$

Corollary 8.5. *Let K be a natural number and let s be a series of $\mathbb{Z}^{\mathrm{rat}}\langle\langle X^* \rangle\rangle$ such that*

$$|(s, w)| \leq k^{\lg w} < K^{\lg w}$$

when lg *w is large. Then the series S obtained by replacing all negative coefficients of* $\sum (K^{\lg w} + (s, w))w$ *with zeroes is* N-*rational.*

PROOF. By modifying finitely many coefficients in *s* we may assume that $S = \sum (K^{\lg w} + (s, w))w$. Applying now Theorems 8.4 and 6.3 we see that S is N-rational. $\qquad\square$

Theorem 8.6. *Let r be a series of* $\mathbb{N}^{\text{rat}}\langle\langle X^* \rangle\rangle$ *and assume that* (r, w) *is never zero. Then the series* $\sum ((r, w) - 1)w$ *is* N-*rational.*

PROOF. We express *r* in the form $\sum \alpha\mu w(1\ 0 \cdots 0)^{\mathrm{T}}w$ (see Corollary 8.2). For any vector *v* we introduce a vector v_B as follows:

$$(v_B)_i = 1 \quad \text{if } v_i \neq 0,$$

$$(v_B)_i = 0 \quad \text{otherwise.}$$

Let $V_1, \ldots, V_M$ be all the different vectors $(\alpha\mu w)_B$.

Define now

$$\bar{\alpha} = (\gamma; \delta)$$

and

$$\bar{\mu}x = \begin{pmatrix} \mu x & 0 \\ \eta x & \chi x \end{pmatrix}$$

where

$$\gamma_i = \alpha_i - 1 \quad \text{if } \alpha_i > 0,$$

$$\gamma_i = 0 \quad \text{otherwise,}$$

$$\delta_i = 1 \quad \text{if } (\alpha)_B = V_i,$$

$$\delta_i = 0 \quad \text{otherwise}$$

and

$$(\chi x)_{ij} = 1 \quad \text{if } (V_i\mu x)_B = V_j,$$

$$(\chi x)_{ij} = 0 \quad \text{otherwise,}$$

$$(\eta x)_{ij} = (V_i\mu x)_j - 1 \quad \text{if } (V_i\mu x)_j > 0$$

$$(\eta x)_{ij} = 0 \quad \text{otherwise.}$$

We claim that the components of

$$\bar{\alpha}\bar{\mu}w = (\gamma(w); \delta(w))$$

are the following:

$$\gamma(w)_i = (\alpha\mu w)_i - 1 \quad \text{if } (\alpha\mu w)_i > 0,$$

$$\gamma(w)_i = 0 \quad \text{otherwise,}$$

$$\delta(w)_i = 1 \quad \text{if } (\alpha\mu w)_B = V_i,$$

$$\delta(w)_i = 0 \quad \text{otherwise.}$$

Assume that this has been proved for a word w and let x be a letter. Then

$$\gamma(wx)_j = \sum_i \gamma(w)_i(\mu x)_{ij} + \sum_i \delta(w)_i(\eta x)_{ij}$$

$$= [(\alpha\mu w\mu x)_j - ((\alpha\mu w)_B\mu x)_j] + ((\alpha\mu w)_B\mu x)_j - 1$$

$$= (\alpha\mu wx)_j - 1 \quad \text{if } ((\alpha\mu w)_B\mu x)_j > 0$$

and

$$\gamma(wx)_j = [(\alpha\mu w\mu x)_j - ((\alpha\mu w)_B\mu x)_j] + 0$$

$$= (\alpha\mu wx)_j = 0 \quad \text{if } ((\alpha\mu w)_B\mu x)_j = 0.$$

Further,

$$\delta(wx)_j = \sum_i \delta(w)_i(\chi x)_{ij} = 1 \quad \text{if } ((\alpha\mu w)_B\mu x)_B = V_j$$

and

$$\delta(wx)_j = 0 \quad \text{otherwise.}$$

Obviously we have $((\alpha\mu w)_B\mu x)_B = (\alpha\mu wx)_B$. Therefore our claim holds true for the word wx.

It is seen now that

$$\sum ((r, w) - 1)w = \sum \overline{\alpha\mu}w(1\ 0\cdots 0)^{\mathsf{T}}w. \qquad \square$$

Corollary 8.7. *Let r be a series of $\mathbb{Q}_+^{\text{rat}}\langle\langle X^*\rangle\rangle$ such that (r, w) is never zero. Then there is a positive number d with the following property: if $s \in \mathbb{Q}^{\text{rat}}\langle\langle X^*\rangle\rangle$ and $|(s, w)| \le d^{1+\lg w}$ then $r + s \in \mathbb{Q}_+^{\text{rat}}\langle\langle X^*\rangle\rangle$.*

PROOF. Lemma 6.5 gives a positive integer q such that $\sum q^{1+\lg w}(r, w)w \in \mathbb{N}^{\text{rat}}\langle\langle X^*\rangle\rangle$. Using now Theorem 8.6 we see that the series

$$r - \sum q^{-1-\lg w} = \sum q^{-1-\lg w}w \odot \sum (q^{1+\lg w}(r, w) - 1)w$$

is $\mathbb{Q}_+$-rational. Further, if $|(s, w)| \le (2q)^{-1-\lg w}$ then

$$\sum q^{-1-\lg w}w + s$$

is a $\mathbb{Q}_+$-rational series by Theorem 8.4. Hence we may choose $d = 1/2q$. $\quad\square$

EXERCISES

1. Show that if $P: \mathbb{N} \to \mathbb{N}$ is a polynomial then the series $\sum P(n)t^n$ is $\mathbb{N}$-rational. Hint: It suffices to show that for a natural number k the series

$$\sum_{n \ge k} (P(n) - P(n - 1))t^n$$

is $\mathbb{N}$-rational.

2. Prove that $\sum (n - m)^2 x^n y^m$ is not $\mathbb{N}$-rational.

3. Assume that $r \in \mathbb{N}^{\mathrm{rat}}\langle\langle X^* \rangle\rangle$, $s \in \mathbb{Z}^{\mathrm{rat}}\langle\langle X^* \rangle\rangle$ and (r, w) is never zero. Prove that for every large natural number K we have

$$\sum (K^{1 + \lg w}(r, w) + (s, w))w \in \mathbb{N}^{\mathrm{rat}}\langle\langle X^* \rangle\rangle.$$

4. Define

$$n_1 \overset{\cdot}{-} n_2 = n_1 - n_2 \quad \text{if } n_1 \geqslant n_2,$$

$$n_1 \overset{\cdot}{-} n_2 = 0 \quad \text{otherwise.}$$

Prove that if $r \in \mathbb{N}^{\mathrm{rat}}\langle\langle X^* \rangle\rangle$ and L is a regular language then

$$\sum ((r, w) \overset{\cdot}{-} (\mathrm{char}\, L, w))w \in \mathbb{N}^{\mathrm{rat}}\langle\langle X^* \rangle\rangle.$$

II.9 Rational sequences

A series over a one-letter alphabet, i.e., belonging to $A\langle\langle x^* \rangle\rangle$ can be identified in a natural way with a sequence of elements of A. Such sequences will be discussed in the present and in the following section. We assume in this section that A is a commutative ring. Of course, the monoid x^* is also commutative, as is necessary in considerations concerning generating functions. A reader familiar with the theory of linear difference equations will notice in this section many similarities.

This section deals most with generating functions. We draw the reader's attention to the following points. Corollary 9.3 shows the interconnection between A-rational series and functions rational in the sense of classical analysis. Theorem 9.5 establishes another Fatou property. The fundamental characterization result for A-rational sequences is given in Theorem 9.8—this result will be useful in many connections. The same holds true with respect to the so-called Skolem–Mahler–Lech Theorem, Lemma 9.10. Its proof lies, however, beyond the scope of this book.

Let A be a commutative ring. A sequence (r_n) of elements of A is called *A-rational* iff the series $\sum r_n x^n$ belongs to $A^{\mathrm{rat}}\langle\langle x^* \rangle\rangle$.

If p and q are polynomials in $A\langle x^* \rangle$ and if $r = \sum r_n x^n$ is a series in $A\langle\langle x^* \rangle\rangle$ then we say that the formal rational function $p(x)/q(x)$ is a *generating function* of the series r, or the sequence (r_n), if $p = qr$.

Theorem 9.1. *Let A be a commutative ring. If r is a series of $A^{\mathrm{rat}}\langle\langle x^* \rangle\rangle$ then r has a generating function*

(1)
$$\frac{p(x)}{1 - q(x)}$$

where $p, q \in A\langle x^* \rangle$ and q is quasiregular. On the other hand, any series of $A\langle\langle x^* \rangle\rangle$, which has a generating function of the form (1), belongs to $A^{\mathrm{rat}}\langle\langle x^* \rangle\rangle$.

PROOF. Suppose that the series r_i has a generating function $p_i(x)/(1 - q_i(x))$ $(i = 1, 2)$. Then an easy calculation shows that

$$\frac{p_1(x) + p_2(x) - p_1(x)q_2(x) - p_2(x)q_1(x)}{1 - (q_1(x) + q_2(x) - q_1(x)q_2(x))}$$

is a generating function of $r_1 + r_2$ and

$$\frac{p_1(x)p_2(x)}{1 - (q_1(x) + q_2(x) - q_1(x)q_2(x))}$$

is a generating function of $r_1 r_2$. Suppose next that the series r is quasiregular and has a generating function $p(x)/(1 - q(x))$. Then we have

$$(1 - q - p)r^+ = ((1 - q) - p)r(1 + r^+) = (p - pr)(1 + r^+)$$
$$= p(1 + r^+ - r - rr^+) = p(1 + r^+ - r^+) = p$$

and hence

$$\frac{p(x)}{1 - (q(x) + p(x))}$$

is a generating function of r^+ (note that p is now quasiregular).

We have seen that the family of those series of $A\langle\langle x^*\rangle\rangle$ which have a generating function of the form (1) is rationally closed. This immediately implies the first assertion of the theorem.

If the series r has a generating function $p(x)/(1 - q(x))$ then $r = p + qr$. This equation implies that $r = (1 + q^+)p$ is A-rational. ☐

Corollary 9.2. *Let A be a commutative ring and let (r_n) be a sequence of elements of A. Then (r_n) is A-rational iff for large values of n a recursion formula*

$$r_n = q_1 r_{n-1} + \cdots + q_k r_{n-k} \qquad (q_i \in A)$$

holds.

PROOF. If (r_n) is A-rational then it has a generating function

$$\frac{p_0 + p_1 x + \cdots + p_l x^l}{1 - (q_1 x + \cdots + q_k x^k)}$$

and this immediately implies that $r_n - q_1 r_{n-1} - \cdots - q_k r_{n-k} = 0$ when $n > 1$.

Conversely, if the recursion formula mentioned holds when $n > 1$ then $(1 - q_1 x - \cdots - q_k x^k) \sum r_n x^n$ is a polynomial whose degree does not exceed 1 and hence r has a generating function of the form (1). ☐

Corollary 9.3. *Let A be a subring of $\mathbb{C}$ (the field of complex numbers). Then a series r of $A\langle\langle x^*\rangle\rangle$ is A-rational iff it is the Maclaurin expansion of a rational function*

$$\frac{p(x)}{1 - q(x)}$$

where p and q are polynomials with coefficients in A and $q(0) = 0$.

Lemma 9.4. *Let K be an integral domain and let r be a series of $K^{\mathrm{rat}}\langle\langle x^*\rangle\rangle$.*

(i) *If $p_1(x)/(1 - q_1(x))$ and $p_2(x)/(1 - q_2(x))$ are generating functions of r then they coincide in the quotient field of $K\langle x^*\rangle$, i.e., $p_1(x)(1 - q_2(x)) = p_2(x)(1 - q_1(x))$. Hence we may speak of the generating function of r.*

(ii) *If r can be expressed in the form $\sum \alpha\mu x^n \beta x^n$ and if $x^k - q_1 x^{k-1} - \cdots - q_k$ is the characteristic polynomial of μx then the generating function of r has the form*

$$\frac{p_0 + p_1 x + \cdots + p_{k-1} x^{k-1}}{1 - q_1 x - \cdots - q_k x^k}$$

PROOF. Assertion (i) is true because

$$p_1(1 - q_2) = (1 - q_1) r (1 - q_2) = (1 - q_2) r (1 - q_1) = p_2(1 - q_1).$$

Assertion (ii) is a consequence of the Cayley–Hamilton theorem. Indeed, since

$$r_n = \alpha\mu x^n \beta = q_1 \alpha\mu x^{n-1} \beta + \cdots + q_k \alpha\mu x^{n-k} \beta = q_1 r_{n-1} + \cdots + q_k r_{n-k}$$

when $n \geq k$ the product $(1 - q_1 x - \cdots - q_k x^k) r$ is a polynomial whose degree does not exceed $k - 1$. $\qquad\square$

Theorem 9.5. *Assume that L is a field and r belongs to $L^{\mathrm{rat}}\langle\langle x^*\rangle\rangle$. If K is a subring of L which is either a field or a principal ideal domain, if the coefficients of r lie in K and if $p(x)/(1 - q(x))$ is the generating function of r written in lowest terms then p and q have their coefficients in K.*

PROOF. Let l be larger than the degree of p and consider the series

$$s = \sum s_n x^n = \sum r_{n+l} x^n.$$

Denote $q(x) = q_1 x + \cdots + q_k x^k$. Because

$$s_n = q_1 s_{n-1} + \cdots + q_k s_{n-k} \qquad (n \geq k)$$

every column of $H(s)$ is an L-linear combination of the k first columns of $H(s)$. Hence the rank of s is at most k.

Using Theorem 6.1, or Theorem 6.2, we write s_n in the form $\alpha\mu x^n \beta$ where $\alpha \in K^{1 \times N}$, $\mu x \in K^{N \times N}$, $\beta \in K^{N \times 1}$ and $N \leq k$. Lemma 9.4 shows now that the generating function of r has the form $P(x)/(1 - Q(x))$ where $\deg Q \leq N$ and the coefficients of Q lie in K. Because p and $1 - q$ have no nontrivial common factors and $\deg Q \leq \deg q$ the equation $p(1 - Q) = P(1 - q)$ implies that $1 - Q = 1 - q$. Consequently, also $p = (1 - q) r$ has its coefficients in K. $\qquad\square$

Lemma 9.6. *Let $\alpha_1, \ldots, \alpha_k$ be distinct nonzero complex numbers and let $P_1, \ldots, P_k$ be complex polynomials. If*

$$\sum_i P_i(n) \alpha_i^n = 0$$

for every large n then all the P_i's are zero polynomials.

PROOF. We claim at first that the sum of the series $\sum_{n=0}^{\infty} n^k z^n$ in the unit circle of the complex plane can be written in the form

$$\frac{a_1}{z-1} + \cdots + \frac{a_{k+1}}{(z-1)^{k+1}} \qquad (a_{k+1} \neq 0).$$

Since $\sum z^n = -1/(z-1)$ this assertion is true when $k = 0$. We have also the formulas

$$\sum n^{k+1} z^n = z \frac{d}{dz} \sum n^k z^n$$

and

$$z \frac{d}{dz} \frac{a_j}{(z-1)^j} = \frac{-ja_j}{(z-1)^j} + \frac{-ja_j}{(z-1)^{j+1}}.$$

Hence the assertion is easily proved by using induction.

By the assumption made in the lemma the series

$$s = \sum_n \left(\sum_i P_i(n)\alpha_i^n \right) z^n = \sum_i \left(\sum_n P_i(n)(\alpha_i z)^n \right)$$

is a polynomial. If there is a nonzero polynomial P_i then the above assertion implies that s is the Maclaurin expansion of a rational function which has a pole at $1/\alpha_i$. This being impossible all the P_i's must be zero. □

Lemma 9.7. *Let A be a subfield of $\mathbb{C}$ and let (r_n) be an A-rational sequence which is not terminating, i.e., $\sum r_n x^n$ is not a polynomial. Then we have for large values of n*

$$r_n = \sum_{i=1}^{k} P_i(n)\alpha_i^n$$

where the numbers α_i are the inverses of the distinct poles of the generating function G of (r_n) and each P_i is a polynomial whose coefficients are algebraic over A and whose degree is equal to the multiplicity of the pole α_i^{-1} subtracted by one.

PROOF. We know that G can be written as the sum of a polynomial and partial fractions

$$\frac{\beta_{ij}}{(x - \alpha_i^{-1})^j} \qquad (j = 1, \ldots, m_i; \beta_{im_i} \neq 0)$$

where the numbers α_i^{-1} are the distinct poles of G and m_i is the multiplicity of α_i^{-1}. If $|x| < |\alpha_i|$ then we have

$$\frac{\beta_{ij}}{(x - \alpha_i^{-1})^j} = \frac{(-\alpha_i)^j \beta_{ij}}{(1 - \alpha_i x)^j} = (-\alpha_i)^j \beta_{ij} \sum_n \binom{-j}{n}(-1)^n \alpha_i^n x^n.$$

But here

$$(-1)^n \binom{-j}{n} = (-1)^n \frac{(-j)(-j-1)\cdots(-j-n+1)}{n!}$$

$$= \frac{j(j+1)\cdots(j+n-1)}{n!} = \frac{(j+n-1)!}{n!\,(j-1)!} = \frac{(n+1)\cdots(n+j-1)}{(j-1)!}$$

and hence

$$r_n = \sum_{i=1}^{k} \left(\sum_{j=1}^{m_i} \beta_{ij}(-\alpha_i)^j \frac{(n+1)\cdots(n+j-1)}{(j-1)!} \right) \alpha_i^n$$

for large values of n. The coefficients of the P_i's are algebraic over A because the numbers β_{ij} and α_i are (e.g., $\beta_{im_i} = [(x-\alpha_i^{-1})^{m_i}G(x)]_{x=\alpha_i^{-1}}$). $\qquad \square$

Theorem 9.8. *Let A be the ring $\mathbb{Z}$ or a subfield of $\mathbb{C}$. If (r_n) is a nonterminating sequence of elements of A then the following three conditions are equivalent:*

(i) *(r_n) is A-rational;*

(ii) *for large values of n we have an expression*

$$r_n = \sum_i P_i(n)\alpha_i^n$$

where the P_i's are nonzero complex polynomials and the α_i's are distinct nonzero complex numbers;

(iii) *for large values of n we have an expression*

$$r_n = \sum_i (P_i(n)r_i^n \cos 2\pi n\varphi_i + Q_i(n)r_i^n \sin 2\pi n\varphi_i)$$

where the P_i's and Q_i's are complex polynomials, the r_i's are positive numbers and the φ_i's are real numbers.

Moreover, in condition (ii) the numbers α_i are the inverses of the distinct poles of the generating function of (r_n), the coefficients of the P_i's are algebraic over A and the degree of P_i is equal to the multiplicity of the pole α_i^{-1} subtracted by one.

PROOF. The equivalence of (ii) and (iii) is easy to prove by using the Eulerian formulas

$$e^{\pm i\varphi} = \cos \varphi \pm i \sin \varphi.$$

If condition (i) holds then Lemma 9.7 implies the validity of condition (ii).

If condition (ii) holds then the sequence (r_n) is $\mathbb{C}$-rational because the sequences (n) and (α_i^n) are $\mathbb{C}$-rational and Hadamard products of $\mathbb{C}$-rational sequences are $\mathbb{C}$-rational. Hence condition (i) is a consequence of Theorem 6.1 or 6.2.

The last assertion of the theorem is implied by Lemmas 9.6 and 9.7. $\qquad \square$

Theorem 9.9. *Let* (r_n) *be a polynomially bounded* $\mathbb{Z}$-*rational sequence. Then there are natural numbers* m *and* p *and polynomials* $P_0, \ldots, P_{p-1}$ *with rational coefficients such that*

$$r_{m+i+np} = P_i(n) \qquad (0 \le i \le p - 1).$$

PROOF. If the sequence (r_n) is not terminating and if $|r_n| \le P(n)$ where P is a polynomial then the convergence radius of the series $\sum r_n x^n$ must be equal to 1. Hence any pole of the generating function

$$\frac{p_0 + \cdots + p_l x^l}{1 - q_1 x - \cdots - q_k x^k} \quad \text{(in lowest terms)}$$

of (r_n) has a modulus greater than or equal to 1. By Theorem 9.5 the numbers q_i are integers.

We see now that the zeroes $\alpha_1, \ldots, \alpha_k$ of the polynomial $x^k - q_1 x^{k-1} - \cdots - q_k$, which are the inverses of the poles, satisfy the inequalities $|\alpha_i| \le 1$. Since this polynomial is monic a lemma of Kronecker implies that every α_i is a root of unity. We choose p to be a natural number such that $\alpha_i^p = 1$ for every i.

If $\beta_1, \ldots, \beta_K$ are the distinct numbers of the set $\{\alpha_1, \ldots, \alpha_k\}$ then Lemma 9.7 gives us an expression

$$r_n = \sum_j Q_j(n) \beta_j^n \qquad (n \ge m).$$

Therefore

$$r_{m+i+np} = \sum_j \beta_j^{m+i} Q_j(m + i + np) = P_i(n).$$

It is a general fact that if a polynomial P with degree l maps $l + 1$ rational numbers into rational numbers then its coefficients are rational. □

Lemma 9.10. *Let* (r_n) *be a* $\mathbb{C}$-*rational sequence and suppose that* $r_n = 0$ *infinitely often. Then there are natural numbers* m *and* p *such that* $r_{m+np} = 0$ *for every* n.

The proof is difficult and is based on non-Archimedian analysis.

Lemma 9.11. *Define*

$$r_n = \sum_{i=1}^{k} P_i(n) \alpha_i^n$$

where the α_i's *are distinct nonzero complex numbers and the* P_i's *are nonzero polynomials. Define also*

$$U = \{\alpha_i / \alpha_j \mid \alpha_i / \alpha_j \ne 1 \quad \text{is a root of unity}\}.$$

If $r_{m+np} = 0$ *for every large* n *then the set* U *is nonvoid. Further, if* q *denotes the smallest positive integer such that* $u^q = 1$ *for every element* u *of* U *then* $r_{m+nq} = 0$ *for every* n.

PROOF. Let $A_1, \ldots, A_K$ be the distinct numbers of the set $\{\alpha_1^p, \ldots, \alpha_k^p\}$ and denote

$$E_j = \{i \mid \alpha_i^p = A_j\}.$$

Now

$$r_{m+np} = \sum_{j=1}^{K} \left(\sum_{i \in E_j} \alpha_i^m P_i(m+np) \right) A_j^n = \sum_{j=1}^{K} Q_j(m+np) A_j^n.$$

According to Lemma 9.6 the polynomials $\bar{Q}_j(n) = Q_j(m+np)$ and hence also the polynomials Q_j must be identically zero. This implies that every class E_j contains at least two indexes. If i_1 and i_2 belong to E_j then $\alpha_{i_1}/\alpha_{i_2} \in U$ because $(\alpha_{i_1}/\alpha_{i_2})^p = 1$. Therefore, the set U is not empty.

The definition of q implies now that if i_1 and i_2 belong to E_j then $(\alpha_{i_1}/\alpha_{i_2})^q = 1$. Letting B_j denote the common value of the numbers α_i^q where $i \in E_j$ we obtain

$$r_{m+nq} = \sum_{j=1}^{K} \left(\sum_{i \in E_j} \alpha_i^m P_i(m+nq) \right) B_j^n = \sum_{j=1}^{K} Q_j(m+nq) B_j^n = 0$$

for every n. □

Lemma 9.12. *Let (r_n) be a K-rational sequence where K is a subfield of $\mathbb{R}$. If k is an element of K and the series $\sum r_n k^n$ converges then its sum lies in K.*

PROOF. Let $p(x)/(1 - q(x))$ be the generating function of (r_n). Then we have

$$\sum r_n k^n = \frac{p(k)}{1 - q(k)}.$$

If $|k|$ is smaller than the converge radius ρ of $\sum r_n x^n$ then this equation is implied by Corollary 9.3 and if $|k| = \rho$ then the equation is a consequence of a well-known theorem of Abel (as a matter of fact, this latter case never occurs).

Because the coefficients of p and q belong to K we see that $\sum r_n k^n \in K$. □

EXERCISES

1. Let K be a field and let (r_n) be a K-rational sequence. Then there is a polynomial $1 - q(x)$ with the following property: if a recursion formula

$$r_n = Q_1 r_{n-1} + \cdots + Q_m r_{n-m}$$

holds for large values of n then we have

$$1 - Q_1 x - \cdots - Q_m x^m = P(x)(1 - q(x))$$

for a polynomial P.

2. Let A be a commutative ring and let (r_n) be a sequence of elements of A satisfying the recursion formula

$$r_n = q_1 r_{n-1} + \cdots + q_k r_{n-k} \qquad (n \geq k).$$

59

Show that r_n can be expressed in the form $\alpha \mu x^n \beta$ where $\mu x \in A^{k \times k}$. Show also that every subsequence (r_{m+np}) satisfies a recursion formula whose length is at most k.

Hint: See the proof of Theorem 3.1.

3. Let K be a field and let r be a series of $K^{\text{rat}}\langle\langle x^* \rangle\rangle$ whose generating function written in lowest terms is

$$\frac{p_0 + \cdots + p_l x^l}{1 - q_1 x - \cdots - q_k x^k} \qquad (p_l, q_k \neq 0).$$

Define

$$N = \begin{cases} k & \text{if } k > l, \\ l + 1 & \text{if } k \leq l. \end{cases}$$

Show that N is the rank of r.

4. If $r = \sum \alpha \mu x^n \beta x^n$ is a $\mathbb{Z}$-rational series then the sequence (r_n) is ultimately periodic mod p for any positive integer p. If $\det \mu x$ and p are relatively prime then this sequence is periodic mod p.

5. Show that the sequence $(((1 + \sqrt{5})/2)^n + ((1 - \sqrt{5})/2)^n)$ is $\mathbb{Z}$-rational. Show also that the sequence

$$\left(c_1 \left(\frac{2 + \sqrt{5}}{2} \right)^n + c_2 \left(\frac{2 - \sqrt{5}}{2} \right)^n \right)$$

is not $\mathbb{Z}$-rational unless $c_1 = c_2 = 0$.

6. Let (r_n) be an $\mathbb{R}$-rational sequence. Show that the set of those real numbers which occur infinitely often in (r_n) is finite.

7. If (r_n) is a K-rational sequence where K is a subfield of $\mathbb{R}$ and if the subsequence (r_{m+np}) is convergent then its limit lies in K.

8. If $\cos 2\pi\alpha = 3/5$ and $\sin 2\pi\alpha = 4/5$ then the series $\sum 5^n \cos (2\pi n\alpha) x^n$ is $\mathbb{Z}$-rational but the series $\sum 5^n |\cos 2\pi n\alpha| x^n$ and $\sum \max\{0, 5^n \cos 2\pi n\alpha\} x^n$ are not.

Hints: The imaginary part of $(3 + 4i)^n$ is congruent to 4 mod 5 when n is a positive integer. This implies the irrationality of α. It is known that if α is irrational then the numbers $n\alpha$ are everywhere dense mod 1 (in fact, they are uniformly distributed).

II.10 Positive sequences

We now consider sequences positive in the sense of Section II.8, i.e., sequences of coefficients in series belonging to $A_+^{\text{rat}}\langle\langle x^* \rangle\rangle$. In most cases, we deal with sequences of real numbers. A necessary condition for positiveness, Theorem 10.1, is that the poles of the generating function with minimum modulus are of the form $\rho\xi$ where $\rho > 0$ and ξ is a root of unity (excluding sequences obtained from polynomials). This gives the possibility to get rid of the roots of unity in the dominating term by decomposing the sequence into parts with "growth order" $n^l \alpha^n$ (Theorem 10.2 and Corollary 10.3). The converse of Theorem 10.2 is given in Theorem 10.5 whose proof is based on a technical lemma, Lemma 10.4. It is also very illustrative to compare the situations in Theorems 10.1, 10.5, and exercise 10.2.

A sequence (r_n) is called *positive* iff the series $\sum r_n x^n$ is positive, i.e., if $\sum r_n x^n \in A_+^{\text{rat}}\langle\langle x^*\rangle\rangle$ where A is a subring of $\mathbb{R}$. We may also say that the sequence (r_n) is A_+-rational.

Theorem 10.1. *Assume that r is a series of $\mathbb{R}_+^{\text{rat}}\langle\langle x^*\rangle\rangle$ and let G be its generating function. If r is not a polynomial then the poles of G with minimum modulus are of the form $\rho\zeta$ where $\rho > 0$ and ζ is a root of unity. The number ρ is among these poles and the multiplicity of any pole $\rho\zeta$ is at most the multiplicity of ρ.*

PROOF. We start by proving the second assertion of the theorem. Let z be one of the poles of G with minimum modulus. If $0 < t < 1$ then

$$|G(tz)| = \left|\sum r_n(tz)^n\right| \le \sum r_n|tz|^n = G(t|z|).$$

This inequality shows that $\lim_{x\to|z|-} G(x) = \infty$ which implies that $|z| = $ Rad r is a pole of G. Further, if m is the multiplicity of $|z|$ then the inequality

$$|(tz - z)^m G(tz)| \le (|z| - t|z|)^m G(t|z|)$$

shows that $(tz - z)^m G(tz)$ remains bounded when $t \to 1-$. This implies that the multiplicity of z is at most m.

Let now U consist of those series of $\mathbb{R}_+\langle\langle x^*\rangle\rangle$ whose generating function is either a polynomial or satisfies the condition mentioned. We have to show that U is rationally closed.

Take two series r and s of U and let G and F be their generating functions. We may assume that Rad $r \le$ Rad s, Rad $r < \infty$ and $s \ne 0$ where Rad denotes the convergence radius.

Because $(r + s)_n \ge r_n$ we must have Rad$(r + s) \le$ Rad r. Further, if s_k is a nonzero coefficient of s then $(rs)_n \ge s_k \cdot r_{n-k}$ and hence we must have Rad$(rs) \le$ Rad r. On the other hand the inequalities

$$\text{Rad}(r + s), \text{Rad}(rs) \ge \text{Rad } r$$

hold. Therefore

$$\text{Rad}(r + s) = \text{Rad}(rs) = \text{Rad } r.$$

Since the poles of $G + F$ and GF are among the poles of G and F the series $r + s$ and rs must belong to U.

Take next a quasiregular nonzero series r of U and let G be its generating function. Because $G/(1 - G)$ is the generating function of r^+ we have to examine the zeroes of $1 - G$. When x grows from 0 to Rad r the function G grows from 0 to ∞. Hence there is between 0 and Rad r exactly one number ρ such that $G(\rho) = 1$.

Suppose now that $|z| \le \rho$ and $G(z) = 1$. Then

$$1 = \sum r_n z^n = \text{Re} \sum r_n z^n = \sum r_n \, \text{Re} \, z^n \le \sum r_n|z^n| \le \sum r_n\rho^n = 1$$

61

and this is possible only if $r_n \operatorname{Re} z^n = r_n \rho^n$ for every n. If now p is an index such that $r_p \neq 0$ then we have $\rho^p = \operatorname{Re} z^p = z^p$. Therefore z has the form $\rho \zeta$ where ζ is a pth root of unity. □

Theorem 10.2. *If* $r \in \mathbb{R}_+^{\mathrm{rat}}\langle\langle x^* \rangle\rangle$ *then there are natural numbers* m *and* p *such that if* $0 \leq j \leq p - 1$ *then*

$$r_{m+j+np} = P_j(n)\alpha_j^n + \sum_i P_{ji}(n)\alpha_{ji}^n$$

where $\alpha_j \geq 0$, $\alpha_j > \max_i |\alpha_{ji}|$ *and the* P_j's *and* P_{ji}'s *are nonzero polynomials.*

PROOF. If r is not a polynomial then Lemma 9.7 gives us an expression

$$r_{m+n} = \sum_i Q_i(n)\beta_i^n \qquad (n \geq 0).$$

Denote

$$U = \{\beta_i/|\beta_i| \mid \beta_i/|\beta_i| \text{ is a root of unity}\}$$

and choose p to be the smallest positive integer such that $u^p = 1$ for every $u \in U$. Let $\alpha_1, \ldots, \alpha_K$ be the distinct values of the numbers β_i^p and define $E_k = \{i \mid \beta_i^p = \alpha_k\}$. Then

$$r_{m+j+np} = \sum_k \left(\sum_{i \in E_k} \beta_i^j Q_i(j + np) \right) \alpha_k^n = \sum_k Q_{jk}(n)\alpha_k^n.$$

By Theorem 9.8 the numbers of the set $A_j = \{\alpha_k \mid Q_{jk} \neq 0\}$ are the inverses of the poles of the generating function of the series $\sum_n r_{m+j+np} x^n$. Using now Theorem 10.1 we conclude that every number of A_j whose modulus is maximal is of the form $\alpha \zeta$ where $\alpha > 0$ and ζ is a root of unity. The definition of the number p immediately implies that $\zeta = 1$. □

Corollary 10.3. *Let* (r_n) *be a positive sequence. Then there is a positive integer* p *such that*

$$r_{j+np} \sim c_j n^{l_j} \alpha_j^n \quad \text{as } n \to \infty \qquad (j = 0, \ldots, p - 1)$$

where $c_j > 0$, $l_j \in \mathbb{N}$ *and* $\alpha_j \geq 0$.

Lemma 10.4. *There is a function* $S: \mathbb{N} \to \mathbb{N}$ *with the following property:* *If* K *is a subfield of* $\mathbb{R}$, (r_n) *is a sequence of elements of* K_+ *and*

$$r_n = P(n)\alpha^n + \sum_i P_i(n)\beta_i^n$$

where $\alpha > S(\sum_i \deg P_i) \cdot \max_i |\beta_i|$, P *and the* P_i's *are nonzero polynomials* *and the* β_i's *are pairwise distinct, then the sequence* (r_n) *is* K_+-*rational.*

PROOF. Let

$$\frac{p_0 + \cdots + p_l x^l}{1 - q_1 x - \cdots - q_m x^m}$$

be the generating function of (r_n) written in lowest terms. By Theorem 9.8 the numbers α and β_i are the distinct zeroes of $q(x) = x^m - q_1 x^{m-1} - \cdots - q_m$ and, moreover, the difference of the multiplicity of α (respectively β_i) and the degree of P (respectively P_i) equals one.

Now we define $g(x) = x^k - g_1 x^{k-1} - \cdots - g_k$ as follows: if $\deg P = 0$ then $g = q$ and if $\deg P > 0$ then g is the minimal polynomial of α with respect to K. Thus α is a simple zero of g. Let $\alpha_1, \ldots, \alpha_{k-1}$ be the remaining zeroes of g.

We know that

$$g_1 = \alpha + \alpha_1 + \cdots + \alpha_{k-1},$$

$$-g_2 = \alpha(\alpha_1 + \cdots + \alpha_{k-1}) + \prod_{i<j} \alpha_i \alpha_j,$$

$$\vdots$$

$$(-1)^{k+1} g_k = \alpha \alpha_1 \cdots \alpha_{k-1}.$$

Assume that the inequalities $\alpha > MB$ and $B > M \max|\alpha_i|$ ($B \in K$, $M > 1$) are satisfied and define then

$$G_0 = \frac{g_1}{\alpha} + \cdots + \frac{k g_k}{\alpha^k},$$

$$G_1 = g_1 - B = \left(\frac{g_1}{B} - 1 \right) B,$$

$$G_2 = g_2 + B g_1 - B^2 = \left(\frac{g_2}{B^2} + \frac{g_1}{B} - 1 \right) B^2,$$

$$\vdots$$

$$G_k = g_k + \cdots + B^{k-1} g_1 - B^k = \left(\frac{g_k}{B^k} + \cdots + \frac{g_1}{B} - 1 \right) B^k.$$

It is easy to see that the numbers $G_0, \ldots, G_k$ are positive when M exceeds a positive number $M(k)$ which depends only on k. We prove now that $\sum r_n x^n$ is K_+-rational if $M > M(k)$.

At first we introduce the numbers

$$R_n = r_n - g_1 r_{n-1} - \cdots - g_k r_{n-k}$$

$$= (r_n - B r_{n-1}) - G_1(r_{n-1} - B r_{n-2}) - \cdots$$

$$\quad - G_{k-1}(r_{n-k+1} - B r_{n-k}) - G_k r_{n-k}$$

$$= s_n - G_1 s_{n-1} - \cdots - G_{k-1} s_{n-k+1} - G_k r_{n-k}.$$

If $n > h + k$ ($h \geq k - 1$) then we have

$$R_n = s_n - G_1 s_{n-1} - \cdots - G_k s_{n-k} - B G_k s_{n-k-1} - \cdots$$

$$\quad - B^{n-h-k-1} G_k s_{h+1} - B^{n-h-k} G_k r_h$$

and hence

$$\sum_{n>h} R_n x^n = (1 - G_1 x - \cdots - G_k x^k - BG_k x^{k+1} - B^2 G_k x^{k+2} - \cdots)$$

$$\cdot \sum_{n>h} S_n x^n - \sum_{n>h+k} B^{n-h-k} G_k r_h x^n$$

$$- (G_1 S_h + \cdots + G_{k-1} S_{h-k+2} + G_k r_{h-k+1}) x^{h+1} - \cdots$$

$$- (G_{k-1} S_h + G_k r_{h-1}) x^{h+k-1} - G_k r_h x^{h+k}$$

i.e.,

(1)
$$\sum_{n>h} S_n x^n = \frac{\displaystyle\sum_{n>h} R_n x^n + \frac{BG_k r_h x^{h+k+1}}{1 - Bx} + Q_h(x)}{1 - \left(G_1 x + \cdots + G_{k-1} x^{k-1} + \dfrac{G_k x^k}{1 - Bx} \right)}$$

Since $r_{n+1}/r_n \to \alpha$ as $n \to \infty$ the numbers s_n are positive for large values of n. Therefore the coefficients of the polynomial Q_h lie in K_+ when h is large. Because

$$\sum r_n x^n = r_0 + \cdots + r_{k-1} x^{k-1} + \frac{1}{1 - Bx} \left(r_h x^h + \sum_{n>h} S_n x^n \right)$$

it is sufficient to prove that the series $\sum_{n>h} S_n x^n$ is K_+-rational when h is large.

If $\deg P = 0$ then the numbers R_n are ultimately equal to 0 because g is the denominator of the generating function of (r_n). The K_+-rationality of $\sum_{n>h} S_n x^n$ for large values of h is now implied by formula (1).

Next we make the induction hypothesis that $\sum r_n x^n$ is K_+-rational if $\deg P < l$ and consider the case when $\deg P = l$. We note that

$$n^j \alpha^n - g_1 (n-1)^j \alpha^{n-1} - \cdots - g_k (n-k)^j \alpha^{n-k}$$

$$= n^j (\alpha^n - g_1 \alpha^{n-1} - \cdots - g_k \alpha^{n-k})$$

$$+ jn^{j-1} (g_1 \alpha^{n-1} + \cdots + kg_k \alpha^{n-k}) + \cdots = G_0 jn^{j-1} \alpha^n + \cdots$$

Using this formula and the induction hypothesis we see that $\sum_{n>h} R_n x^n$ is K_+-rational when h is large. The induction step is now completed by applying formula (1).

The function S can be calculated by using the numbers $M(k)$. □

Theorem 10.5. *Let A be a subfield of $\mathbb{R}$ or the ring $\mathbb{Z}$ and let r be a series of $A_+\langle\langle x^*\rangle\rangle$. If the coefficients of r have expressions such as given in Theorem 10.2 then r is A_+-rational.*

PROOF. It suffices to prove that for a large natural number q all the series

$$\sum_n r_{j+nq} x^n \qquad (j = 0, \ldots, q-1)$$

are A_+-rational (because then all the series $\sum_n r_{j+nq} x^{j+nq} = x^j \sum_n r_{j+nq}(x^q)^n$ are A_+-rational).

If A is a field this is immediately proved with the aid of Lemma 10.4. Also in the case $A = \mathbb{Z}$ we may utilize Lemma 10.4. Indeed, if $\alpha = 1$ in Lemma 10.4 then there are no numbers α_j (see the proof of Theorem 9.9); if $\alpha > 1$ then we consider subsequences (r_{i+nt}) where t is large and choose the number B from $\mathbb{N}$.

Another possibility to prove the theorem in the case $A = \mathbb{Z}$ is to apply Theorem 6.3. □

Corollary 10.6. *Assume that (r_n) and (s_n) are $\mathbb{Z}$-rational sequences, (t_n) is a $\mathbb{Z}$-rational sequence, $s_n > 0$ for every n and $r_n = s_n t_n$. Then the sequence (t_n) is $\mathbb{N}$-rational.*

Remark. It is known that if (r_n) and (s_n) are $\mathbb{N}$-rational sequences and the numbers r_n/s_n are integers then the sequence (r_n/s_n) is $\mathbb{Z}$-rational. See [Bel] and exercise 4.

PROOF. Suppose that

$$r_{m+j+np} = P(n)\alpha^n + \sum P_i(n)\alpha_i^n$$

and

$$s_{m+j+np} = Q(n)\beta^n + \sum Q_i(n)\beta_i^n$$

where

$$\alpha > \max|\alpha_i| \quad \text{and} \quad \beta > \max|\beta_i|$$

and

$$t_{m+j+np} = \sum S_i(n)\gamma_i^n.$$

Using Lemma 9.6 we conclude that if $|\gamma_i|$ is maximal then i is uniquely determined, $P(n) = Q(n)S_i(n)$ and $\alpha = \beta\gamma_i$. Hence the sequence (t_{m+j+np}) is $\mathbb{N}$-rational. □

EXERCISES

1. If K is a subfield of $\mathbb{R}$ and $r \in \mathbb{Q}\langle\langle x^*\rangle\rangle \cap K_+^{\text{rat}}\langle\langle x^*\rangle\rangle$ then $r \in \mathbb{Q}_+^{\text{rat}}\langle\langle x^*\rangle\rangle$.

2. Define $r_{2n} = 30^n$, $r_{1+2n} = 25^n \cos^2 2\pi n\alpha$ where $\cos 2\pi\alpha = 3/5$ and $\sin 2\pi\alpha = 4/5$. Show that the sequence (r_n) is $\mathbb{Z}$-rational but not $\mathbb{N}$-rational. Investigate the poles of the generating function of (r_n).

3. Show that any polynomially bounded $\mathbb{Z}$-rational sequence with nonnegative terms is $\mathbb{N}$-rational.

4. Prove the result mentioned after Corollary 10.6 assuming that

$$s_n = p_0\alpha^n + \sum P_i(n)\alpha_i^n \quad (\alpha > \max|\alpha_i|).$$

Hints: We have

$$\frac{r_n}{s_n} = \frac{r_n}{p_0\alpha^n}\left(1 - \frac{\sum P_i(n)\alpha_i^n}{p_0\alpha^n} + \cdots + (-1)^k\left(\frac{\sum P_i(n)\alpha_i^n}{p_0\alpha^n}\right)^k\right) + T_{n,k}$$

$$= \frac{r_n}{p_0\alpha^n} S_{n,k} + T_{n,k}$$

where $\lim_{n\to\infty} T_{n,k} = 0$ if k is large. The sequence $(r_n/p_0\alpha^n)S_{n,k}$ is rational and its terms are algebraic. Therefore it satisfies a recursion formula with rational coefficients (see Lemma 6.6). The sequence (r_n/s_n) satisfies the same formula from a point on.

5. The series $\sum(2\cdot 4^n + (-2)^n + (-3)^n)x^n$ is $\mathbb{N}$-rational but it cannot be expressed in the form $\sum \alpha\mu x^n\beta x^n$ where $\mu x \in R_+^{3\times 3}$ although its rank equals 3. Hint: Consider the trace of μx.

II.11 On series in product monoids

We now return to the discussion of series over direct products. More specifically, we consider in this section the family $A\langle\langle X_1^* \otimes X_2^*\rangle\rangle$. The results are of basic importance for the theory of rational transductions, Section III.1.

Several results are obtained concerning the representation of series belonging to $A^{\mathrm{rec}}\langle\langle X_1^* \otimes X_2^*\rangle\rangle$ and $A^{\mathrm{rat}}\langle\langle X_1^* \otimes X_2^*\rangle\rangle$ in terms of rational series over a free monoid. Of special interest in the sequel will be the notion of a regulated representation and the corresponding characterization result, Theorem 11.8.

In Theorem 11.1, A being commutative is essential, whereas this is not required in Theorem 11.2. The additional assumption in Theorem 11.3 concerning the homomorphisms h_1 and h_2 is needed because, otherwise, (r, v) might remain undefined in some cases.

Theorem 11.1 *If A is a commutative semiring and r belongs to $A\langle\langle X_1^* \otimes X_2^*\rangle\rangle$ then the following two conditions are equivalent:*

(i) $r \in A^{\mathrm{rec}}\langle\langle X_1^* \otimes X_2^*\rangle\rangle$;
(ii) $r = \sum_{i=1}^m s_{1i} \otimes s_{2i}$ *where* $s_{1i} \in A^{\mathrm{rat}}\langle\langle X_1^*\rangle\rangle$ *and* $s_{2i} \in A^{\mathrm{rat}}\langle\langle X_2^*\rangle\rangle$ *($i = 1,\ldots,m$).*

PROOF. Suppose first that condition (i) is valid and $r = \sum \alpha\mu w\beta w$ where $\mu w \in A^{m\times m}$. Define

$$s_{1i} = \sum_{u\in X_1^*} (\alpha\mu u)_i u$$

and

$$s_{2i} = \sum_{v\in X_2^*} (\mu v\beta)_i v.$$

The series s_{1i} and s_{2i} are rational and

$$(r, u \otimes v) = \alpha\mu u\mu v\beta = \sum_{i=1}^{m} (\alpha\mu u)_i(\mu v\beta)_i = \sum_{i=1}^{m} (s_{1i}, u)(s_{2i}, v).$$

Hence condition (ii) is valid.

Suppose next that condition (ii) holds. By Theorem 4.3 the series

$$t_{1i} = \sum (s_{1i}, u)u \otimes v$$

and

$$t_{2i} = \sum (s_{2i}, v)u \otimes v$$

belong to $A^{\text{rec}}\langle\langle X_1^* \otimes X_2^* \rangle\rangle$. But we have

$$r = \sum_{i=1}^{m} t_{1i} \odot t_{2i}.$$

Therefore, condition (i) is implied by Theorem 4.4. $\qquad\square$

Theorem 11.2. *If r is a series of $A\langle\langle X_1^* \otimes X_2^* \rangle\rangle$ then the following three conditions are equivalent:*

(i) $r \in A^{\text{rat}}\langle\langle X_1^* \otimes X_2^* \rangle\rangle$;
(ii) $r \in (A^{\text{rat}}\langle\langle X_1^* \rangle\rangle)^{\text{rat}}\langle\langle X_2^* \rangle\rangle \ (= (A^{\text{rat}}\langle\langle X_1^* \rangle\rangle)^{\text{rec}}\langle\langle X_2^* \rangle\rangle)$;
(iii) $r \in (A^{\text{rat}}\langle\langle X_2^* \rangle\rangle)^{\text{rat}}\langle\langle X_1^* \rangle\rangle$.

PROOF. Assume that (i) holds and let $Z = P + QZ$ be the linear system given by Theorem 1.4. The natural isomorphism of $A\langle\langle X_1^* \otimes X_2^* \rangle\rangle$ and $(A\langle\langle X_1^* \rangle\rangle)\langle\langle X_2^* \rangle\rangle$ transforms this system into the form

(1) $$Z = P + (s + S)Z$$

where the entries of s have the form $\sum_i a_i x_{1i}$ and the entries of S have the form $\sum_i a_i x_{2i}$ $(x_{1i} \in X_1, x_{2i} \in X_2, a_i \in A)$.

Consider now the system

(2) $$Z = (i + s^+)P + (i + s^+)SZ$$

where s^+ is the quasi-inverse of s in $A\langle\langle X_1^* \rangle\rangle^{m \times m}$. If Y is the solution of (2) then

$$P + (s + S)Y = P + SY + s(i + s^+)P + s(i + s^+)SY$$
$$= P + SY + s^+P + s^+SY = (i + s^+)(P + SY) = Y$$

and hence Y is a solution of (1). But since (1) is equivalent with the original system $Z = P + QZ$ there cannot be any other solutions for (1). Therefore r is the first entry of Y.

By Corollary 1.3 the entries of s^+ lie in the semiring $A^{\text{rat}}\langle\langle X_1^* \rangle\rangle$. Using now Theorem 1.2 we see that the components of Y belong to

$$(A^{\text{rat}}\langle\langle X_1^* \rangle\rangle)^{\text{rat}}\langle\langle X_2^* \rangle\rangle.$$

Assume next that (ii) holds and let $Z = P + QZ$ be the linear system given by Theorem 1.4. Applying the natural isomorphism of $(A\langle\langle X_1^* \rangle\rangle)\langle\langle X_2^* \rangle\rangle$ and $A\langle\langle X_1^* \otimes X_2^* \rangle\rangle$ we obtain an equivalent system $Z = P + SZ$ where the entries of S are quasiregular series of $A^{\mathrm{rat}}\langle\langle X_1^* \otimes X_2^* \rangle\rangle$ (as a matter of fact, they are series of $A^{\mathrm{rec}}\langle\langle X_1^* \otimes X_2^* \rangle\rangle$). Therefore the entries of the solution vector belong to $A^{\mathrm{rat}}\langle\langle X_1^* \otimes X_2^* \rangle\rangle$.

Thus we have proved the equivalence of (i) and (ii). The equivalence of (i) and (iii) is proved in the same manner. □

Theorem 11.3. *Let X_1, X_2 and Z be alphabets, let s belong to $A^{\mathrm{rat}}\langle\langle Z^* \rangle\rangle$ and let $h_i: Z^* \to X_i^*$ ($i = 1, 2$) be homomorphisms. If, moreover, $h_1 w = h_2 w = \lambda$ for no word w of Z^+ then the series defined by*

$$(r, v) = h_1(h_2^{-1} v \odot s) \qquad (v \in X_2^*)$$

belongs to $A^{\mathrm{rat}}\langle\langle X_1^* \otimes X_2^* \rangle\rangle$. If the semiring A is complete then the extra assumption is not needed.

PROOF. Denote by h the homomorphism mapping w ($w \in Z^*$) into $h_1 w \otimes h_2 w$. Because h is λ-free the series hs is rational by Theorem 4.2. But

$$(hs, v) = \sum_u (hs, u \otimes v)u$$

$$= \sum_u \left(\sum_{\substack{h_1 w = u \\ h_2 w = v}} (s, w) \right) u = h_1 \left(\sum_{h_2 w = v} (s, w)w \right) = h_1(h_2^{-1} v \odot s)$$

and hence $r = hs$.

If A is complete and h is not λ-free then we use Theorem 4.7 instead of Theorem 4.2. □

Theorem 11.4. *Let X_1 and X_2 be two alphabets and let $\bar{X}_1$ and $\bar{X}_2$ be mutually disjoint copies of X_1 and X_2. If $r \in A^{\mathrm{rat}}\langle\langle X_1^* \otimes X_2^* \rangle\rangle$ then there is a series s of $A^{\mathrm{rat}}\langle\langle (\bar{X}_1 \cup \bar{X}_2)^* \rangle\rangle$ such that*

$$(r, v) = \pi_1(\pi_2^{-1} v \odot s) \qquad (v \in X_2^*)$$

where π_i is the natural projection of $(\bar{X}_1 \cup \bar{X}_2)^*$ onto X_i^*.

PROOF. Define $\pi w = \pi_1 w \otimes \pi_2 w$ ($w \in (\bar{X}_1 \cup \bar{X}_2)^*$). We know (see Corollary 2.4) that $r = \pi s$ for a series s of $A^{\mathrm{rat}}\langle\langle (\bar{X}_1 \cup \bar{X}_2)^* \rangle\rangle$. The calculations we made in the preceding proof show now that $(r, v) = \pi_1(\pi_2^{-1} v \odot s)$. □

We say that a representation $\mu: X_1^* \to (A\langle\langle X_2^* \rangle\rangle)^{m \times m}$ is *regulated* iff there is a natural number k such that all entries of the matrices μw where $\lg w \geq k$ are quasiregular. A series of $(A\langle\langle X_2^* \rangle\rangle)\langle\langle X_1^* \rangle\rangle$ is called *rational regulated* iff it can be written in the form

$$r_0 + \sum_{w \in X_1^+} (\mu w)_{1m} w$$

where $r_0 \in A^{\text{rat}}\langle\langle X_2^* \rangle\rangle$ and $\mu\colon X_1^* \to (A^{\text{rat}}\langle\langle X_2^* \rangle\rangle)^{m \times m}$ is a regulated representation. The family of the rational regulated series of $(A\langle\langle X_2^* \rangle\rangle)\langle\langle X_1^* \rangle\rangle$ is denoted by $(A^{\text{rat}}\langle\langle X_2^* \rangle\rangle)^{\text{reg}}\langle\langle X_1^* \rangle\rangle$.

Lemma 11.5. *Let A_1 and A_2 be subsemirings of B and assume that the elements of A_1 commute with those of A_2. If r is a series of $A_1^{\text{rat}}\langle\langle X_1^* \rangle\rangle$ and if $\mu\colon X_1^* \to (A_2^{\text{rat}}\langle\langle X_2^* \rangle\rangle)^{m \times m}$ is a regulated representation then the entries of $\mu r = \sum (r, w)\mu w$ belong to $B^{\text{rat}}\langle\langle X_2^* \rangle\rangle$.*

PROOF. We at first suppose that the matrices μx ($x \in X_1$) have quasiregular entries. The commutativity assumption made implies that the mapping

$$\mu s = \sum (s, w)\mu w$$

is a semiring homomorphism from $A_1\langle\langle X_1^* \rangle\rangle$ into $(B\langle\langle X_2^* \rangle\rangle)^{m \times m}$. Therefore, if r is the first component of the solution of the system $Z = P + QZ$ (Theorem 1.4) then the first component of the solution of $Z = \mu P + \mu QZ$ is μr. If we now replace each component z_i of Z with a matrix

$$\begin{pmatrix} z_{i11} & \cdots & z_{i1m} \\ & \vdots & \\ z_{im1} & \cdots & z_{imm} \end{pmatrix}$$

then we obtain a new system which is equivalent with the original one and whose unknowns are the symbols z_{ijk}. Using Theorem 1.2 we see that the solution of this system is B-rational. Thus we have proved our lemma using the extra assumption made at the beginning. $\square$

Assume now that the matrices μw where $\lg w = k$ have quasiregular entries. Let $y_1, \ldots, y_l$ be the words of X_1^k and let $h\colon Y^* = \{y_1, \ldots, y_l\}^* \to X_1^*$ be the natural homomorphism. It is easy to see (cf. Theorem 4.3) that all the series

$$r_w = \sum_{v \in Y^*} (r, whv)v$$

are A_1-rational. Hence the entries of

$$\mu r_w = \sum (r, whv)(\mu h)v$$

and

$$\mu r = \sum_{\lg w < k} \mu w \cdot \mu r_w$$

are B-rational.

Lemma 11.6. *The family $(A^{\text{rat}}\langle\langle X_2^* \rangle\rangle)^{\text{reg}}\langle\langle X_1^* \rangle\rangle$ is a subsemiring of $(A^{\text{rat}}\langle\langle X_2^* \rangle\rangle)^{\text{rat}}\langle\langle X_1^* \rangle\rangle$ and contains the semiring $(A^{\text{rat}}\langle\langle X_2^* \rangle\rangle)\langle X_1^* \rangle$.*

PROOF. Let

$$r = r_0 + \sum (\mu w)_{1m} w = r_0 + \sum \alpha \mu w \beta w$$

and

$$s = s_0 + \sum (\chi w)_{1n} w = s_0 + \sum \gamma \chi w \delta w$$

be two series of $(A^{\text{rat}}\langle\langle X_2^*\rangle\rangle)^{\text{reg}}\langle\langle X_1^*\rangle\rangle$.

The sum $r + s$ is rational regulated since

$$r + s = r_0 + s_0 + \sum (\rho w)_{1, m+n+2} w$$

where

$$\rho w = \begin{pmatrix} 0 & \alpha\mu w & \gamma\chi w & \alpha\mu w\beta + \gamma\chi w\delta \\ 0 & \mu w & 0 & \mu w\beta \\ 0 & 0 & \chi w & \chi w\delta \\ 0 & 0 & 0 & 0 \end{pmatrix}.$$

Next we prove that

$$rs = r_0 s_0 + r_0 \cdot \sum (\chi w)_{1n} w + \sum (\mu w)_{1m} w \cdot s_0 + \sum (\mu w)_{1m} w \cdot \sum (\chi w)_{1n} w$$

is rational regulated. Because

$$r_0 \cdot \sum (\chi w)_{1n} w = \sum \begin{pmatrix} 0 & r_0 \chi w \\ 0 & \chi w \end{pmatrix}_{1,2n} w$$

and

$$\sum (\mu w)_{1m} w \cdot s_0 = \sum \begin{pmatrix} \mu w & \mu w \cdot s_0 \\ 0 & 0 \end{pmatrix}_{1,2m} w$$

these two series are rational regulated. Further, we know (see exercise 3 of II.2) that

$$\sum (\mu w)_{1m} w \cdot \sum (\chi w)_{1n} w = \sum (\rho w)_{1, m+n} w$$

where ρ is defined by the matrices

$$\rho z = \begin{pmatrix} \mu z & \beta\gamma\chi z \\ 0 & \chi z \end{pmatrix} \qquad (z \in X_1).$$

This representation ρ is regulated because the "diagonal" representations are. It is now seen that rs is a sum of rational regulated series. Hence rs is itself rational regulated.

Thus we have proved that $(A^{\text{rat}}\langle\langle X_2^*\rangle\rangle)^{\text{reg}}\langle\langle X_1^*\rangle\rangle$ is a subsemiring of $(A^{\text{rat}}\langle\langle X_2^*\rangle\rangle)^{\text{rat}}\langle\langle X_1^*\rangle\rangle$. The semiring $(A^{\text{rat}}\langle\langle X_2^*\rangle\rangle)\langle X_1^*\rangle$ is generated by polynomials of the form $r \in A^{\text{rat}}\langle\langle X_2^*\rangle\rangle$ and $z \in X_1$. Since

$$r = r + \sum 0 w$$

and

$$z = 0 + \sum (\mu w)_{12} w$$

where $\mu z = \begin{pmatrix} 0 & 1 \\ 0 & 0 \end{pmatrix}$ and $\mu x = \begin{pmatrix} 0 & 0 \\ 0 & 0 \end{pmatrix}$ if $z \neq z$ these polynomials are rational regulated. Hence $(A^{\text{rat}}\langle\langle X_2^* \rangle\rangle)^{\text{reg}}\langle\langle X_1^* \rangle\rangle$ contains $(A^{\text{rat}}\langle\langle X_2^* \rangle\rangle)\langle X_1^* \rangle$. $\qquad \square$

Lemma 11.7. *If r is a series of $(A^{\text{rat}}\langle\langle X_2^* \rangle\rangle)^{\text{reg}}\langle\langle X_1^* \rangle\rangle$ whose coefficients are quasiregular in $A\langle\langle X_2^* \rangle\rangle$ then r^+, the quasi-inverse of r in $A\langle\langle X_1^* \otimes X_2^* \rangle\rangle$, is a series of $(A^{\text{rat}}\langle\langle X_2^* \rangle\rangle)^{\text{reg}}\langle\langle X_1^* \rangle\rangle$.*

PROOF. Let

$$s = \sum (\mu w)_{1m} w = \sum \alpha \mu w \beta w$$

be a series of $(A^{\text{rat}}\langle\langle X_2^* \rangle\rangle)^{\text{reg}}\langle\langle X_1^* \rangle\rangle$ whose coefficients are quasiregular in $A\langle\langle X_2^* \rangle\rangle$. We know (see again exercise 3 of II.2) that the quasi-inverse of s in $(A\langle\langle X_2^* \rangle\rangle)\langle\langle X_1^* \rangle\rangle$ can be expressed in the form

$$\sum (\chi w)_{1m} w$$

where the representation χ is defined by the matrices

$$\chi z = \beta \alpha \mu z + \mu z = (M + I)\mu z \qquad (z \in X_1).$$

We have

$$\chi w = (M + I)\mu w + \sum_{\substack{w_1 w_2 = w \\ w_i \neq \lambda}} (M + I)\mu w_1 M \mu w_2$$

$$+ \sum_{n \geq 3} \sum_{\substack{w_1 \cdots w_n = w \\ w_i \neq \lambda}} (M + I)\mu w_1 M \cdots M \mu w_n.$$

If $\lg w$ is large then $(M + I)\mu w$ and the terms of the second sum have quasi-regular entries. Moreover, each term in the third sum has a factor

$$M\mu w_k M = \begin{pmatrix} 0 & 0 & \cdots & 0 \\ \vdots & \vdots & & \vdots \\ 0 & 0 & \cdots & 0 \\ (\mu w_k)_{1m} & 0 & \cdots & 0 \end{pmatrix}.$$

Hence the representation χ is regulated.

Now we write r in the form $r_0 + r_1$ where $r_0 \in A^{\text{rat}}\langle\langle X_2^* \rangle\rangle$ and r_1 is quasiregular in $(A\langle\langle X_2^* \rangle\rangle)\langle\langle X_1^* \rangle\rangle$. The series r^+ satisfies the equation

$$r^+ = (r_0 + r_1) + (r_0 + r_1)r^+$$

which is seen to be equivalent with the equation

$$r^+ = (1 + r_0^+)(r_0 + r_1) + (1 + r_0^+)r_1 r^+$$

(cf. the proof of Theorem 11.2). Therefore

$$r^+ = (1 + ((1 + r_0^+)r_1)^+)(1 + r_0^+)(r_0 + r_1)$$

where $((1 + r_0^+)r_1)^+$ is calculated in $(A\langle\langle X_2^* \rangle\rangle)\langle\langle X_1^* \rangle\rangle$. Using now the first part of this proof and Lemma 11.6 we obtain the desired conclusion. $\qquad \square$

Theorem 11.8. *If A is a semiring then*

$$(A\langle X_1^*\rangle)^{\mathrm{rat}}\langle\langle X_2^*\rangle\rangle = (A^{\mathrm{rat}}\langle\langle X_2^*\rangle\rangle)^{\mathrm{reg}}\langle\langle X_1^*\rangle\rangle.$$

PROOF. Let $r = r_0 + \sum (\mu w)_{1m} w$ be a series of $(A^{\mathrm{rat}}\langle\langle X_2^*\rangle\rangle)^{\mathrm{reg}}\langle\langle X_1^*\rangle\rangle$ where $r_0 \in A^{\mathrm{rat}}\langle\langle X_2^*\rangle\rangle$ and define

$$\chi w = (\mu w)w.$$

Then obviously $r_0 \in (A\langle X_1^*\rangle)^{\mathrm{rat}}\langle\langle X_2^*\rangle\rangle$ and $\chi w \in ((A\langle X_1^*\rangle)^{\mathrm{rat}}\langle\langle X_2^*\rangle\rangle)^{m \times m}$. Because χ is a regulated representation and char$(X_1^+) \in A_1^{\mathrm{rat}}\langle\langle X_1^*\rangle\rangle$ where A_1 is the subsemiring of A generated by the element 1 (Theorem 5.1), Lemma 11.5 implies that

$$(\chi \, \mathrm{char}(X_1^+))_{1m} = \sum_{w \neq \lambda} (\mu w)_{1m} w \in (A\langle X_1^*\rangle)^{\mathrm{rat}}\langle\langle X_2^*\rangle\rangle.$$

Hence also r belongs to $(A\langle X_1^*\rangle)^{\mathrm{rat}}\langle\langle X_2^*\rangle\rangle$.

We have now to prove the converse inclusion $(A\langle X_1^*\rangle)^{\mathrm{rat}}\langle\langle X_2^*\rangle\rangle \subseteq (A^{\mathrm{rat}}\langle\langle X_2^*\rangle\rangle)^{\mathrm{reg}}\langle\langle X_1^*\rangle\rangle$. By Lemma 11.6 $(A\langle X_1^*\rangle)\langle X_2^*\rangle = (A\langle X_2^*\rangle)\langle X_1^*\rangle$ is contained in $(A^{\mathrm{rat}}\langle\langle X_2^*\rangle\rangle)^{\mathrm{reg}}\langle\langle X_1^*\rangle\rangle$. By this same lemma we have that $(A^{\mathrm{rat}}\langle\langle X_2^*\rangle\rangle)^{\mathrm{reg}}\langle\langle X_1^*\rangle\rangle$ is closed with respect to sum and product. Further, if s is quasiregular in $(A\langle X_1^*\rangle)^{\mathrm{rat}}\langle\langle X_2^*\rangle\rangle$ then its quasi-inverses calculated in $(A\langle\langle X_1^*\rangle\rangle)\langle\langle X_2^*\rangle\rangle$ and $A\langle\langle X_1^* \otimes X_2^*\rangle\rangle$ coincide. Using Lemma 11.7 we see now that if the series s belongs to $(A^{\mathrm{rat}}\langle\langle X_2^*\rangle\rangle)^{\mathrm{reg}}\langle\langle X_1^*\rangle\rangle$ then s^+ belongs to

$$(A^{\mathrm{rat}}\langle\langle X_2^*\rangle\rangle)^{\mathrm{reg}}\langle\langle X_1^*\rangle\rangle,$$

too. The above facts immediately imply the inclusion desired. □

EXERCISES

1. If the semiring A is commutative then $A^{\mathrm{rec}}\langle\langle X_1^* \otimes X_2^*\rangle\rangle$ is a semiring containing $A\langle X_1^* \otimes X_2^*\rangle$.

2. If the semiring A is positive then $A^{\mathrm{rat}}\langle\langle X^*\rangle\rangle$ is a Fatou extension of $A\langle X^*\rangle$. Hence $A^{\mathrm{rat}}\langle\langle X_1^* \otimes X_2^*\rangle\rangle \cap (A\langle X_1^*\rangle)\langle X_2^*\rangle = (A^{\mathrm{rat}}\langle\langle X_2^*\rangle\rangle)^{\mathrm{reg}}\langle\langle X_1^*\rangle\rangle$.

3. If $\mu: X^* \to (A\langle\langle Y^*\rangle\rangle)^{m \times m}$ is a representation, $v \in Y^*$ and $1 \leq i, j \leq m$ then $\sum (\mu w, v)_{ij} w \in A^{\mathrm{rat}}\langle\langle X^*\rangle\rangle$.
Hint: Obviously we may assume that $\mu x \in (A\langle Y^*\rangle)^{m \times m}$.

4. Call a series r *commutative* iff $(r, w_1) = (r, w_2)$ holds for all words w_1 and w_2 with the same Parikh vector. In case $A = \mathbb{N}$ commutative series over an alphabet with m letters may be regarded as functions from $\mathbb{N}^m$ into $\mathbb{N}$. An instance of such a function (for $m = 2$) is the polynomial $n_1^2 - n_1 n_2 + n_2^2$. It defines the commutative series r, where $(r, w) = n_1^2 - n_1 n_2 + n_2^2$ if the Parikh vector of w equals (n_1, n_2). Show by Theorem 11.1 that r is not $\mathbb{N}$-rational. Conclude that there exist $\mathbb{N}$-rational (and even commutative) series r_1 and r_2 such that the series r defined by $(r, w) = (r_1, w)/(r_2, w)$ is integer-valued but not $\mathbb{N}$-rational.

II.12 Decidability questions

In this final section of the present chapter, we prove some decidability and undecidability results concerning $\mathbb{Z}$-rational series. The undecidability results of Theorem 12.1 will be our basic tool for proving similar results concerning growth in L systems, cf. Section III.8. Theorem 12.1 can be established also using the Post correspondence problem rather than Hilbert's tenth problem (Exercise III.8.3). Also the decidability result of Theorem 12.4 will be very useful in Section III.8.

The decidability status of (i), (iii), and (iv) in Theorem 12.1 is open in case the alphabet X contains only one letter. This will be discussed further in Section III.8. Also the decidability status of the following problem is open: Is there a finite upper bound for (the absolute values of) the coefficients in a given $\mathbb{Z}$-rational series? In one-letter case this is decidable (Exercise 12.4).

When we speak in this section of a "given" series, we of course mean that the series is given by some effective way, such as a matrix representation.

Theorem 12.1. *Let X be an alphabet containing at least two letters. Then it is undecidable whether a given series r of $\mathbb{Z}^{\mathrm{rat}}\langle\langle X^* \rangle\rangle$*

(i) *has a zero coefficient,*
(ii) *has infinitely many zero coefficients,*
(iii) *has a positive coefficient,*
(iv) *has infinitely many positive coefficients.*

PROOF. Let P be an integer polynomial of k variables. We claim that we can construct a $\mathbb{Z}$-rational series r such that

$$(r, x^{n_1}yx^{n_2}y \cdots yx^{n_k}) = P(n_1, \ldots, n_k).$$

For any index j $(1 \le j \le k)$ we define

$$r_j = \left(\sum_{n_1, \ldots, n_{j-1}} x^{n_1}y \cdots x^{n_{j-1}}y \right)\left(\sum n_j x^{n_j} \right)$$
$$\left(\sum_{n_{j+1}, \ldots, n_k} yx^{n_{j+1}}y \cdots yx^{n_k} \right).$$

These series r_j are obviously $\mathbb{N}$-rational and

$$(r_j, x^{n_1}y \cdots yx^{n_k}) = n_j.$$

The series r is now easily constructed by forming Hadamard products, sums and differences.

Next we introduce the series

$$r^{(1)} = r \odot r + \mathrm{char}((x^*y)^{k-1}x^*)^C,$$
$$r^{(2)} = \left(r \cdot y \sum x^{n_k+1} \right) \odot \left(r \cdot y \sum x^{n_k+1} \right) + \mathrm{char}((x^*y)^k x^*)^C,$$
$$r^{(3)} = \mathrm{char}\, X^* - r^{(1)}$$

and

$$r^{(4)} = \text{char } X^* - r^{(2)}.$$

By considering these series it is immediately seen that if we were able to solve any one of the questions (i)–(iv) then we would be able to solve Hilbert's tenth problem which is known to be impossible. ☐

Theorem 12.2. *It is decidable whether a given $\mathbb{Z}$-rational series $\sum r_n x^n$*

    (i) *is identically zero*,
    (ii) *is a polynomial*,
    (iii) *has infinitely many zero coefficients*.

PROOF. To decide (i) and (ii) we have only to calculate the generating function $G(x)$.

If $\sum r_n x^n$ is not a polynomial then Lemma 9.11 gives us a number q such that condition (iii) is valid iff one of the series $\sum r_{j+nq} x^n$ $(j = 0, \ldots, q - 1)$ is a polynomial. Thus our problem is to find the integer q effectively.

Obviously this number q can be calculated if we know the roots of unity appearing among the quotients β_i/β_j of the poles of $G(x)$. By using symmetric polynomials we can construct the integer polynomial

$$Q(x) = \sum_{i,j} (\beta_j x - \beta_i).$$

But the degree of a primitive nth root of unity is $\varphi(n)$ where φ is Euler's function and it is possible to find an index n_Q such that $n > n_Q$ implies $\varphi(n) > \deg Q$. If we now divide Q by the first n_Q cyclotomic polynomials we obtain the roots of unity which satisfy the equation $Q(x) = 0$. ☐

Corollary 12.3. *It is possible to decide whether a given series r of $\mathbb{Z}^{\text{rat}}\langle\langle X^* \rangle\rangle$ is identically zero or a polynomial.*

PROOF. We need only consider the series $h(r \odot r)$ where $hx = z$ for every $x \in X$. ☐

Theorem 12.4. *It is decidable whether a given $\mathbb{Z}$-rational series $\sum r_n x^n$ is $\mathbb{N}$-rational.*

PROOF. Let $\sum s_n x^n$ be a nonpolynomial series of $\mathbb{Z}^{\text{rat}}\langle\langle x^* \rangle\rangle$ and suppose that no one of the poles of its generating function is of the form $\rho\zeta$ where $\rho > 0$ and ζ is a root of unity different from 1. By the results of Section II.10 the series $\sum s_n x^n$ is $\mathbb{N}$-rational iff the following two conditions hold:

(i) there is only one pole with minimum modulus;
(ii) $s_n \geq 0$ for every n.

    It is known that the validity of (i) can be effectively tested. In the presence of condition (i) also the validity of (ii) can be solved (because the behavior of s_n is mainly determined by the minimal pole). For all technical details we refer to Stolarsky [St].

If now $\beta_1, \ldots, \beta_k$ are the poles of the generating function of $\sum r_n x^n$ then Lemmas 9.7 and 9.6 imply that the poles of the generating function of $\sum r_{j+np} x^n$ are among the numbers $\beta_1^p, \ldots, \beta_k^p$. Therefore, if we can find a number p such that no one of the numbers β_i^p is of the form $\rho \zeta$ where $\rho > 0$ and ζ is a root of unity different from 1 then we can decide the $\mathbb{N}$-rationality of $\sum r_n x^n$ by investigating the series $\sum r_{j+np} x^n$ $(j = 0, \ldots, p - 1)$.

By the proof of Theorem 12.2 we can find an integer q such that no one of the quotients $(\beta_i/\beta_j)^q$ is a root of unity differing from 1. It is now seen that the number $p = 2q$ has the desired property. Indeed, if $\beta_i^{2q} = \rho \zeta$ where ζ is a complex root of unity then

$$(\beta_i/\bar{\beta}_i)^{2q} = \zeta/\bar{\zeta} = \zeta^2$$

and hence

$$(\beta_i/\bar{\beta}_i)^q = \pm \zeta;$$

further, if $\beta_i^{2q} = -\rho$ then $\beta_i^q = \pm i\sqrt{\rho}$ and hence

$$(\beta_i/\bar{\beta}_i)^q = -1. \qquad \square$$

EXERCISES

1. If X contains at least two letters then it is undecidable whether a given series r of $\mathbb{Z}^{\text{rat}}\langle\langle X^* \rangle\rangle$

   (i) has its coefficients ultimately nonnegative,
   (ii) has a regular support,
   (iii) has two equal coefficients.

2. It is decidable whether a given series r of $\mathbb{Z}^{\text{rat}}\langle\langle X^* \rangle\rangle$ is ultimately constant.

3. It is decidable whether a given series $r \in \mathbb{Z}^{\text{rat}}\langle\langle x^* \rangle\rangle$ has the form $p + s$ where $p \in \mathbb{Z}\langle x^* \rangle$ and $s \in \mathbb{N}^{\text{rat}}\langle\langle x^* \rangle\rangle$.

4. It is decidable whether a given series $r \in \mathbb{Z}^{\text{rat}}\langle\langle x^* \rangle\rangle$ is bounded, or polynomially bounded.

5. If $r \in \mathbb{N}^{\text{rat}}\langle\langle X^* \rangle\rangle$ is given then all the languages $L_j = \{w \mid (r, w) = j\}$ can be effectively found.

Note added in proof. The part concerning boundedness in Exercise 4 can be extended to concern arbitrary alphabets. This has been shown recently by G. Jacob (Springer-Verlag Lecture Notes in Computer Science, Vol. 48, 1977, pp. 259–269), and A. Mandel and I. Simon (unpublished manuscript).

III
Applications of rational series

The applications considered in this chapter range from rational transductions and density of regular languages to various aspects concerning
probabilistic automata and stochastic languages, as well as concerning growth
in L systems. The whole machinery developed in the previous chapter will be
used, at least indirectly.

III.1 On rational transductions

One of the most widely studied topics in formal language theory is the notion
of a generalized sequential machine (gsm) mapping, as well as a rational
transduction of languages. From the point of view of formal power series,
such mappings can be considered as mappings from $\mathbb{B}\langle\langle X^* \rangle\rangle$ into $\mathbb{B}\langle\langle Y^* \rangle\rangle$.
In the general case of transductions between families of power series, the
Boolean semiring $\mathbb{B}$ is replaced by an arbitrary commutative one, A. However,
if the direct generalization of a rational transduction of languages is considered, then some difficulties are caused by the fact that in the transduced
series infinite sums over A might occur. Therefore, we must assume that
A is complete. Then, for instance, a result (Theorem 1.3) analogous to
Nivat's Theorem concerning rational transductions of languages is obtained.

Such difficulties do not arise when regulated rational transductions are
considered because then we do not get any infinite sums over A. We can also
decompose (Theorem 1.4) a rational transduction into a projection and a
regulated rational transduction, generalizing the corresponding results for
homomorphisms obtained in Section II.4. The composition theorems (Theorems 1.2 and 1.6) could also be established by considering "nested" matrix
representations.

Definition. Let A be a commutative semiring. A mapping $\tau: A\langle\langle X^*\rangle\rangle \to$ $A\langle\langle Y^*\rangle\rangle$ is called a *regulated rational transduction* iff

$$\tau s = (s, \lambda)r_0 + \sum_{w \neq \lambda} (s, w)(\mu w)_{1m}$$

where $r_0 \in A^{\mathrm{rat}}\langle\langle Y^*\rangle\rangle$ and $\mu: X^* \to (A^{\mathrm{rat}}\langle\langle Y^*\rangle\rangle)^{m \times m}$ is a regulated representation.

It is easy to see that a mapping $\tau: A\langle\langle X^*\rangle\rangle \to A\langle\langle Y^*\rangle\rangle$ is a regulated rational transduction iff $\sum w \otimes \tau w \in (A^{\mathrm{rat}}\langle\langle Y^*\rangle\rangle)^{\mathrm{reg}}\langle\langle X^*\rangle\rangle$ and $\tau s = \sum (s, w)\tau w$.

Theorem 1.1. *If $\tau: A\langle\langle X^*\rangle\rangle \to A\langle\langle Y^*\rangle\rangle$ is a regulated rational transduction and $s \in A^{\mathrm{rat}}\langle\langle X^*\rangle\rangle$ then $\tau s \in A^{\mathrm{rat}}\langle\langle Y^*\rangle\rangle$.*

PROOF. We need only Lemma II.11.5.

Theorem 1.2. *If $\tau_1: A\langle\langle X^*\rangle\rangle \to A\langle\langle Y^*\rangle\rangle$ and $\tau_2: A\langle\langle Y^*\rangle\rangle \to A\langle\langle Z^*\rangle\rangle$ are regulated rational transductions then also $\tau_2\tau_1$ is.*

PROOF. Denote

$$t_1 = \sum_{w \in X^*} w \otimes \tau_1 w,$$

$$t_2 = \sum_{u \in Y^*} u \otimes \tau_2 u = \lambda \otimes r_0 + \sum_{u \neq \lambda} u \otimes (\mu u)_{1m}$$

and

$$t = \sum_{w \in X^*} w \otimes \tau_2\tau_1 w = \sum_{\substack{w \in X^* \\ v \in Z^*}} \left(\sum_{u \in Y^*} (t_1, w \otimes u)(t_2, u \otimes v) \right) w \otimes v.$$

Using Theorem II.11.8 we see that t_1 lies in $(A\langle X^*\rangle)^{\mathrm{rat}}\langle\langle Y^*\rangle\rangle$. Obviously, it suffices to show that t belongs to $(A\langle X^*\rangle)^{\mathrm{rat}}\langle\langle Z^*\rangle\rangle$. But we have

$$t = (t_1, \lambda)r_0 + \sum_{u \neq \lambda} (t_1, u)(\mu u)_{1m}.$$

Here the second term belongs to $(A\langle X^*\rangle)^{\mathrm{rat}}\langle\langle Z^*\rangle\rangle$ because of Lemma II.11.5. The first term is also a member of this family since $(t_1, \lambda) \in A\langle X^*\rangle$ and $r_0 \in A^{\mathrm{rat}}\langle\langle Z^*\rangle\rangle$. $\qquad\square$

Definition. Let A be a complete commutative semiring and let $\tau: A\langle\langle X^*\rangle\rangle \to$ $A\langle\langle Y^*\rangle\rangle$ be a mapping. If

$$\tau s = \sum (s, w)\tau w$$

and

$$\sum w \otimes \tau w \in A^{\mathrm{rat}}\langle\langle X^* \otimes Y^*\rangle\rangle$$

then τ is said to be a *rational transduction*.

Theorem 1.3. *If A is a complete commutative semiring and $\tau: A\langle\langle X^*\rangle\rangle \to A\langle\langle Y^*\rangle\rangle$ is a mapping then the following conditions are equivalent:*

(i) *τ is a rational transduction;*

(ii) *there is a series $t \in A^{\mathrm{rat}}\langle\langle X^* \otimes Y^*\rangle\rangle$ such that $\tau s = \sum_w (s, w)(t, w)$;*

(iii) *there are an alphabet Z, homomorphisms $\varphi: Z^* \to X^*$ and $\psi: Z^* \to Y^*$ and a series r of $A^{\mathrm{rat}}\langle\langle Z^*\rangle\rangle$ such that $\tau s = \psi((\varphi^{-1}s) \odot r)$;*

(iv) *there are a series $r_0 \in A^{\mathrm{rat}}\langle\langle Y^*\rangle\rangle$ and a representation $\mu: X^* \to (A^{\mathrm{rat}}\langle\langle Y^*\rangle\rangle)^{m \times m}$ such that $\tau s = (s, \lambda)r_0 + \sum_{w \neq \lambda} (s, w)(\mu w)_{1m}$.*

PROOF. The equivalence of (i) and (ii) is obvious by the above definition and the equivalence of (ii), (iii) and (iv) is an immediate consequence of Theorems II.11.2, 11.3 and 11.4. $\qquad\square$

Remark. By Theorem II.11.4 we may suppose that in (iii) ψ and φ are projections.

Theorem 1.4. *Let A be a complete commutative semiring. Then every regulated rational transduction is a rational transduction and every rational transduction τ has a factorization $p\sigma$ where p is a projection and σ is a regulated rational transduction.*

PROOF. The first assertion is immediately implied by Theorem 1.3 (iv).

Also the second assertion is quickly proved by using Theorem 1.3 (iv). Indeed, if we define

$$\bar{Y} = Y \cup \{\bar{y}\},$$

$$\chi w = (\mu w, \lambda)\bar{y} + \sum_{u \neq \lambda} (\mu w, u)u,$$

$$\sigma s = (s, \lambda)r_0 + \sum_{w \neq \lambda} (s, w)(\chi w)_{1m}$$

and

$$p\bar{y} = \lambda, \qquad py = y \qquad (y \in Y)$$

then $\tau = p\sigma$. $\qquad\square$

Theorem 1.5. *If $\tau: A\langle\langle X^*\rangle\rangle \to A\langle\langle Y^*\rangle\rangle$ is a rational transduction and $s \in A^{\mathrm{rat}}\langle\langle X^*\rangle\rangle$ then $\tau s = A^{\mathrm{rat}}\langle\langle Y^*\rangle\rangle$.*

PROOF. We write $\tau = p\sigma$ as in Theorem 1.4 and apply then Theorems 1.1 and II.4.7. $\qquad\square$

Theorem 1.6. *If $\tau_1: A\langle\langle X^*\rangle\rangle \to A\langle\langle Y^*\rangle\rangle$ and $\tau_2: A\langle\langle Y^*\rangle\rangle \to A\langle\langle Z^*\rangle\rangle$ are rational transductions then also $\tau_2\tau_1$ is.*

Proof. We suppose that τ_2 is regulated and denote

$$t_1 = \sum w \otimes \tau_1 w,$$

$$t_2 = \sum u \otimes \tau_2 u = \lambda \otimes r_0 + \sum_{u \neq \lambda} u \otimes (\mu u)_{1m}$$

and

$$t = \sum w \otimes \tau_2 \tau_1 w.$$

Since $t_1 \in (A^{\mathrm{rat}}\langle\langle X^*\rangle\rangle)^{\mathrm{rat}}\langle\langle Y^*\rangle\rangle$ and

$$t = (t_1, \lambda)r_0 + \sum_{u \neq \lambda} (t_1, u)(\mu u)_{1m},$$

Lemma II.11.5 implies that $t \in (A^{\mathrm{rat}}\langle\langle X^*\rangle\rangle)^{\mathrm{rat}}\langle\langle Z^*\rangle\rangle$. Therefore $\tau_2\tau_1$ is a rational transduction if τ_2 is regulated.

In the general case we apply Theorem 1.4 and write $\tau_2 = p\sigma_2$. Because

$$t = \sum w \otimes \tau_2 \tau_1 w = \bar{p}\Big(\sum w \otimes \sigma_2 \tau_1 w\Big)$$

where $\bar{p}(w \otimes v) = w \otimes pv$, Theorem II.4.7 shows that $t \in A^{\mathrm{rat}}\langle\langle X^* \otimes Z^*\rangle\rangle$. Hence $\tau_2\tau_1$ is a rational transduction. $\square$

Examples. Assume that A is a commutative semiring, $h: Z^* \to X^*$ is a homomorphism, $r \in A^{\mathrm{rat}}\langle\langle Z^*\rangle\rangle$ and $k: Z^* \to Y^*$ is a λ-free homomorphism. Then the mappings $\tau_1 s = h^{-1} s$, $\tau_2 s = s \odot r$ and $\tau_3 s = ks$ are regulated rational transductions. In fact, we have

$$\sum_{w \in X^\bullet} w \otimes \tau_1 w = \sum_{u \in Z^\bullet} hu \otimes u \in (A\langle X^*\rangle)^{\mathrm{rat}}\langle\langle Z^*\rangle\rangle$$

and

$$\sum_{u \in Z^\bullet} u \otimes \tau_3 u = \lambda \otimes \lambda + \sum_{u \neq \lambda} u \otimes (ku) \in (A^{\mathrm{rat}}\langle\langle Y^*\rangle\rangle)^{\mathrm{reg}}\langle\langle Z^*\rangle\rangle.$$

Further, if $r = (r, \lambda)\lambda + \sum_{u \neq \lambda} (\mu u)_{1m} u$ then

$$\sum_{u \in Z^\bullet} u \otimes \tau_2 u = (r, \lambda)\lambda \otimes \lambda + \sum_{u \neq \lambda} u \otimes ((\mu u)u)_{1m} \in (A^{\mathrm{rat}}\langle\langle Z^*\rangle\rangle)^{\mathrm{reg}}\langle\langle Z^*\rangle\rangle.$$

We know that any rational transduction has an expression $\tau s = \psi(\varphi^{-1} s \odot r)$ where ψ and φ are projections. Hence τ can be written in the form $\psi\tau'$ where $\tau' s = \varphi^{-1} s \odot r$. The above examples and Theorem 1.2 imply that τ' is a regulated rational transduction. Thus we have obtained a new proof for Theorem 1.4.

Also the mapping $\tau s = sr$ where $r \in A^{\mathrm{rat}}\langle\langle X^*\rangle\rangle$ is a regulated rational transduction since

$$\tau s = (s, \lambda)r + \sum_{w \neq \lambda} (s, w)\begin{pmatrix} w & wr \\ 0 & 0 \end{pmatrix}_{12}.$$

A transduction $\tau: \mathbb{B}\langle\langle X^*\rangle\rangle \to \mathbb{B}\langle\langle Y^*\rangle\rangle$ is often called a *transduction of languages*.

We say that S is a *family of series* iff S is a set of pairs (X, r) where X is an alphabet, $r \in A\langle\langle X^*\rangle\rangle$ and the semiring A is fixed. A family of series S is called a *regulated rational cone* (respectively *rational cone*) iff for every pair (X, r) of S and every regulated rational (respectively rational) transduction $\tau: A\langle\langle X^*\rangle\rangle \to A\langle\langle Y^*\rangle\rangle$ the pair $(Y, \tau r)$ belongs to S.

We observe that if A is a commutative semiring then the pairs (X, r) where $r \in A^{\mathrm{rat}}\langle\langle X^*\rangle\rangle$ form a regulated rational cone; if A is also complete then these pairs form a rational cone.

EXERCISES

1. Let $\tau: A\langle\langle X^*\rangle\rangle \to A\langle\langle Y^*\rangle\rangle$ be a rational transduction. Then the rational transduction $\tau': A\langle\langle Y^*\rangle\rangle \to A\langle\langle X^*\rangle\rangle$ satisfying the equation

$$\sum w \otimes \tau w = \sum \tau' v \otimes v$$

is called the *inverse* of τ. Show that if A is positive then τ is regulated iff τ' is polynomial, i.e., $\tau' v \in A\langle X^*\rangle$ for every $v \in Y^*$.

2. If $s \in \mathbb{N}^{\mathrm{rat}}\langle\langle X^*\rangle\rangle$, $\tau: \mathbb{N}^{(\infty)}\langle\langle X^*\rangle\rangle \to \mathbb{N}^{(\infty)}\langle\langle Y^*\rangle\rangle$ is a rational transduction and $\tau s \in \mathbb{N}\langle\langle Y^*\rangle\rangle$ then $\tau s \in \mathbb{N}^{\mathrm{rat}}\langle\langle Y^*\rangle\rangle$.

3. If $\tau: \mathbb{B}\langle\langle X^*\rangle\rangle \to \mathbb{B}\langle\langle Y^*\rangle\rangle$ is a rational transduction of languages and L is a regular language over Y then the languages

$$\{w \mid \tau w \cap L \neq \varnothing\} \quad \text{and} \quad \{w \mid \tau w \subseteq L\}$$

are regular.

4. If L is a regular language over X then the mapping

$$\tau s = \sum (s, w)\left(\sum_{\substack{u \in L \\ uv = w}} v\right)$$

is a rational transduction of languages.

III.2 Families of rational languages

Assume that a language L over the alphabet X equals the support of some series in $A^{\mathrm{rat}}\langle\langle X^*\rangle\rangle$. Such (so-called A-rational) languages and their complements (A-corational languages) are discussed in this section which continues the investigations begun in Section II.5. For most semirings A, the family of regular languages is a proper subfamily of A-rational languages. In some cases (Theorem 2.5), although the inclusion is proper for general alphabets, the families are identical if only one-letter languages are considered. Note that the pumping lemma (Theorem 2.6) holds for $\mathbb{R}$-rational languages and that strong closure properties (Theorem 2.3) are obtained for the family of K-rational languages where K is a subfield of $\mathbb{R}$. A number of open problems remain in this area, notably the problem of whether every $\mathbb{R}$-rational language is $\mathbb{Q}$-rational.

We say that a language L over X is *A-rational* iff there is a series r of $A^{\text{rat}}\langle\langle X^*\rangle\rangle$ such that $L = \{w \mid (r, w) \neq 0\}$. Complements of A-rational languages are called *A-corational*. By Theorem II.5.1 regular languages are A-rational for every semiring A.

Theorem 2.1. *If A is a positive semiring or a finite commutative semiring then a language is A-rational iff it is regular.*

This theorem is a consequence of Theorem II.5.2 and Corollary II.5.3.

Theorem 2.2. *If A is an integral domain and K its quotient field then the families of A-rational and K-rational languages coincide.*

This theorem is implied by Lemma II.6.5.

Theorem 2.3. *The family of K-rational languages when K is a subfield of $\mathbb{R}$ is closed with respect to sum, intersection, catenation and iteration but not with respect to complement.*

PROOF. Let L_i be a K-rational language defined by the series r_i ($i = 1, 2$). We may assume that r_i has nonnegative coefficients (if not we replace r_i by $r_i \odot r_i$). Then obviously

$$L_1 \cup L_2 = \{w \mid (r_1 + r_2, w) \neq 0\},$$
$$L_1 \cap L_2 = \{w \mid (r_1 \odot r_2, w) \neq 0\}$$

and

$$L_1 L_2 = \{w \mid (r_1 r_2, w) \neq 0\}.$$

Further, if $s_1 = r_1 - (r_1, \lambda)\lambda$ then
$$L_1^* = \{w \mid (\lambda + s_1^+, w) \neq 0\}.$$

The series $\sum (\mu w)_{12} w$ where

$$\mu x = \begin{pmatrix} 1 & 1 \\ 0 & 1 \end{pmatrix}, \quad \mu y = \begin{pmatrix} 1 & -1 \\ 0 & 1 \end{pmatrix}$$

defines a K-rational language L whose complement is not K-rational. Indeed, if s were a series of $K^{\text{rat}}\langle\langle\{x, y\}^*\rangle\rangle$ defining L^C then $(s, x^n y^m) \neq 0$ iff $n = m$ and this is impossible by Lemma II.7.6. □

Theorem 2.4. *Let K be a subfield of $\mathbb{R}$. If L is a K-rational language over X and $\tau: \mathbb{B}\langle\langle X^*\rangle\rangle \to \mathbb{B}\langle\langle Y^*\rangle\rangle$ is a rational transduction of languages then τL is K-rational.*

PROOF. Assume that $L = \{w \mid (t, w) \neq 0\}$ where t has nonnegative coefficients and express τ in the form

$$\tau s = \psi(\varphi^{-1} s \odot r)$$

where ψ is a projection. The series r is K-rational because it is the characteristic series of a regular language. Since $\varphi^{-1}t$ is K-rational by Theorem II.4.3 also the series $\varphi^{-1}t \odot r$ is K-rational. Now Corollary II.7.2 gives a number k of K_+ such that the family of the coefficients of the K-rational series

$$\bar{t} = \sum k^{\lg w}(\varphi^{-1}t \odot r, w)w$$

is summable. Hence the series $\psi\bar{t}$ exists. Because $\tau L = \{w \mid (\psi\bar{t}, w) \neq 0\}$ we have to show that $\psi\bar{t}$ is K-rational.

Consider the proof of Theorem II.4.6. We have

$$\sigma = \sum_{\psi w = \lambda} \mu w = I + \sum_{n=1}^{\infty} \left(\sum_{\substack{\psi z = \lambda \\ \lg z = 1}} \mu z \right)^n$$

and therefore

$$\sigma_{ij} = I_{ij} + \sum_{n>0} (\chi^n)_{ij} 1^n$$

where χ has its entries in K. Using now Lemma II.9.12 we see that also σ has its entries in K which immediately implies that $\psi\bar{t}$ is K-rational. $\quad\square$

Theorem 2.5. *Every one-letter $\mathbb{R}$-rational language is regular.*

This is a direct consequence of Lemmas II.9.10 and 9.11.

Theorem 2.6. *Let L be an $\mathbb{R}$-rational language. Then there is a natural number k such that if $w \in L$ and $\lg w \geq k$ then w can be written in the form $w_1 w_2 w_3$ where $w_2 \neq \lambda$ and $w_1 w_1^n w_3 \in L$ for infinitely many values of n.*

This is simply a reformulation of Lemma II.7.7.

EXERCISES

1. If K is a subfield of $\mathbb{R}$ then the family of K-corational languages is closed with respect to sum and intersection but not with respect to complement.

2. Let us call a transduction of languages τ injective if $w_1 \neq w_2$ implies $\tau(w_1) \cap \tau(w_2) = \varnothing$. Prove that the family of K-corational languages where K is a subfield of $\mathbb{R}$ is closed with respect to injective rational transductions.

3. Show that the language $L = \{x^n y^{n^2} \mid n \in N\}$ is $\mathbb{Q}$-corational. Show also that hL where $hx = hy = x$ is not $\mathbb{R}$-corational and L has not the property mentioned in Theorem 2.6.

4. Suppose that K is a subfield of $\mathbb{R}$ and F is an algebraic extension of K. Show that every F-rational language is K-rational.

5. It is decidable whether a given $\mathbb{Q}$-rational language is empty or finite but it is undecidable whether a given $\mathbb{Q}$-corational language is empty or finite.

III.3 Rational series and stochastic automata

The purpose of this section is to establish Turakainen's result to the effect that every language of the form $\{w \mid (r, w) > 0\}$, where r is an $\mathbb{R}$-rational series, is stochastic. Consequently, the family of stochastic languages equals the family of languages of the form mentioned. The result is also extended to concern subfields K of $\mathbb{R}$.

Theorem 3.1. *Let r be a series of $\mathbb{R}^{\text{rat}}\langle\langle X^*\rangle\rangle$ with rank N. Then there is for any large real number b an actual double stochastic automaton A with $N + 3$ states such that*

$$(r, w) = b^{\lg w}\left(p_A(w) - \frac{1}{N + 3}\right) \qquad (w \neq \lambda).$$

The automaton A has only one final state which is the same as the initial state. If K is a subfield of $\mathbb{R}$, $r \in K^{\text{rat}}\langle\langle X^*\rangle\rangle$ and $b \in K$ then A will be a K-stochastic automaton.

PROOF. We write $r = \sum \alpha\mu w\beta w$ where $\mu w \in \mathbb{R}^{N \times N}$ and define

$$\mu_1 x = \begin{pmatrix} 0 & \alpha\mu x \\ 0 & \mu x \end{pmatrix},$$

$$\alpha_1 = (1\, 0 \cdots 0), \qquad \beta_1 = (1, \beta)^{\mathrm{T}}.$$

Then

$$\alpha_1\mu_1 w\beta_1 = \alpha_1 \begin{pmatrix} 0 & \alpha\mu w \\ 0 & \mu w \end{pmatrix} \beta_1 = \alpha\mu w\beta = (r, w) \qquad (w \neq \lambda).$$

In addition we have $\alpha_1\beta_1 = 1$.

Let $\{\beta_1, v_2, \ldots, v_{N+1}\}$ be an orthogonal basis of $\mathbb{R}^{N+1}$ (it can be constructed by using the Gram-Schmidt process). Then the vectors $\alpha_1, v_2, \ldots, v_{N+1}$ are linearly independent as in the opposite case α_1 were a linear combination of the vectors v_i and therefore $\alpha_1\beta_1$ were equal to zero. Hence the matrix

$$D = \begin{pmatrix} \alpha_1 \\ v_1 \\ \vdots \\ v_{N+1} \end{pmatrix}$$

is nonsingular. Obviously

$$\alpha_2 = \alpha_1 D^{-1} = \alpha_1 = (1\, 0 \cdots 0)$$

and

$$\beta_2 = D\beta_1 = (1\, 0 \cdots 0)^{\mathrm{T}}$$

(note that $(1\, 0 \cdots 0)D = \alpha_1$). Defining further

$$\mu_2 x = D\mu_1 x D^{-1}$$

we obtain

$$(\mu_2 w)_{1,1} = \alpha_2 \mu_2 w \beta_2 = \alpha_1 \mu_1 w \beta_1 = (r, w) \qquad (w \neq \lambda).$$

Next we introduce a representation μ_3 which has the property that in the matrices

$$\mu_3 x = \begin{pmatrix} 0 & 0 & 0 \\ t(x) & \mu_2 x & 0 \\ s(x) & u(x) & 0 \end{pmatrix}$$

all the row and column sums are zero (of course $s(x)$ is the sum of the entries of $\mu_2 x$). It is immediately seen that every matrix $\mu_3 w$ where $w \neq \lambda$ has this same property. Denoting now

$$\alpha_3 = (0, \alpha_2, 0), \qquad \beta_3 = (0, \beta_2, 0)^{\mathrm{T}}$$

we obtain

$$(\mu_3 w)_{2,2} = \alpha_3 \mu_3 w \beta_3 = (r, w) \qquad (w \neq \lambda).$$

Let generally $M(a)$ denote the $(N + 3) \times (N + 3)$ matrix all of whose entries are equal to a. Then

$$\mu_3 w \cdot M(a) = M(a) \cdot \mu_3 w = 0 \qquad (w \neq \lambda).$$

This implies that if

$$\mu_4 x = \mu_3 x + M(a)$$

then

$$\mu_4 w = \mu_3 w + M(a)^{\lg w} = \mu_3 w + M((N + 3)^{\lg w - 1} a^{\lg w})$$

for any nonempty word w.

Choose now a to be so large that all the entries of the matrices $\mu_4 x$ are positive. Then the matrices

$$\mu_5 x = \frac{1}{(N + 3)a} \mu_4 x$$

are actual double stochastic matrices. If we define $\alpha_5 = \alpha_3$, $\beta_5 = \beta_3$ then

$$
\begin{aligned}
(\mu_5 w)_{2,2} = \alpha_5 \mu_5 w \beta_5 &= \alpha_3 \frac{\mu_3 w + M((N + 3)^{\lg w - 1} a^{\lg w})}{((N + 3)a)^{\lg w}} \beta_3 \\
&= \frac{1}{((N + 3)a)^{\lg w}} \alpha_3 \mu_3 w \beta_3 + \frac{1}{N + 3} \alpha_3 M(1) \beta_3 \\
&= \frac{1}{((N + 3)a)^{\lg w}} (r, w) + \frac{1}{N + 3}
\end{aligned}
$$

i.e.,

$$(r, w) = ((N + 3)a)^{\lg w} \left((\mu_5 w)_{22} - \frac{1}{N + 3} \right)$$

for all nonempty words w. Thus we have proved the first assertion.

It should be clear that in the above constructions we may use any subfield of $\mathbb{R}$ instead of $\mathbb{R}$. Hence also the second assertion is true.

Corollary 3.2. *A language L is K-stochastic iff there is a K-rational series r such that*

$$L = \{w \mid (r, w) > 0\}.$$

PROOF. Let $L = \{w \mid p_A(w) > \alpha\}$ be a K-stochastic language. Then $L = \{w \mid (r, w) > 0\}$ where $r = \Sigma (p_A(w) - \alpha)w$.

Let next L be a language given in the form $\{w \mid (r, w) > 0\}$ where the series r is K-rational. By Theorem 3.1

$$L + \{\lambda\} = \left\{ w \mid p_A(w) > \frac{1}{m} \right\}$$

for a K-stochastic automaton A with m states (note that $p_A(\lambda) = 1$). Hence, if $\lambda \in L$ the proof is ready. If $\lambda \notin L$ then we join to A a new state which shall be the initial state. □

Corollary 3.3. *A language L is K-rational iff*

$$L - \{\lambda\} = \{w \mid p_A(w) \neq \alpha, w \neq \lambda\}$$

where A is a K-stochastic automaton and $\alpha \in K$.

PROOF. Let $L = \{w \mid (r, w) \neq 0\}$ be a K-rational language. Then Theorem 3.1 gives us a K-stochastic automaton A with m states such that

$$L - \{\lambda\} = \left\{ w \mid p_A(w) \neq \frac{1}{m}, w \neq \lambda \right\}.$$

Conversely, if $L - \{\lambda\} = \{w \mid p_A(w) \neq \alpha, w \neq \lambda\}$ then

$$L = \{w \mid (r, w) \neq 0\} \quad \text{where } r = \operatorname{char}(L \cap \{\lambda\}) + \sum_{w \neq \lambda} (p_A(w) - \alpha)w. \quad □$$

EXERCISES

1. If $r \in K_+^{\mathrm{rat}}\langle\langle X^* \rangle\rangle$ (K a subfield of $\mathbb{R}$) then we have for any large number b of K a K-stochastic automaton A such that $(r, w) = b^{\lg w} p_A(w)$ $(w \neq \lambda)$.

2. We say that a stochastic automaton is *ε-deterministic* if every row in its transition matrices contains an entry $> 1 - \varepsilon$.

 Show that if L is a stochastic language and $\varepsilon > 0$ then there is an ε-deterministic stochastic automaton accepting L.

 Hint: If $L = \{w \mid \pi\mu wf > \alpha\}$, $\pi_1 = (\pi, 0)$, $f_1 = (f - (\alpha, \ldots, \alpha), 0)$ and

$$\mu_1 x = \begin{pmatrix} \beta\mu x & & 1 - \beta \\ & & \vdots \\ & & 1 - \beta \\ 0 & \cdots & 0 & 1 \end{pmatrix}$$

then $L = \{w \mid \pi_1\mu_1 wf_1 > 0\}$. Defining next $\pi_2 = (\pi, 0, 0)$, $f_2 = (f, 1, 0)$ and

$$
\mu_2 x = \begin{pmatrix} \beta\mu x & & \alpha(1-\beta) & (1-\alpha)(1-\beta) \\ & & \vdots & \vdots \\ & & \alpha(1-\beta) & (1-\alpha)(1-\beta) \\ 0 & \cdots & 0 & \alpha & 1-\alpha \\ 0 & \cdots & 0 & \alpha & 1-\alpha \end{pmatrix}
$$

we obtain $L = \{w \mid \pi_2\mu_2 wf_2 > \alpha\}$.

III.4 On stochastic languages

In general, stochastic languages have very weak closure properties. Some closure properties are established in Theorems 4.1–4.4 below. The injectivity assumption in Theorem 4.4 is quite essential, as seen clearly from exercise 4.7. It is an open problem whether or not Theorems 4.2 and 4.3 hold for $\mathbb{R}$-stochastic languages as well. The most important tools for proving that a given language is not stochastic are Theorem 4.7 (based on a geometric lemma, Lemma 4.6) and the techniques used in the proof of Theorem 4.5.

Theorem 4.1. *The union of a K-stochastic and a $\mathbb{Q}$-rational language is K-stochastic. Further, the intersection of a K-stochastic and a K-rational language is K-stochastic.*

PROOF. Let $L_1 = \{w \mid (r_1, w) > 0\}$ be a K-stochastic language and let $L_2 = \{w \mid (r_2, w) \neq 0\}$ be a rational language. Replacing (r_1, w) with $(r_1, w)/M^{1+\lg w}$ where M is a large natural number we may assume that $|(r_1, w)| < 1$ (Theorem II.7.1) and replacing r_2 with $r_2 \odot r_2$ we may assume that $(r_2, w) \geq 0$.

If L_2 is $\mathbb{Q}$-rational then Theorem 2.2 implies that r_2 can be chosen to be $\mathbb{Z}$-rational. Since now

$$L_1 \cup L_2 = \{w \mid (r_1 + r_2, w) > 0\}$$

we see that $L_1 \cup L_2$ is K-stochastic.

If L_2 is K-rational then the formula

$$L_1 \cap L_2 = \{w \mid (r_1 \odot r_2, w) > 0\}$$

shows that $L_1 \cap L_2$ is K-stochastic. $\qquad\square$

Theorem 4.2. *The symmetric difference of two $\mathbb{Q}$-stochastic languages is $\mathbb{Q}$-stochastic.*

PROOF. Let $L_i = \{w \mid (r_i, w) > 0\}$ $(i = 1, 2)$ be $\mathbb{Q}$-stochastic languages. By Theorem 2.2 we may assume that the series r_i are $\mathbb{Z}$-rational. Replacing (r_i, w) with $2(r_i, w) - 1$ we may also assume that (r_i, w) is never zero. But now

$$L_1 \bigtriangleup L_2 = \{w \mid (-r_1 \odot r_2, w) > 0\}$$

and hence $L_1 \bigtriangleup L_2$ is $\mathbb{Q}$-stochastic. $\qquad\square$

Corollary 4.3. *The complement of a $\mathbb{Q}$-stochastic language (and especially every $\mathbb{Q}$-corational language) is $\mathbb{Q}$-stochastic. If L_1 is $\mathbb{Q}$-stochastic and L_2 is $\mathbb{Q}$-rational or $\mathbb{Q}$-corational then $L_1 \cup L_2$ and $L_1 \cap L_2$ are $\mathbb{Q}$-stochastic.*

PROOF. We have $X^* - L = X^* \triangle L$, $L_1 \cup L_2 = (L_1^c \cap L_2^c)^c$ and $L_1 \cap L_2 = (L_1^c \cup L_2^c)^c$. $\qquad\qquad\square$

Theorem 4.4. *Let τ be a rational transduction of languages which is injective in the sense that $w_1 \neq w_2$ implies $\tau w_1 \cap \tau w_2 = \varnothing$. Then τ preserves K-stochasticity.*

PROOF. We consider the language τL where $\tau s = \psi(\varphi^{-1} s \odot r)$ (ψ is a projection) and $L = \{w \mid (t, w) > 0\}$. Since τ is injective φ must have a constant value on each set $L_w = \{v \mid \psi v = w, (r, v) = 1\}$. Using this fact it is easy to observe that

$$\tau L = \{w \mid (\psi \tilde{t}, w) > 0\}$$

where $\psi \tilde{t}$ is the K-rational series constructed in the proof of Theorem 2.4. $\quad\square$

Theorem 4.5. *There is a $\mathbb{Q}$-corational (and hence $\mathbb{Q}$-stochastic) language L such that the languages LL and L^+ are neither stochastic nor costochastic.*

PROOF. It is seen (cf. the proof of Theorem II.12.1) that the language

$$L = \bigcup_{n=1}^{\infty} x^n y (x^* y)^* x^n y$$

is $\mathbb{Q}$-corational. Assume now that LL is stochastic and is determined by the series r. By Lemma II.7.6 there are constants $c_1, \ldots, c_n$ such that at least one of them is positive and

$$c_1(r, xw) + \cdots + c_n(r, x^n w) = 0$$

for all words w. Define

$$w = yx^{i(1)}yx^{n+1}yx^{i(2)}yx^{n+1}y \cdots yx^{i(k)}yx^{n+1}yx^{n+1}y$$

where $i(1), \ldots, i(k)$ are those indexes for which $c_i > 0$. If $1 \leq i \leq n$ then $(r, x^i w) > 0$ iff i has one of the values $i(1), \ldots, i(k)$. Thus

$$c_1(r, xw) + \cdots + c_n(r, x^n w) > 0$$

which is impossible.

The above argumentation shows also that L^+ is nonstochastic.

When proving that LL and L^+ cannot be costochastic we choose $i(1), \ldots, i(k)$ to be those indexes for which $c_i \leq 0$. $\qquad\qquad\square$

Lemma 4.6. *Let $C(n, h)$ denote the maximal number of regions into which $\mathbb{R}^n$ is divided by h hyperplanes. If $n, h \geq 2$ then $C(n, h) \leq h^n$.*

Remark. Obviously $C(1, h) = h + 1$.

PROOF. Clearly $C(n, 2) = 4 \le 2^n$. Suppose now that the estimate holds when $h < H$ and let $\alpha_1, \ldots, \alpha_H$ be hyperplanes in $\mathbb{R}^n$. The planes $\alpha_1, \ldots, \alpha_{H-1}$ divide α_H in at most $C(n - 1, H - 1)$ regions. Every one of these is contained in a region of $\mathbb{R}^n$ determined by the planes $\alpha_1, \ldots, \alpha_{H-1}$ and divides this in two parts. Hence

$$C(n, H) \le C(n, H - 1) + C(n - 1, H - 1) \le (H - 1)^n + (H - 1)^{n-1}$$
$$= (H - 1)^{n-1}H < H^n$$

if $n > 2$ and

$$C(2, H) \le (H - 1)^2 + H < H^2. \qquad \square$$

Theorem 4.7. *For any stochastic language L there is a polynomial P with the following property: if χ_L denotes the characteristic function of L and if $v_1, \ldots, v_h$ are distinct words then the number of different sequences $(\chi_L(v_1 v), \ldots, \chi_L(v_h v))$ is majorized by $P(h)$.*

PROOF. Express L in the form $\{w \mid \alpha \mu w \beta > 0\}$ and introduce the hyperplanes $\alpha_i = \{\bar{x} \mid (\alpha \mu v_i)\bar{x} = 0\}$. Since the number of the possible sequences $(\chi_L(v_1 v), \ldots, \chi_L(v_h v))$ is at most the number of the regions into which the space is divided by the planes α_i our theorem is implied by Lemma 4.6. $\qquad \square$

EXERCISES

1. The intersection of a K-stochastic and a $\mathbb{Q}$-corational language is K-stochastic.

2. If L is a K-stochastic language and w is a word then the language Lw is also K-stochastic. The same holds if K-stochastic is replaced with K-corational.

3. If card $X > 1$ then the symmetric words of X^* form a language which is $\mathbb{Q}$-stochastic but not $\mathbb{R}$-rational.
   Hint: If $Z = \{z_0, \ldots, z_{k-1}\}$ then the series
   $$\sum (i(1)k^{n-1} + \cdots + i(n - 1)k + i(n))z_{i(1)} \cdots z_{i(n-1)}z_{i(n)}$$
   is $\mathbb{N}$-rational. This fact makes it easy to show that the above language is $\mathbb{Q}$-corational.

4. The language $\{x^m y^n z^l \mid m > n > l\}$ is $\mathbb{Q}$-stochastic.
   Hint: Consider the inequality $q^{m-n} + q^{n-l} < 1$ where $0 < q < 1$.

5. The language $\{x^n y^{mn}\}$ is nonstochastic.
   Hint: Apply Theorem 4.7 choosing $v_i = x^{p_i}$ where the p_i's are pairwise relatively prime integers.

6. Every $\mathbb{Q}$-stochastic language can be written in the form hL where h is a coding homomorphism and L is a $\mathbb{Q}$-corational language. Show also that the language of exercise 5 can be written in this same form.
   Hint: Define the language by an inequality $(r, w) \ge 0$ where $r \in \mathbb{Z}^{rat}\langle\langle X^* \rangle\rangle$ and use the hint given in exercise 3.

7. Given any language L over $\{0\}$ there is a stochastic language L_s over $\{0, 1\}$ such that $L = hL_s$ where $h0 = h1 = 0$.
Hint: Choose

$$\alpha = 0 \cdot d_1 d_2, \ldots \quad \text{where} \quad \begin{cases} d_i = 1 & \text{if } 0^{i-1} \in L, \\ d_i = 0 & \text{otherwise,} \end{cases}$$

and consider the language

$$\{i_1 \cdots i_n \mid \tfrac{1}{2} < 2^n\alpha - i_1 \cdot 2^{n-1} - \cdots - i_{n-1}2 - i_n < 1\}.$$

8. It is impossible to decide whether a given $\mathbb{Q}$-stochastic language is empty or finite.

III.5 On one-letter stochastic languages

Stochastic languages over a one-letter alphabet may behave in a very strange way. For instance, such a language may have arbitrarily large "gaps" in the following sense. Let $x^{n_1}, x^{n_2}, \ldots$ be the words in the language, ordered according to their length. Then, no matter how rapidly increasing a function $f(i)$ we choose, there are stochastic languages for which the difference $x_{n_{i+1}} - x_{n_i}$ is not bounded by $f(i)$.

Our chief aim in this section is to establish Theorem 5.3. This theorem yields immediately a number of nonclosure results. The proof of the classical result, Lemma 5.5, needed for Theorem 5.3 is omitted.

Theorem 5.1. *The symmetric difference of two K-stochastic languages over $\{x\}$ is K-stochastic.*

PROOF. Let $L = \{x^n \mid (r, x^n) > 0\}$ be a K-stochastic language. Since the language $L_0 = \{x^n \mid (r, x^n) = 0\}$ is regular by Theorem 2.5 the series $r - \operatorname{char} L_0$ is K-rational, has no zero coefficients and determines the language L. We can now prove the theorem as we proved Theorem 4.2. $\square$

Corollary 5.2. *The complement of a K-stochastic language over $\{x\}$ is K-stochastic.*

Theorem 5.3. *There is a $\mathbb{Q}$-stochastic language L over $\{x\}$ such that $\{\lambda, x\}L$ is not stochastic.*

Corollary 5.4. *There are $\mathbb{Q}$-stochastic languages L_1 and L_2 over $\{x\}$ such that $L_1 \cup L_2$ and $L_1 \cap L_2$ are not stochastic.*

PROOF. If we choose $L_1 = L$ and $L_2 = xL$ then $L_1 \cup L_2 = \{\lambda, x\}L$. Further, the formula

$$L_1 \cup L_2 = (L_1 \triangle L_2) \triangle (L_1 \cap L_2)$$

and Theorem 5.1 imply that $L_1 \cap L_2$ cannot be stochastic. $\square$

Lemma 5.5. *Let* $\{1, \alpha_1, \ldots, \alpha_k\}$ *be a set of numbers which is linearly independent over* $\mathbb{Q}$ *and let* P *be a nonconstant integer polynomial. Then the vectors* $P(n)\bar{\alpha} = P(n)(\alpha_1, \ldots, \alpha_k)$ *are uniformly distributed* mod 1 *in the following sense:*

Let V *be a subset of* $(0, 1)^k$ *with Jordan content. We say that a vector* $\bar{v}$ *belongs to* V mod 1 *if there is a vector* $\bar{z}$ *of* Z^k *such that* $\bar{v} + \bar{z} \in V$. *If now* $C(N, V)$ *is the number of the vectors* $P(1)\bar{\alpha}, \ldots, P(N)\bar{\alpha}$ *belonging to* V mod 1 *then*

$$\lim_{N \to \infty} \frac{C(N, V)}{N} = \text{cont}(V).$$

Lemma 5.6. *Let the function* $f(x_1, x_2)$ *have a power series expansion in a neighborhood of the origin. Suppose that in this neighborhood* $f(x_1, x_2) \leq 0$ *if* $x_1 < 0$ *and* $x_2 < 0$ *while* $f(x_1, x_2) \geq 0$ *if* $x_1 > 0$ *or* $x_2 > 0$. *Then* f *is identically zero.*

PROOF. If x_1 appears in the power series expansion then we can write this expansion in the form

$$x_1^k(f_k(x_2) + x_1 f_{k+1}(x_2) + \cdots) = x_1^k F(x_1, x_2)$$

where $f_k \neq 0$. Because $f_k(x_2)$ is a power series in x_2 there must be a small positive number y such that $f_k(x_2) \neq 0$ when $0 < |x_2| \leq y$. The continuity of F gives a small positive number z such that $F(x_1, y)$ and $F(x_1, -y)$ do not change their sign on the interval $[-z, z]$. This means that if k is odd then $f(-z, y)$ and $f(z, y)$ have opposite signs and if k is even then $f(-z, -y)$ and $f(z, -y)$ have a common sign. Both of these cases being impossible x_1 cannot appear in the power series expansion.

In the same way we can prove that x_2 does not appear in the expansion of f. □

PROOF OF THEOREM 5.3. Let the numbers 1, α_1, α_2 be linearly independent over $\mathbb{Q}$ and define

$$e(t_1, t_2) = \cos 2\pi(t_1 + t_2) + \cos 2\pi(t_1 - t_2),$$
$$L = \{x^n \mid e(n\alpha_1, n\alpha_2) > 0\}.$$

The positivity set of e on the plane consists of all those open squares whose middle point is of the form (i, j) or $(i + \frac{1}{2}, j + \frac{1}{2})$ where $i, j \in \mathbb{Z}$ and whose sides have length $\frac{1}{2}$ (the sides are parallel to the coordinate axes). The positivity set of $e(t_1 - \alpha_1, t_2 - \alpha_2)$ is a translate of the previous set. Let U denote the union of these two sets. Then obviously

$$x^n \in \{\lambda, x\}L \quad \text{iff} \quad n(\alpha_1, \alpha_2) \in U \quad (n > 0).$$

We note that U has "corner points". For example a point (c_1, c_2) with the following property will be called a corner point: in a small neighborhood of (c_1, c_2), if $t_1 < c_1$ and $t_2 < c_2$ then $(t_1, t_2) \notin U$, and if $t_1 > c_1$ or $t_2 > c_2$ then $(t_1, t_2) \in U$.

We note also that if $(t_1, t_2) \in U$ mod 1 then $(t_1, t_2) \in U$.

Let now $r = \sum r_n x^n$ be an $\mathbb{R}$-rational series and let L_r be the stochastic language $\{x^n \mid r_n > 0\}$. We know by Theorem II.9.8 that for large values of n the coefficient r_n is a sum of terms which have the form $cn^l A^n \cos 2\pi n\beta$ or $cn^l A^n \sin 2\pi n\beta$. If $\{1, \alpha_1, \alpha_2, \beta_1, \ldots, \beta_m\}$ is a basis for the linear $\mathbb{Q}$-space generated by $1, \alpha_1, \alpha_2$ and all the numbers β then we have for each β a representation

$$q_0 + q_1\alpha_1 + q_2\alpha_2 + p_1\beta_1 + \cdots + p_m\beta_m$$

where the q_i's and p_i's are rational numbers. Therefore, if p is chosen so that all the numbers pq_i and pp_i are integers then each of the functions $\cos 2\pi np\beta$ and $\sin 2\pi np\beta$ is a polynomial in $\cos 2\pi n\alpha_1, \ldots, \sin 2\pi n\alpha_2, \cos 2\pi n\beta_1, \ldots, \sin 2\pi n\beta_m$ (addition formulas of trigonometry are needed here).

Consider the sequence (r_{np}). If it is not ultimately zero then we gather together those terms $cp^l n^l (A^p)^n \cos 2\pi np\beta$ and $cp^l n^l (A^p)^n \sin 2\pi np\beta$ which have the largest growth order $n^l (A^p)^n$. Hence

$$r_{np} = n^l (A^p)^n E(n\alpha_1, \ldots, n\beta_m) + T(n)$$

where $E(t_1, \ldots, t_{m+2})$ is a polynomial in $\cos 2\pi t_1, \ldots, \sin 2\pi t_{m+2}$ and $T(n)$ consists of terms with lower growth order.

Let next (c_1, c_2) be a corner point of U such as described above and assume that there is a point $\bar{t} = (t_1, \ldots, t_{n+2})$ such that (t_1, t_2) is very near $(c_1/p, c_2/p)$, $t_1 < c_1/p$, $t_2 < c_2/p$ and $E(\bar{t}) > 0$. Then $E(\bar{y}) > a > 0$ in a small neighborhood V of $\bar{t}$.

By Lemma 5.5 the vector $(n\alpha_1, \ldots, n\beta_m)$ belongs to V mod 1 infinitely often. But if $(n\alpha_1, \ldots, n\beta_m)$ belongs to V mod 1 then $(np\alpha_1, np\alpha_2)$ does not belong to U and hence $x^{np} \notin \{\lambda, x\}L$; moreover, if n is large then $r_{np} > 0$ and hence $x^{np} \in L_r$. Thus $L_r \triangle \{\lambda, x\}L$ is infinite.

If we assume the existence of a point $\bar{t} = (t_1, \ldots, t_{m+2})$ such that (t_1, t_2) is very near $(c_1/p, c_2/p)$, $t_1 > c_1/p$ or $t_2 > c_2/p$, and $E(\bar{t}) < 0$ then we obtain the same conclusion.

If points $\bar{t}$ of the above kinds do not exist then Lemma 5.6 implies that the function E is identically zero. Hence this situation cannot occur.

If the sequence (r_{np}) is ultimately zero then the language $L_r \cap (x^p)^*$ is finite. But Lemma 5.5 applied to the vectors $pn(\alpha_1, \alpha_2)$ implies that $\{\lambda, x\}L \cap (x^p)^*$ is infinite.

Thus we have shown that the language $\{\lambda, x\}L$ cannot be stochastic. The problem is now to choose α_1 and α_2 so that the language L becomes $\mathbb{Q}$-stochastic. Define α_1 and α_2 by

$$e^{2\pi i\alpha_1} = \frac{3 + 4i}{5}, \qquad e^{2\pi i\alpha_2} = \frac{8 + 15i}{17}.$$

Since $\cos 2\pi\alpha_1$, $\sin 2\pi\alpha_1$, $\cos 2\pi\alpha_2$ and $\sin 2\pi\alpha_2$ are rational the numbers $e(n\alpha_1, n\alpha_2)$ are rational, too, and this implies that L is $\mathbb{Q}$-stochastic. Therefore the proof is finished by showing that the numbers $1, \alpha_1, \alpha_2$ are linearly independent over $\mathbb{Q}$.

Assume now that $n_0 + n_1\alpha_1 + n_2\alpha_2 = 0$ where the n_i's are integers. Then we have

$$\left(\frac{3 + 4i}{5}\right)^{n_1}\left(\frac{8 + 15i}{17}\right)^{n_2} = e^{2\pi i(n_0 + n_1\alpha_1 + n_2\alpha_2)} = 1.$$

It is easy to see that if $n > 0$ then

$$(3 \pm 4i)^n = a(n) \pm b(n)i$$

and

$$(8 \pm 15i)^n = A(n) \pm B(n)i$$

where $a(n) \equiv 3 \bmod 5$, $b(n) \equiv 4 \bmod 5$, $A(n) \not\equiv 0 \bmod 5$, $B(n) \equiv 0 \bmod 5$ and $B(n) \equiv 2$ or $15 \bmod 17$. Using these facts we can prove that the left side of the above equation is real only if $n_1 = n_2 = 0$. For example if $n_1 > 0$ and $n_2 < 0$ then

$$\left(\frac{3 + 4i}{5}\right)^{n_1}\left(\frac{8 + 15i}{17}\right)^{n_2} = \left(\frac{1}{5}\right)^{n_1}\left(\frac{1}{17}\right)^{-n_2}(3 + 4i)^{n_1}(8 - 15i)^{-n_2}$$

$$= 5^{-n_1}17^{n_2}((a(n_1)A(-n_2) + b(n_1)B(-n_2))$$
$$+ (-a(n_1)B(-n_2) + b(n_1)A(-n_2))i)$$
$$= 5^{-n_1}17^{n_2}(x(n_1, n_2) + y(n_1, n_2)i)$$

where $y(n_1, n_2) \not\equiv 0 \bmod 5$. $\qquad\square$

EXERCISES

1. Let L_1 and L_2 be K-stochastic languages over $\{x\}$. Then $L_1 \cup L_2$ is K-stochastic iff $L_1 \cap L_2$ is.

2. Show that if $\alpha > 1$ is irrational then the language $\{x^{(n\alpha)}\}$, where $(n\alpha)$ denotes the integer nearest to $n\alpha$, is stochastic. Investigate the union of two languages which have this form.

3. Let $x^{k_1}, x^{k_2}, \ldots$ ($k_1 < k_2 < \cdots$) be the words of $\{x^n \mid n^2 \sin^2 2\pi n\alpha < 1\}$ where α is irrational. Show that $k_{n+1} - k_n \to \infty$ as $n \to \infty$.
   Hint: It is known that $|n\alpha - m| < 1/\sqrt{5}n$ for infinitely many pairs $(n, m) \in \mathbb{Z}^2$. Further, the number $2(k_{n+1} - k_n)\alpha$ must be very near an integer.

III.6 Densities of regular languages

Consider a language L over the alphabet X. Denote by $C(L, n)$ the number of words in L of length $\leq n$, and by $D(n)$ the number of all words over X of length $\leq n$. If the limit of the sequence $C(L, n)/D(n)$, $n = 0, 1, 2, \ldots$, exists, it is referred to as the density of L. This notion of the density can be generalized in various ways. Instead of the limit, one may consider accumulation points. Instead of $D(n)$ which gives the number of all words, one may take the number of words of length $\leq n$ in another language L_1, thus obtaining the relative density of L with respect to L_1. From the point of view of power series, this means that we consider the characteristic series of L_1. A further generalization (chosen in the definition below) is to replace the characteristic series by an arbitrary $\mathbb{Q}_+$-rational series.

Results about densities can be applied, for instance, to show that a given language does not belong to a given family of languages. An example of this is provided by the family of k-recognizable languages discussed below (cf. also exercise 6.4).

Let L be a language over X (card $X > 1$) and let r be a series of $\mathbb{Q}_+^{\text{rat}}\langle\langle X^* \rangle\rangle$. Define

$$c(L, r, n) = \sum_{\lg w = n} (r, w)(\text{char } L, w), \qquad d(r, n) = \sum_{\lg w = n} (r, w),$$

$$C(L, r, n) = \sum_{i=0}^{n} c(L, r, i), \qquad D(r, n) = \sum_{i=0}^{n} d(r, i).$$

We shall assume that the numbers $d(r, n)$ are positive. Then obviously

$$0 \leq \frac{c(L, r, n)}{d(r, n)}, \frac{C(L, r, n)}{D(r, n)} \leq 1.$$

Theorem 6.1. *If L is a regular language then the sequences*

$$\left(\frac{c(L, r, n)}{d(r, n)} \right) \quad and \quad \left(\frac{C(L, r, n)}{D(r, n)} \right)$$

have only finitely many accumulation points and these are algebraic numbers. If

$$r = \sum w \quad or \quad r = \sum (\text{card } X)^{-\lg w} w$$

then the accumulation points are rational numbers. Moreover, if $r = \sum (\text{card } X)^{-\lg w} w$ then the sequence $(C(L, r, n)/D(r, n))$ has only one accumulation point.

PROOF. Define $hx = t$ for every $x \in X$. Then

$$\sum d(r, n) t^n = hr,$$

$$\sum c(L, r, n) t^n = h(r \odot \text{char } L),$$

$$\sum D(r, n) t^n = (1 + t^+) \sum d(r, n) t^n$$

and

$$\sum C(L, r, n) t^n = (1 + t^+) \sum c(L, r, n) t^n.$$

Hence these four series are $\mathbb{Q}_+$-rational and the first assertion is implied by Theorems II.9.8 and 10.2.

Before continuing we make the following general remark: if $\sum s_n t^n$ is $\mathbb{Q}_+$-rational and its coefficients remain bounded then there are rational numbers $q_0, \ldots, q_{p-1}$ such that

$$s_{i+np} \to q_i \quad \text{as} \quad n \to \infty \qquad (i = 0, \ldots, p-1).$$

The existence of the q_i's is guaranteed by Corollary II.10.3. Because

$$q_i = s_i + \sum_{n=1}^{\infty} (s_{i+np} - s_{i+(n-1)p})1^n$$

Lemma II.9.12 shows that these numbers are rational.

If $r = \sum w$ then $d(r, n) = (\text{card } X)^n$ and

$$D(r, n) = ((\text{card } X)^{n+1} - 1)/(\text{card } X - 1).$$

Because the series

$$\sum \frac{c(L, r, n)}{(\text{card } X)^n} t^n \quad \text{and} \quad \sum \frac{C(L, r, n)(\text{card } X - 1)}{(\text{card } X)^{n+1}} t^n$$

are $\mathbb{Q}_+$-rational the above remark becomes applicable.

If $r = \sum (\text{card } X)^{-\lg w} w$ then $d(r, n) = 1$ and $D(r, n) = n + 1$. By the remark made there are rational numbers $q_0, \ldots, q_{p-1}$ such that

$$c(L, r, i + np) \to q_i \quad \text{as} \quad n \to \infty \qquad (i = 0, \ldots, p-1).$$

This immediately implies that

$$\frac{C(L, r, n)}{n+1} \to \frac{q_0 + \cdots + q_{p-1}}{p} \quad \text{as} \quad n \to \infty. \qquad \square$$

The accumulation points of the sequence

$$\left(\frac{C(L, r, n)}{D(r, n)} \right)$$

are called the *densities* of L with respect to r. If $r = \sum w$ then we speak of the *natural densities*.

We note that the following facts were established during the preceding proof:

If L is regular and r is $\mathbb{Q}_+$-rational ($\mathbb{N}$-rational) then the series $\sum c(L, r, n)t^n$ and $\sum C(L, r, n)t^n$ are $\mathbb{Q}_+$-rational ($\mathbb{N}$-rational). If the sequence $(c(L, r, n))$ remains bounded then its accumulation points are rational and the sequence $(C(L, r, n)/n)$ converges to a rational limit.

EXAMPLE. If n and k are integers, $n > 0$ and $k > 1$ then n can be uniquely written in the form $i_l k^l + \cdots + i_1 k + i_0$ ($0 \le i, j \le k - 1$, $i_l > 0$). Hence to n corresponds the word

$$\sigma_k(n) = i_l \cdots i_1 i_0 \in \{0, \ldots, k-1\}^+.$$

We set also $\sigma_k(0) = \lambda$.

A set M consisting of natural numbers is said to be *k-recognizable* iff the language $\sigma_k M$ is regular.

Choose now

$$M = \left\{ \frac{1}{\sqrt{5}} \left(\left(\frac{1 + \sqrt{5}}{2}\right)^n - \left(\frac{1 - \sqrt{5}}{2}\right)^n \right) \right\}.$$

If $r = \sum w$ then we see that the sequence $(c(\sigma_k M, r, n))$ is bounded and

$$\frac{C(\sigma_k M, r, n)}{n} \to \ln k / \ln \frac{1 + \sqrt{5}}{2} \quad \text{as} \quad n \to \infty$$

(note that $c(\sigma_k M, r, n) = \text{card}(M \cap [k^{n-1}, k^n)))$.

But the number

$$\ln k / \ln \frac{1 + \sqrt{5}}{2}$$

is irrational since in the opposite case an equation

$$k^{m_1} = \left(\frac{1 + \sqrt{5}}{2}\right)^{m_2} \quad (m_1, m_2 \in N \backslash \{0\})$$

holds. Hence M is k-recognizable for no value of k.

EXERCISES

1. Choose $L = y(x^2 + y)^*$ and $r = \text{char}(x^2 + y)^*$. Show that $d(r, n) = d(r, n - 1) + d(r, n - 2)$ and $c(L, r, n) = d(r, n - 1)$. Conclude then that the sequences

$$\left(\frac{c(L, r, n)}{d(r, n)}\right) \quad \text{and} \quad \left(\frac{C(L, r, n)}{D(r, n)}\right)$$

converge to $2/(1 + \sqrt{5})$.

2. Discuss Theorem 6.1 in the case $r = \sum \mu w w$ where

$$\mu w \in \mathbb{Q}_+^{1 \times 1} = \mathbb{Q}_+ \quad \text{and} \quad \sum_{x \in X} \mu x = 1.$$

3. Define

$$L = \{i_1 \cdots i_k \in \{0, 1\}^+ \mid 0 \cdot i_1, \ldots, i_k < \alpha\} \quad (0 < \alpha < 1).$$

Show that L_α is regular iff α is rational.

4. Show that the set $\{3^n + 2^n\}$ is neither 2-recognizable nor 3-recognizable.

III.7 Growth functions of L systems: characterization results

The purpose of the subsequent two sections is to apply the theory of $\mathbb{Z}$-rational formal power series to the study of growth functions of L systems, mainly DOL and DTOL systems. This study is not interested in the generated words themselves but only in the length of the words. The theory of growth functions is of interest, apart from many direct applications, also because a number of important problems concerning languages can be reduced to problems concerning growth functions.

Consider a DOL system $G = (X, w, h)$. The function

$$f_G(n) = \lg(h^n(w)) \qquad n \geq 0$$

is termed the *growth function* of G, and the sequence

(1) $$\lg(h^n(w)), \qquad n = 0, 1, 2, \ldots,$$

its *growth sequence*. Sequences of the form (1) are called *DOL sequences*.

One can also visualize growth functions as mappings of the set of words over the alphabet $\{h\}$ into nonnegative integers, simply by representing the integer n in $f_G(n)$ as the sequence of n h's. This point of view is needed to understand the generalization to DTOL systems.

Consider, next, a DTOL system $G = (X, w, h_1, \ldots, h_t)$. The mapping f_G of $\{h_1, \ldots, h_t\}^*$ into $\mathbb{N}$ defined by

$$f_G(h_{i_1} \cdots h_{i_u}) = \lg(h_{i_u} \cdots h_{i_1}(w)), \qquad u \geq 0, 1 \leq i_j \leq t,$$

is termed the growth function of G. Functions defined in this way are termed *DTOL functions*.

Thus, $f_G(h_{i_1} \cdots h_{i_u})$ indicates the length of the word generated by the system G through the sequence of tables $h_{i_1}, \ldots, h_{i_u}$.

If the system we are dealing with is propagating, we may add the letter P to the abbreviations involved. We may, thus, speak of PDOL sequences or PDTOL functions. In what follows, we shall be mostly concerned with DOL and PDOL systems although analogous results hold for systems with tables as well.

For a DOL system $G = (X, w, h)$, let

$$X = \{x_1, \ldots, x_m\}.$$

For any word α over X, let $\lg_i \alpha$ denote the number of occurrences of x_i in α, $1 \leq i \leq m$. Then the *growth matrix* associated to G is defined by

(2) $$M = \begin{pmatrix} \lg_1 hx_1 & \cdots & \lg_m hx_1 \\ & \vdots & \\ \lg_1 hx_m & \cdots & \lg_m hx_m \end{pmatrix}.$$

Denoting

$$\pi = (\lg_1 w, \ldots, \lg_m w), \qquad \eta = (1, \ldots, 1)^T,$$

we see that the following matrix representation holds for the growth function:

(2)′ $$f_G(n) = \pi M^n \eta.$$

In case of DTOL systems, we have a matrix M_i associated to each of the homomorphisms h_i, $i = 1, \ldots, t$. The matrix representation corresponding to (2)' is for DTOL systems:

$$f_G(h_{i_1} \cdots h_{i_u}) = \pi M_{i_1} \cdots M_{i_u} \eta.$$

EXAMPLE 7.1. In each of the following systems, the axiom is a, and the homomorphisms are given by listing the productions $x \to hx$, $x \in X$. Consider first DOL systems. The systems defined by the following productions have the associated growth functions as indicated:

$G: a \to ab, b \to b;$ $\qquad\qquad\qquad f_G(n) = n + 1,$

$G: a \to aa;$ $\qquad\qquad\qquad\qquad\quad f_G(n) = 2^n,$

$G: a \to abc^2, b \to bc^2, c \to c;$ $\quad f_G(n) = (n + 1)^2,$

$G: a \to abd^6, b \to bcd^{11}, c \to cd^6, d \to d;$ $\quad f_G(n) = (n + 1)^3,$

$G: a \to b, b \to ab;$ $\qquad\qquad\qquad f_G(n) = n$th Fibonacci number.

Consider next the DTOL system G with two homomorphisms defined by

$$h_1: a \to aa; \qquad h_2: a \to aaa.$$

Then for any $\alpha \in \{h_1, h_2\}^*$,

$$f_G(\alpha) = 2^i 3^j,$$

where i (respectively j) equals the number of occurrences of h_1 (respectively h_2) in α. Thus, $f_G(\alpha)$ does not depend on the order of letters in α but only on the Parikh vector of α. For the DTOL system G with two homomorphisms defined by

$$h_1: a \to ab, b \to b; \qquad h_2: a \to a, b \to bb,$$

$f_G(\alpha)$ assumes its maximal value for the word α in $h_1^* h_2^*$ when α ranges over a set of words with the same Parikh vector. Note that all systems in this example are propagating.

After these preliminary remarks and examples, the motivation behind the terminology introduced in the next definition should be apparent.

Definition. A series r in $\mathbb{N}^{\mathrm{rec}}\langle\langle X^* \rangle\rangle$ (or, equivalently, in $\mathbb{N}^{\mathrm{rat}}\langle\langle X^* \rangle\rangle$) is termed a *DTOL series* iff there is a representation $\mu: X^* \to N^{m \times m}$, a row vector α with entries in $\mathbb{N}$ and a column vector β consisting entirely of 1's such that

$$(r, w) = \alpha(\mu w)\beta$$

holds for all words w. A DTOL series is termed a *PDTOL series* iff no row in any of the matrices μx, for $x \in X$, consists entirely of 0's. In the special case where the alphabet X consists of one letter only, a DTOL (respectively PDTOL) series is also referred to as *DOL* (respectively *PDOL*) *series* and its sequence of coefficients (taken in the natural order) as a *DOL* (respectively *PDOL*) *sequence.*

Before we proceed, we make the following two remarks concerning growth in more general L systems. (i) Every $\mathbb{N}$-rational series (respectively every $\mathbb{N}$-rational series over a one-letter alphabet) defines the growth function of an HDTOL system (respectively HDOL system), and vice versa. (ii) No mathematical characterization corresponding to the matrix representation is known for growth functions of L systems with interactions. Consequently, very few results are known as regards growth functions of the latter type.

We now turn to the discussion of characterization results for series and sequences defined above. More specifically, we are looking for characterizations as a subclass of $\mathbb{N}$-rational series and sequences, as well as results that show what types of modifications turn, for instance, an arbitrary $\mathbb{Z}$-rational sequence into a DOL sequence. Results of both kinds are very useful in constructions involving growth functions, such as the solution of the analysis and synthesis problem. (Vaguely stated, the analysis problem consists of determining the growth function of a given system—the synthesis problem is the converse one: realizing a given function as the growth function of a system of a certain type. The results in Section II.8 are directly applicable to the analysis problem.) Moreover, we obtain a necessary and sufficient condition for a DOL sequence to be a PDOL sequence.

Our first theorem indicates how arbitrary $\mathbb{Z}$-rational series can be expressed in terms of DTOL series.

Theorem 7.1. *Every $\mathbb{Z}$-rational series can be expressed as the difference of two DTOL series. Consequently, every $\mathbb{Z}$-rational sequence can be expressed as the difference of two DOL sequences.*

PROOF. By Corollary II.8.2, every $\mathbb{Z}$-rational series can be expressed as the difference of two $\mathbb{N}$-rational series. Since clearly the sum of two DTOL series is again a DTOL series, it suffices to show that every $\mathbb{N}$-rational series can be expressed as the difference of two DTOL series.

Let r be the given $\mathbb{N}$-rational series. Without loss of generality, we assume that r is defined by the row and column vectors

$$\pi = (1, 0, \ldots, 0), \qquad \eta = (0, \ldots, 0, 1)^{\mathrm{T}}$$

and a representation μ, i.e., for any word w,

$$(r, w) = \pi(\mu w)\eta.$$

For each of the matrices M_i defining the representation μ, we define a new matrix M_i^1 by

$$M_i^1 = \begin{pmatrix} M_i & & \begin{matrix} \alpha_{1m} \\ \vdots \\ \alpha_{mm} \end{matrix} \\ 0 \quad \cdots \quad 0 & 0 \end{pmatrix},$$

where the α's constitute the last column of M_i. Let μ_1 be the representation thus obtained. Now, for any nonempty w,

$$(r, w) = (\pi, 0)(\mu_1 w)(1, \ldots, 1)^\mathrm{T} - \pi(\mu w)(1, \ldots, 1)^\mathrm{T},$$

which proves the theorem. (An alternative proof is obtained by applying exercise 7.6 to the identity

$$\pi(\mu w)\eta = (\pi + (1, \ldots, 1))(\mu w)\eta - (1, \ldots, 1)(\mu w)\eta.) \qquad \square$$

The result of Theorem 7.1 can be further strengthened by the following lemma which is very useful in other constructions as well.

Lemma 7.2. *For any $\mathbb{Z}$-rational series r, there exists an integer α_0 such that, for all integers $\alpha \geq \alpha_0$, the series r_1 defined by*

$$(r_1, w) = \alpha^{\lg(w)+1} + (r, w)$$

is a PDTOL series.

PROOF. We express, by Theorem 7.1, r in the form

$$r = s - t,$$

where s and t are DTOL series. It will be more convenient to present the following argument in the terminology of DTOL systems than directly in terms of matrices. Thus, let

$$G_s = (X_s, w_s, h_s^1, \ldots, h_s^k), \qquad G_t = (X_t, w_t, h_t^1, \ldots, h_t^k)$$

be two DTOL systems generating s and t, respectively. Without loss of generality, we assume that the alphabets X_s and X_t are disjoint. Define

$$\alpha_0 = \max\{\lg(h_j^i(x)), \lg(w_s) + 2\lg(w_t), 1\} + 1,$$

where $1 \leq i \leq k$; $j = s, t$; and x ranges over the appropriate alphabets. Fix an integer $\alpha \geq \alpha_0$. Let X_s' be an auxiliary alphabet consisting of primed versions of letters of X_s. For any word w over X_s, we denote by w' the word over X_s' obtained from w by providing each letter with a prime.

Consider now the PDTOL system

$$G_1 = (X_s \cup X_t \cup X_s' \cup \{y\}, w_s w_s' w_t y^{\alpha - 2\lg(w_t) - \lg(w_s)}, h^1, \ldots, h^k),$$

where, for $1 \leq i \leq k$, the homomorphism h^i is defined by the following productions:

$$y \to y^\alpha,$$
$$x \to h_s^i(x)y, \qquad\qquad \text{for } x \in X_s,$$
$$x \to (h_s^i(x))'y^{\alpha - \lg(h_s^i(x)) - 1}, \qquad \text{for } x \in X_s',$$
$$x \to h_t^i(x)y^{2\alpha - 2\lg(h_t^i(x))}, \qquad \text{for } x \in X_t.$$

99

Denoting by r_1 the PDTOL series defined by G_1, we have to show that

$$(3) \qquad (r_1, w) = \alpha^{\lg(w)+1} + (s, w) - (t, w)$$

is satisfied for all words w. (In these considerations, we identify the letters h^i, h^i_s and h^i_t.) To prove (3), we establish a more general statement concerning words generated by the systems G_1, G_s and G_t. For a word w over the alphabet consisting of the homomorphisms, we denote by

$$(G_i, w), \qquad i = 1, s, t,$$

the word generated by the system G_i when the sequence w of homomorphisms is applied to the axiom. We now claim that, for any word w,

$$(4) \qquad (G_1, w) = (G_s, w)(G_s, w)'(G_t, w)y^{\alpha^{\lg(w)+1} - 2\lg(G_t, w) - \lg(G_s, w)}$$

holds true when the positions of the occurrences of the letter y are disregarded. Clearly, (4) implies (3).

The proof of (4) is by induction on the length of w. For $\lg(w) = 0$, (4) holds by the choice of the axiom for G_1. Assuming that (4) holds for all words of length n, we consider an arbitrary word wx of length $n + 1$ (here x is one of the letters h). Disregarding all y's, we see by the inductive assumption and the definition of G_1 that (G_1, wx) begins with the word

$$(G_s, wx)(G_s, wx)'(G_t, wx)$$

as it should. Because of the same reasons we also see that the total number of y's in (G_1, wx) equals

$$\alpha(\alpha^{n+1} - 2\lg(G_t, w) - \lg(G_s, w)) + \lg(G_s, w)$$
$$+ [(\alpha - 1)\lg(G_s, w) - \lg(G_s, wx)] + [2\alpha\lg(G_t, w) - 2\lg(G_t, wx)]$$
$$= \alpha^{\lg(wx)+1} - 2\lg(G_t, wx) - \lg(G_s, wx).$$

This completes the induction. $\qquad\qquad\qquad\qquad\qquad\qquad\qquad\square$

The following stronger version of Theorem 7.1 is now immediate.

Corollary 7.3. *Every $\mathbb{Z}$-rational series can be expressed as the difference of two PDTOL series. Every $\mathbb{Z}$-rational sequence can be expressed as the difference of two PDOL sequences.*

Most of the subsequent discussions will be restricted to the case of one-letter alphabets. This is because the most important mathematical results (such as the existence of a strictly growing DOL sequence which is not a PDOL sequence) can be established for this case. However, analogous results hold also for general alphabets (for instance, cf. exercise 7.9).

To simplify subsequent assertions, we introduce some auxiliary terminology. Let $r(n)$, $n = 0, 1, 2, \ldots$, be a sequence of one of the four types we are considering (i.e., $\mathbb{Z}$-rational, $\mathbb{N}$-rational, DOL or PDOL). We say that

$r(n)$ can be *decomposed* into sequences of type α iff there exist integers m and p such that each of the sequences

(5) $$s_i(n) = r(m + i + np), \qquad i = 0, \ldots, p - 1,$$

is of type α. Conversely, we say that the sequences $s_i(n)$, $i = 0, \ldots, p - 1$, are *β-mergeable* iff (5) holds for some sequence $r(n)$ of type β and some integer m.

We will be mostly concerned with DOL-mergeability. As regards decomposition, we are, of course, only interested in results where the type α is more restrictive than the type of the sequence $r(n)$, for instance, the decomposition of $\mathbb{N}$-rational sequences into DOL sequences. Clearly, the decomposition relation is transitive in the following sense: if a sequence $r(n)$ can be decomposed into sequences of type α and each of the latter ones can be decomposed into sequences of type β, then $r(n)$ can be decomposed into sequences of type β.

Lemma 7.4. *Every $\mathbb{N}$-rational sequence can be decomposed into DOL sequences.*

PROOF. Consider a matrix representation

$$r(n) = \pi M^n \eta$$

for the given $\mathbb{N}$-rational sequence. Let $G = (X, w, h)$ be an arbitrary DOL system such that M is its growth matrix and π is the Parikh vector of the axiom w. (Thus, G and η define r as an HDOL sequence.) For any word w_1, we denote by $\min(w_1)$ the set of letters occurring in w_1. Then the sequence $\min(h^i(w))$, $i = 0, 1, 2, \ldots$, is almost periodic and, consequently, there are integers m and p such that

$$\min(h^{m+i}(w)) = \min(h^{m+i+np}(w)),$$

for all $n \geq 0$ and $0 \leq i \leq p - 1$. Without loss of generality, we assume that the sets $\min(h^j(w))$ are nonempty.

Let now π_i and M_i ($0 \leq i \leq p - 1$) be the Parikh vector of the axiom and the growth matrix of the DOL system

$$G_i = (\min(h^{m+i}(w)), h^{m+i}(w), h^p),$$

and let η_i be the column vector obtained from η by listing only the entries corresponding to the letters in $\min(h^{m+i}(w))$. By the choice of G_i, all entries in π_i are positive. Clearly,

$$s_i(n) = r(m + i + np) = \pi_i M_i^n \eta_i = \eta_i^T (M_i^T)^n \pi_i^T, \qquad 0 \leq i \leq p - 1,$$

whence the assertion follows by exercise 7.6. □

We are now ready for the result characterizing the family of PDOL sequences.

Theorem 7.5. *A sequence $r(n)$ is a PDOL sequence not identically zero iff the sequence*

$$s(n) = r(n + 1) - r(n)$$

is $\mathbb{N}$-rational and $r(0)$ is a positive integer.

PROOF. Note first that the additional statement concerning $r(0)$ is necessary because the only PDOL sequence for which $r(0) = 0$ is the identically zero sequence.

Consider first the "only if" part. Assume that $r(n)$ is defined by a PDOL system

$$(\{x_1, \ldots, x_k\}, w, h).$$

Clearly, each of the sequences $\lg_i(h^n(w)) = s_i(n)$, $1 \le i \le k$, is $\mathbb{N}$-rational. We now express $s(n)$ in the form

$$s(n) = \sum_{i=1}^{k} s_i(n)(\lg(h(x_i)) - 1)$$

which shows that $s(n)$ is $\mathbb{N}$-rational.

Consider then the "if" part. According to Lemma 7.4, there are integers m and p such that the sequences

$$d_i(n) = s(m + i + np), \qquad i = 0, \ldots, p - 1,$$

are DOL sequences. Assume that the sequence $d_i(n)$ is defined by the DOL system $G_i = (X_i, w_i, h_i)$, $0 \le i \le p - 1$, where the alphabets X_i are mutually disjoint. For each of the alphabets X_i, introduce new alphabets $X_i^{(j)}$, $0 \le j \le p - 1$, and denote by $w^{(j)}$ the word obtained from a word w by providing every letter with the superscript (j). Define now a PDOL system $G = (X, w, h)$ in the following way. The alphabet X equals the union of all of the alphabets $X_i^{(j)}$, $0 \le i, j \le p - 1$, added with a special letter y. The axiom is defined by

$$w = w_0^{(p-1)} w_1^{(p-2)} \cdots w_{p-2}^{(1)} w_{p-1}^{(0)}$$

and the homomorphism h by the productions

$$x^{(j)} \to x^{(j+1)}, \qquad \text{for } x \in X_i, 0 \le i \le p - 1, 0 \le j \le p - 1,$$

$$x^{(p-1)} \to (h_i(x))^{(0)} y, \qquad \text{for } x \in X_i, 0 \le i \le p - 1,$$

$$y \to y.$$

Disregarding the positions of the occurrences for the letter y, we notice that the first few words in the word sequence generated by G are:

$$w, (h_0(w_0))^{(0)} y^{\lg(w_0)} w_1^{(p-1)} \cdots w_{p-2}^{(2)} w_{p-1}^{(1)},$$

$$(h_0(w_0))^{(1)} y^{\lg(w_0)} (h_1(w_1))^{(0)} y^{\lg(w_1)} \cdots w_{p-2}^{(3)} w_{p-1}^{(2)}.$$

From this it is easy to observe that the growth function f_G of G satisfies, for $n \geq m + p$,

$$f_G(n - m - p) = s(m) + \cdots + s(n - 1).$$

(In fact, $f_G(0) = s(m) + \cdots + s(m + p - 1)$, the first derivation step according to G brings to this sum the additional term $s(m + p)$, the second derivation step the additional term $s(m + p + 1)$, and so forth.) Because of the identity

$$r(n) = r(0) + \sum_{j=0}^{n-1} s(j),$$

we may now write

$$r(n) = f_G(n - m - p) + r(0) + \sum_{j=0}^{m-1} s(j), \qquad \text{for } n \geq m + p.$$

But this shows that $r(n)$ is a PDOL sequence because it is easy to modify the system G to a system G' for which $f_{G'}(n) = r(n)$. For this purpose, it suffices to introduce new letters to take care of (i) the initial part of the sequence, and (ii) the constant part in the expression for $r(n)$. □

We now turn to the more difficult problem of characterizing the family of DOL sequences (as a subfamily of the family of N-rational sequences). The following simple result (whose proof is immediate by the definition of a DOL sequence) turns out to be the essential point in the characterization.

Theorem 7.6. *Assume that $r(n)$ is a DOL sequence not becoming ultimately zero. Then there is a constant c such that $r(n + 1)/r(n) \leq c$, for all n.*

Theorem 7.6 implies that a DOL sequence cannot be decomposed into differently growing parts. More explicitly, this means the following. If we consider the decomposition of a DOL sequence $r(n)$ according to Theorem II.10.2 into sequences

$$r(m + i + np) = s_i(n) = P(n)\alpha^n + \sum_j P_j(n)\alpha_j^n, \qquad 0 \leq i \leq p - 1,$$

then for each of the latter sequences, the number α and the degree of P must be the same. We say that $r(n)$ has the *growth order*

$$n^{\deg P}(\alpha^{1/p})^n.$$

Conversely, we are going to see that any finite set of DOL sequences with the same growth order is DOL-mergeable. Our chief aim in the sequel is to establish the following theorem.

Theorem 7.7. *Assume that $s_i(n)$, $0 \leq i \leq p - 1$, are DOL sequences with the same growth order $n^q A^n$. Then the sequences $s_i(n)$ are DOL-mergeable.*

103

Before attacking the proof of Theorem 7.7, we establish two corollaries. A further corollary is given in exercise 7.12. Corollary 7.8 can be considered to be a converse of Theorem 7.6, completing the characterization of the family of DOL sequences as a subfamily of $\mathbb{N}$-rational sequences.

Corollary 7.8. *Assume that $r(n)$ is an $\mathbb{N}$-rational sequence such that (i) $r(n) \neq 0$ for all n, and (ii) there is a constant c such that $r(n + 1)/r(n) \leq c$ for all n. Then $r(n)$ is a DOL sequence.*

PROOF. Decompose $r(n)$ into DOL sequences according to Lemma 7.4. By our assumption, all components of the decomposition have the same growth order, whence the assertion follows by Theorem 7.7. $\square$

Corollary 7.9. *There is a strictly growing DOL sequence which is not a PDOL sequence.*

PROOF. Let $a(n)$ be any $\mathbb{Z}$-rational sequence of positive integers which is not $\mathbb{N}$-rational. (Such a sequence exists by exercise II.10.2.) By Lemma 7.2, the sequence

$$a_1(n) = \alpha^{n+1} + a(n)$$

is a DOL sequence (in fact, even a PDOL sequence) for all integers α large enough. We now construct according to Theorem 7.7 a DOL sequence $b(n)$ by merging the sequences $a_0(n) = \alpha^{n+1}$ and $a_1(n)$. The sequence $b(n)$ is strictly growing (for large enough α). If $b(n)$ were a PDOL sequence, then the sequence $c(n) = b(n + 1) - b(n)$ would be $\mathbb{N}$-rational, by Theorem 7.5. Consequently, the sequence $c(2n) = a(n)$ would be $\mathbb{N}$-rational, a contradiction. $\square$

We now begin the proof of Theorem 7.7. We prove first two lemmas. Lemma 7.10 establishes some growth properties of different letters in a DOL system. In particular, it shows that letters of certain growth types cannot occur without letters of certain other growth types. Lemma 7.11 establishes DOL-mergeability in a "pure exponential" case: all letters involved give rise to the same growth order A^n. It also serves as the basis of induction in the proof of Theorem 7.7.

Consider now a DOL scheme (i.e., a DOL system without axiom) $G = (X, h)$ which gives rise to the growth order

$$n^q A^n \qquad (A \geq 1, q \geq 0)$$

but not to growth of higher order. We decompose the alphabet X into subsets $X_{\text{low}}, X_0, \ldots, X_q$ as follows. The letters of X_{low} generate a growth of order lower than A^n (i.e., for each letter x in X_{low}, the growth order of the DOL system (X, x, h) is smaller than A^n). For $i = 0, \ldots, q$, the letters of X_i generate a growth of order $n^i A^n$.

It is clear that a letter of X_{low} may only vanish or generate letters of X_{low}. A letter of X_i cannot generate (in any number of steps) a letter of X_j with $j > i$, it must generate directly a letter of X_i, and in addition it may generate (in a number of steps) letters of X_{low} and X_j with $j < i$. We prove now that, in fact, it must generate (in a number of steps) letters of X_{i-1}. We also consider the "pure" scheme G_1 obtained from G by omitting all letters in $X - X_q$.

Lemma 7.10. *All letters of X_i $(i > 0)$ generate in G letters of X_{i-1}. In the scheme G_1 all letters generate a growth of order A^n.*

PROOF. Consider a letter x in G_1. We prove first that x generates in G_1 a growth of order at most A^n. Assume the contrary: x generates in G_1 a growth of order at least nA^n. (Clearly, this is the next higher order of DOL growth.) Consider now a derivation of length $2n$ in the original scheme G, starting from x. By our assumption, x generates during the first n steps letters in X_q, their number being of order nA^n. Each of these letters generates during the next n steps a growth of order $n^q A^n$. Hence, x generates in G in $2n$ steps a word whose length is at least of the order

$$nA^n \cdot n^q A^n = (\tfrac{1}{2})^{q+1}(2n)^{q+1}A^{2n}.$$

This is a contradiction because the highest growth order in G was assumed to be $n^q A^n$.

We show now that $x \in X_i$ $(i > 0)$ generates in G a letter of X_{i-1}. Again, assume the contrary. Then the growth order generated by x is majorized by the sum

(6)
$$\sum_{j=0}^{n} A^j(n-j)^{i-2}A^{n-j}.$$

In fact, A^j gives an upper bound for the order of the number of letters belonging to $X_{low} \cup X_0 \cup \cdots \cup X_{i-2}$, generated directly by letters of X_i at the jth step. (This follows by the first paragraph of the proof.) The expression $(n-j)^{i-2}A^{n-j}$ indicates the length of the maximal contribution made by each of the latter letters.

Writing now (6) in the form

$$A^n \sum_{j=0}^{n} j^{i-2},$$

we see that the growth generated by x is at most of the order $n^{i-1}A^n$, a contradiction. Hence, x must generate letters of X_{i-1}.

We still have to show that each letter x in G_1 generates the growth order A^n. By what we have already shown, it suffices to prove that x generates at least the growth order A^n. Proceeding again indirectly, we assume that the growth generated by x in G_1 is majorized by a^n $(a < A)$. As above, we obtain a contradiction with respect to the growth generated by x in G by considering the sum

$$\sum_{j=0}^{n} a^j(n-j)^{q-1}A^{n-j}$$

which is of order lower than $n^q A^n$. $\qquad\square$

Lemma 7.11. *Assume that*

$$G_i = (X_i, w_i, h_i) \qquad (i = 0, \ldots, p - 1)$$

are DOL systems and that $A \geq 1$ is a number such that, for every i and every letter x in X_i, the growth generated by x in G_i is of order A^n. Then the DOL sequences generated by the systems G_i are DOL-mergeable.

PROOF. Assume that x_j is a letter in X_i and that the growth generated by x_j in G_i equals asymptotically $g_{ij} A^n$ ($g_{ij} > 0$). For a word w over X_i, define

$$g_i(w) = \sum_j \lg_j(w) g_{ij}.$$

Denote by Y the collection of all p-tuples

$$(\alpha_0, \ldots, \alpha_{p-1}), \qquad \alpha_i \in X_i^+,$$

such that $g_i(\alpha_i)/g_i(w_i)$ assumes the same value for every i. Since we are interested only in growth, the order of letters does not matter. In the elements of Y, we replace the components α_i by their Parikh vectors $\pi(\alpha_i)$. In this fashion we obtain a set of vectors $\pi(Y)$, closed with respect to addition. Thus, we may regard $\pi(Y)$ as an additive subsemigroup of $\mathbb{N}^K$ where K is the sum of the cardinalities of the alphabets X_i.

It is easy to see (for instance, by using König's lemma) that $\pi(Y)$ has only finitely many minimal elements with respect to the natural componentwise ordering. Let $\{\beta_1, \ldots, \beta_t\}$ be the set of minimal elements. Then it is also a set of generators, i.e., any element of $\pi(Y)$ can be expressed as a sum of the β's. This follows because the definition of $\pi(Y)$ implies that whenever v_1 and v_2 are in $\pi(Y)$ and $v_1 - v_2$ is in $\mathbb{N}^K$, then either $v_1 = v_2$ or $v_1 - v_2$ is in $\pi(Y)$.

To prove our lemma, we now construct a DOL system G merging the sequences generated by the systems G_i. The alphabet of G consists of the letters

$$\beta_i^{(j)}, \qquad 1 \leq i \leq t, 0 \leq j \leq p - 1,$$

and of the additional letter y. Although we treat the β's as letters, their original meaning should not be forgotten. The fact that any element of $\pi(Y)$ can be expressed as a sum of the β's is used for expressing elements $(\alpha_0, \ldots, \alpha_{p-1})$ of Y as "commutative products" of the β's. More explicitly, we use the notation

$$\varepsilon(\alpha_0, \ldots, \alpha_{p-1})$$

to mean a word x over $\{\beta_1, \ldots, \beta_t\}$ such that the sum of the Parikh vectors of the letters of x (taken in their original meaning) equals $(\pi(\alpha_0), \ldots, \pi(\alpha_{p-1}))$. Superscripts (j) are distributed over factors in products. We also use the notation

$$h(\alpha_0, \ldots, \alpha_{p-1}) = (h_0(\alpha_0), \ldots, h_{p-1}(\alpha_{p-1})).$$

Clearly, Y is closed under this operation h. The operation h is defined in the same way for elements of $\pi(Y)$. Finally, the additional letter y is used to cope with the length simulation, similarly as in Lemma 7.2.

We are now ready to complete the definition of G. The axiom is

$$\varepsilon(w_0, \ldots, w_{p-1})^{(0)} y^d,$$

where d is chosen in such a way that the length of the axiom will equal $\lg(w_0)$. The productions are

$$y \rightarrow \lambda,$$

$$\beta_i^{(j)} \rightarrow \beta_i^{(j+1)} y^{d(i,j)}, \qquad j < p - 1,$$

$$\beta_i^{(p-1)} \rightarrow \sum (h\beta_i)^{(0)} y^{d(i,p-1)},$$

where $d(i, j)$ equals the length of the $(j + 1)$st component of β_i (or, more exactly, the length of the $(j + 1)$st component in the element of Y with Parikh vector β_i) subtracted by one, and $d(i, p - 1)$ is chosen in such a way that the length of the right side of the last production will be equal to $\lg(h_0(\alpha_{i0}))$ where α_{i0} is the first component of β_i. It is easy to see that our definitions imply that all of the exponents of y will be nonnegative.

The DOL system G thus constructed has the desired property. The derivations in the systems G_i are simulated at every pth step (up to the length of words). A detailed inductive verification, along the lines of the proof of Lemma 7.2, is omitted. $\qquad\qquad\qquad\qquad\qquad\qquad\qquad\qquad\qquad\qquad\square$

EXAMPLE 7.2. Consider the DOL systems

$$G_0 = (\{a\}, a, \{a \rightarrow a^4\}),$$
$$G_1 = (\{b, c, d\}, b, \{b \rightarrow b^2c^3, c \rightarrow c^2d^4, d \rightarrow bd\}).$$

For these systems the hypothesis of Lemma 7.11 is satisfied with $A = 4$. In fact, the coefficients g_{ij} considered in the proof of Lemma 7.11 are in this case

$$g_{00} = 1, \qquad g_{10} = 27/16, \qquad g_{11} = 18/16, \qquad g_{12} = 9/16.$$

Hence the vectors

(7) $\qquad\qquad (a, b), \qquad (a^2, c^3), \qquad (a, d^3)$

belong to Y. A little reflection shows that the Parikh vectors associated to the vectors (7) generate $\pi(Y)$. Hence, our basic alphabet $\{\beta_1, \ldots, \beta_t\}$ consists of the three letters (7). We now follow the construction in the proof of Lemma 7.11. The axiom of our system G will be

$$(a, b)^{(0)}.$$

The productions are

$$(a, b)^{(0)} \to (a, b)^{(1)},$$
$$(a^2, c^3)^{(0)} \to (a^2, c^3)^{(1)}y^2,$$
$$(a, d^3)^{(0)} \to (a, d^3)^{(1)}y^2,$$
$$(a, b)^{(1)} \to ((a, b)^{(0)})^2(a^2, c^3)^{(0)}y,$$
$$(a^2, c^3)^{(1)} \to ((a^2, c^3)^{(0)})^2((a, d^3)^{(0)})^4y^2,$$
$$(a, d^3)^{(1)} \to (a, d^3)^{(0)}((a, b)^{(0)})^3,$$
$$y \to \lambda. \qquad\qquad\qquad \square$$

We are now in the position to establish Theorem 7.7. We assume that in the common growth order $n^q A^n$ of the sequences $s_i(n)$ we have $A > 1$ because the polynomial case is much easier to handle, cf. exercise 7.11.

Let $G_i = (X_i, w_i, h_i)$, $0 \le i \le p - 1$, be a DOL system generating the sequence $s_i(n)$. For each of the alphabets X_i, we introduce the decomposition

$$X_i = X_{i\,\text{low}} \cup X_{i0} \cup \cdots \cup X_{iq}$$

exactly as above. We denote by H_{ij} the DOL scheme obtained from the scheme (X_i, h_i) by omitting all letters except those of X_{ij}.

The main idea in the proof is the following. We use induction on q. The basis of induction, $q = 0$, is almost the same as Lemma 7.11, we only have to take care of the additional difficulty caused by the alphabet $X_{i\,\text{low}}$. In the inductive step we first apply Lemma 7.11 to the scheme H_{iq}, and then add further components to the letters, simulating by the inductive hypothesis the growth of lower order. In order to be able to do this, we have to assure ourselves of the availability of all letters at each step of the derivation. This is accomplished by decomposing the systems G_i further, i.e., taking a multiple of p. Clearly, a DOL system merging this bigger set of systems also merges the original set.

We now derive some estimates needed to take care of the alphabets $X_{i\,\text{low}}$. Consider a fixed i, $0 \le i \le p - 1$, words $\alpha \in X_{i0}^+$ and $\beta \in X_{i\,\text{low}}^*$, and derivations of some length k according to G_i. The word α generates in k steps a word $\alpha_1 \beta_1$, where α_1 is a nonempty word over X_{i0} and β_1 is a word over $X_{i\,\text{low}}$. (As a matter of fact, the letters of α_1 may be scattered in the word rather than forming a prefix but the order does not matter because we are interested in lengths only.) The word β generates in k steps a word β_2 over $X_{i\,\text{low}}$. Let the growth for letters in $X_{i\,\text{low}}$ be majorized by a^n, $a < A$. Then, by the definition of the alphabets, there are constants c_1, c_2 and c_3 independent of k and i such that

$$\lg(\alpha_1) \ge c_1 A^k \lg(\alpha),$$
$$\lg(\beta_1) \le c_2 A^k \lg(\alpha),$$
$$\lg(\beta_2) \le c_3 a^k \lg(\beta).$$

Choose now k so large that

$$(c_3/c_1)(a/A)^k \leq \tfrac{1}{2}.$$

We are going to prove that if the ratio between the lengths of the original words β and α is bounded by a certain constant, then also the ratio between the lengths of the generated words $\beta_1\beta_2$ and α_1 is bounded by the same constant. This enables us to take care of the letters in the alphabet $X_{i\,\text{low}}$.

Assume, thus, that

$$\lg(\beta)/\lg(\alpha) \leq cc_2/c_1 \qquad (c \geq 2).$$

Then, by the inequalities obtained for the constants c_i and the choice of the number k,

(8) $$\lg(\beta_1\beta_2)/\lg(\alpha_1) \leq c_2/c_1 + (c_3/c_1)(a/A)^k(\lg(\beta)/\lg(\alpha))$$

$$\leq c_2/c_1 + \tfrac{1}{2}cc_2/c_1 \leq cc_2/c_1.$$

We now decompose the systems G_i further, i.e., take a multiple of p such that for the resulting set of systems (for which we still use our original notation) the following three conditions are satisfied:

(i) Any growth in H_{ij} $(i = 0, \ldots, p - 1; j = 0, \ldots, q)$ is asymptotically equal to a constant times A^n.
(ii) Every letter of X_{ij} $(i = 0, \ldots, p - 1; j = 0, \ldots, q)$ generates in G_i in one step letters of all of the alphabets $X_{i,j-1}, \ldots, X_{i,0}$.
(iii) The inequality (8) holds for one-step derivations, i.e., $k = 1$.

Note that conditions (i) and (ii) depend essentially on Lemma 7.10. Moreover, by omitting some words from the beginning of the word sequences generated by G_i (an operation which does not affect mergeability), we can also assume that the following condition is satisfied:

(iv) The axiom of G_i $(i = 0, \ldots, p - 1)$ contains letters of all of the alphabets $X_{i0}, \ldots, X_{iq}$.

We have now all the technical tools needed for the proof of Theorem 7.7 by induction on q. If $q = 0$ we first delete all letters of the alphabets $X_{i\,\text{low}}$ and construct by (i) a system G as in the proof of Lemma 7.11. Then we take p copies $x^{(0)}, \ldots, x^{(p-1)}$ of each letter x deleted, and join these copies as components to the letters of G so that the original systems G_i will be simulated. This can be done because of condition (iii). All the time we add y's in such a way that the correct lengths are obtained.

In the inductive step, we at first delete all letters of the alphabets $X_{i\,\text{low}}$, $X_{i0}, \ldots, X_{i(q-1)}$. We then construct by (i) a system according to Lemma 7.11. Because of conditions (ii) and (iv), the inductive hypothesis can now be applied to complete the induction. $\qquad\square$

EXAMPLE 7.3. This example is a modification of Example 7.2. The letters a, b, c, d correspond to the same letters in Example 7.2. Define

$$G_0 = (\{a, e, f\}, ae, h_0)$$

where

$$e \to e^4 a, \qquad a \to a^4 f, \qquad f \to f$$

and

$$G_1 = (\{g, b, c, d\}, gb, h_1)$$

where

$$g \to g^4 b, \qquad b \to b^2 c^3, \qquad c \to c^2 d^4, \qquad d \to bd.$$

Now the common order of growth is $n \cdot 4^n$, and the alphabets involved are

$$X_{0\,\text{low}} = \{f\}, \qquad X_{00} = \{a\}, \qquad X_{01} = \{e\},$$
$$X_{1\,\text{low}} = \varnothing, \qquad X_{10} = \{b, c, d\}, \qquad X_{11} = \{g\}.$$

Using the constructions in the preceding proof, we obtain, for instance, the following system. The axiom is

$$(e, g)^{(0)} (a, b)^{(0)}$$

and the productions are

$$(e, g)^{(0)} \to (e, g)^{(1)},$$
$$(e, g)^{(1)} \to (e, g)^{(0)4} (a, b)^{(0)},$$
$$(a, b)^{(0)} \to (a, b)^{(1)},$$
$$(a, b)^{(1)} \to (af, b)^{(0)} (a, b)^{(0)} (a^2, c^3)^{(0)} y^2,$$
$$(a^2, c^3)^{(0)} \to (a^2, c^3)^{(1)} y^2,$$
$$(a^2, c^3)^{(1)} \to (a^2 f, c^3)^{(0)2} (a, d^3)^{(0)4} y^4,$$
$$(a, d^3)^{(0)} \to (a, d^3)^{(1)} y^2,$$
$$(a, d^3)^{(1)} \to (af, d^3)^{(0)} (a, b)^{(0)3} y,$$
$$(af, b)^{(0)} \to (af, b)^{(1)},$$
$$(af, b)^{(1)} \to (af, b)^{(0)2} (a^2, c^3)^{(0)} y^3,$$
$$(a^2 f, c^3)^{(0)} \to (a^2 f, c^3)^{(1)} y^2,$$
$$(a^2 f, c^3)^{(1)} \to (a^2 f, c^3)^{(0)2} (af, d^3)^{(0)} (a, d^3)^{(0)3} y^5,$$
$$(af, d^3)^{(0)} \to (af, d^3)^{(1)} y^2,$$
$$(af, d^3)^{(1)} \to (af, d^3)^{(0)} (af, b)^{(0)} (a, b)^{(0)2} y^2,$$
$$y \to \lambda.$$

Note how the productions of Example 7.2 appear as a substructure. In fact, the first three productions of Example 7.2 are exactly as before, whereas in the next three productions the simulation of $X_{0\,\text{low}}$ causes the addition of f and the corresponding increase in the exponent of y to the right sides.

EXERCISES

1. Give an analytical expression of the form $\sum_i P_i(n)\rho_i^n$ for the growth function of the system G_1 in Example 7.2. (This is an instance of the analysis problem.)

2. Construct a PDOL system whose growth function equals $(n + 1)^4 - n^2$. (This is an instance of the synthesis problem.)

3. Construct a matrix representation for the $\mathbb{N}$-rational sequence obtained by merging the sequences

$$d_1(n) = 0, \qquad d_2(n) = 2^n, \qquad d_3(n) = (n + 1)^2.$$

Interpret the matrix representation as an HDOL system.

4. Prove the following so-called "Lemma of long constant intervals": No sequence $r(n)$ having the property that, for every integer n, there are integers m and $i > n$ such that

$$r(m + i) \neq r(m + n) = r(m + n - 1) = \cdots = r(m)$$

is $\mathbb{Z}$-rational. Using this lemma, give an example of a D1L (length) sequence which is not $\mathbb{Z}$-rational.

5. Prove that, for every $\mathbb{N}$-rational series r over an alphabet X, one can find a PDTOL system G with X as the alphabet of tables, and a letter b in the alphabet of G with the following property. For any w, the coefficient (r, w) equals the number of occurrences of b in the word generated by G via the sequence of tables w.

6. Prove that an $\mathbb{N}$-rational series r having a matrix representation $(r, w) = \pi(\mu w)\eta$ with positive entries in η is a DTOL series. (This result is easily obtained by a direct construction. It is also a consequence of the result CDTOL = NDTOL, known in L systems theory, cf. [NRSS].)

7. Show that every DOL sequence $d(n)$ can be decomposed into PDOL sequences. Conclude by Lemma 7.4 that every $\mathbb{N}$-rational sequence can be decomposed into PDOL sequences.
(Hint: If M is the growth matrix of $d(n)$ then, by König's lemma, there are positive integers m and p such that $M^{m+p} \geq M^m$ with respect to the natural elementwise ordering. Apply then Theorem 7.5 to the sequences

$$d_i(n) = d(m + i + np) \qquad (i = 0, \ldots, p - 1).$$

The result can also be obtained by the inclusion DOL $\subseteq$ CPDFOL established in [NRSS].

8. Apply Corollary II.8.5 to obtain a better bound α_0 in Lemma 7.2.

9. Extend Theorem 7.6 to DTOL series r, i.e., deduce an upper bound for $(r, wx)/(r, w)$. Can you obtain also a positive lower bound for this quotient (assuming that always $(r, w) \neq 0$)?

10. Show that, for any $\mathbb{N}$-rational sequence $r(n)$, there is a DTOL series r_1 over the alphabet $\{x, y\}$ such that, for all n, $r(n) = (r_1, x^n y)$.

11. Prove Theorem 7.7 in the polynomially bounded case, i.e., $A = 1$. (One can either use the straightforward approach of merging first growth functions of the form cn^q and then simulating lower growth by suitable components, or proceed inductively. For the latter approach, the reader is referred to [Ru1].)

12. Assume that $r(n)$ and $s(n)$ are DOL sequences such that $s(n) \neq 0$ for every n. Prove that if the sequence $t(n) = r(n)/s(n)$ has integer terms then it is a DOL sequence.

(Hint: Use Corollary 7.8 and a result by Berstel, cf. [Be1], according to which $t(n)$ is $\mathbb{Z}$-rational.)

13. Prove that there is a DOL sequence $r(n)$ such that (i) $r(n) < r(n - 1)$ holds for infinitely many values of n, and (ii) for each natural number n there exists an m such that

$$r(m) < r(m + 1) < \cdots < r(m + n).$$

(Thus, the result corresponding to the lemma of long constant intervals does not hold for inequalities. The sequence $r(n)$ is obtained by merging two DOL sequences $k^n + s(n)$ and $k^n + t(n)$ where (i) k is large, (ii) $s(n) < t(n)$ holds in some arbitrarily long intervals, and (iii) $s(n) > t(n)$ infinitely often. The details can be found in [Ka2].)

14. Generalize the decomposition techniques in this section to show that for any commutative $\mathbb{N}$-rational series r (cf. exercise II.11.4) there exist natural numbers m and n such that, for all letters x and words w whose Parikh vector contains no component less than n, we have $(r, wx^m) \geq (r, w)$. Conclude that if a commutative series r is defined by a function

$$F(n_1, n_2) = f(n_1) + g(n_2) - n_1 n_2,$$

where f and g are any functions, then r is not $\mathbb{N}$-rational. (This exercise, as well as exercise II.11.4 are due to J. Karhumäki.)

III.8 Growth functions of L systems: decidability

The results in the previous section and Chapter II (in particular, Sections II.10 and II.12) enable us to deduce almost directly a number of results concerning decidability and undecidability of problems dealing with DTOL and related series. We consider problems of equivalence (i.e., whether or not two given series coincide), characterization (i.e., whether or not a series given in some class actually belongs to a specified subclass), determining the number of zeros appearing as coefficients, as well as the monotonicity of the coefficients. In some cases there is a remarkable difference depending on whether the alphabet consists of one or more letters. Some of the most important problems in the one-letter case remain open.

Theorem 8.1. *There is an algorithm for deciding whether or not two given DTOL functions (or even HDTOL functions) coincide. The special case of deciding whether or not two given DOL systems, with alphabets of cardinalities k_1 and k_2, generate the same sequences is solved by deciding whether or not the first $k_1 + k_2$ numbers in the sequences are the same.*

PROOF. The first sentence is established by applying Corollary II.12.3 to the difference of the given series. (Clearly, the difference is $\mathbb{Z}$-rational.) The second sentence follows by noting that the degree of the numerator (respectively denominator) of the generating function $F_i(x)$, written in lowest terms, for the sequence is at most $k_i - 1$ (respectively k_i). (Cf. Lemma II.9.4.) Hence, if the difference $F_1(x) - F_2(x)$ does not vanish identically, it must contain a term

$$a_k x^k, \qquad k \leq k_1 + k_2 - 1, a_k \neq 0. \qquad \square$$

Hence considering two DOL systems with the same alphabet of cardinality k, it suffices to compare the first $2k$ numbers in the sequences to decide whether or not the sequences coincide. This is, in fact, the best possible bound, cf. exercise 8.4.

The following simple result is an instance of decidability similar to the previous theorem.

Theorem 8.2. *It is decidable whether or not a given DOL sequence is polynomially bounded.*

PROOF. This is a special case of the matters discussed in Section II.12, cf. especially exercise II.12.4. $\qquad \square$

A polynomially bounded DOL sequence can be decomposed into polynomials. Assuming that the underlying DOL system is reduced (i.e., every letter is reachable from the axiom), one can also give (cf. exercise 8.5) an effective bound α, depending on the cardinality of the alphabet, such that the sequence is not polynomially bounded iff some power M^p with $p \leq \alpha$ of the growth matrix M has a diagonal element greater than 1.

The following theorem gives a positive solution for the decidability of characterization of sequences.

Theorem 8.3. *It is decidable whether or not a given $\mathbb{Z}$-rational sequence is* (i) *$\mathbb{N}$-rational,* (ii) *a DOL sequence,* (iii) *a PDOL sequence.*

PROOF. The theorem follows by Theorems II.12.4, Theorem 7.5, Theorem 7.6, and Corollary 7.8. In fact, (i) and (iii) are immediate consequences of the results mentioned, whereas (ii) requires the additional fact that one can effectively compare growth orders of DOL sequences. This additional fact is a consequence of the result that one can effectively compare the minimal positive roots and their multiplicities of given integer polynomials. $\qquad \square$

EXAMPLE 8.1. A sequence obtained by merging two DOL sequences $r(n)$ and $s(n)$ is a DOL sequence iff $r(n)$ and $s(n)$ have the same growth order. Let $z(n)$ be a $\mathbb{Z}$-rational sequence of positive integers and k an integer sufficiently large. The sequence obtained by merging the sequences k^{n+1} and $k^{n+1} + z(n)$ is a DOL sequence. It is a PDOL sequence iff $z(n)$ is $\mathbb{N}$-rational.

We now turn to the discussion of problems concerning the existence of zeroes and monotonicity among coefficients. In view of Theorem 7.1, the problem of deciding whether for some word w the coefficients (r_1, w) and (r_2, w) coincide in two given DTOL series r_1 and r_2 is the same as deciding the existence of a zero among the coefficients in a given $\mathbb{Z}$-rational series. However, by a simple result (Lemma 8.4 below) which corresponds to merging in the one-letter case, this problem is further reduced to the following one: Given a DTOL series r of which it is known that $(r, w) \leq (r, wx)$ holds for all words w and letters x, decide whether the equality holds for some w and x. Similarly, the problem of deciding whether all coefficients in a given $\mathbb{Z}$-rational series are nonnegative is the same as deciding whether $(r_1, w) \leq (r_2, w)$ holds for all words w in two given DTOL series r_1 and r_2. This problem can also be further reduced to the problem of monotonicity among the coefficients in a given DTOL series, as will be seen below. Of course, these results hold in the one-letter case as well and, thus, corresponding reducibilities are obtained for sequences.

We will first establish a number of undecidability results in the case the alphabet contains (at least) two letters. Our basic tool is Theorem II.12.1. We will also need Lemma 7.2, and the subsequent Lemma 8.4 which is a weak analogy of Theorem 7.7 for the case of an alphabet with more than one letter. We omit the proof of Lemma 8.4. It is similar to that of Lemma 7.2, and is based on Theorem 7.1. In the statement of Lemma 8.4, the operator "odd" is defined for words of odd length by

$$\text{odd}(x_1 x_2 \cdots x_{2n+1}) = x_1 x_3 \cdots x_{2n+1}.$$

Lemma 8.4. *For any $\mathbb{Z}$-rational series r, there exists an integer α_0 such that, for all integers $\alpha \geq \alpha_0$, the series r_1 defined by*

$$(r_1, w) = \alpha^{n+1} \quad \text{for } \lg(w) = 2n,$$
$$(r_1, w) = \alpha^{n+1} + (r, \text{odd}(w)) \quad \text{for } \lg(w) = 2n + 1,$$

is a DTOL series.

Theorem 8.5. *Each of the decision problems (i)–(viii) listed below is undecidable. In the statement of the problems, X is a two-letter alphabet, r (respectively r_P) is a DTOL (respectively PDTOL) series over X, w is a word over X, x is a letter of X, and $s(n)$ is a PDOL sequence.*

    (i) *(Comparison between PDOL and PDTOL growth.) Given s and r_P, decide whether $s(n) \leq (r_P, w)$ holds for all n and w with $\lg(w) = n$.*

114

(ii) (*Monotonicity of* DTOL *growth.*) *Given* r, *decide whether* $(r, w) \leq (r, wx)$ *holds for all* w *and* x.

(iii) (*Equal size between* PDOL *and* PDTOL *growth.*) *Given* s *and* r_P *of which it is known that* $s(n) \leq (r_P, w)$ *holds for all* n *and* w *with* $\lg(w) = n$, *decide whether the equality holds for some such* n *and* w.

(iv) (*Constant level in* DTOL *growth*) *Given* r *of which it is known that* $(r, w) \leq (r, wx)$ *holds for all* w *and* x, *decide whether the equality holds for some* w *and* x.

(v) (*Ultimate comparison between* PDOL *and* PDTOL *growth.*) *Given* s *and* r_P, *decide whether* $s(n) \leq (r_P, w)$ *holds for all sufficiently large* n *and* w *with* $\lg(w) = n$.

(vi) (*Ultimate monotonicity of* DTOL *growth.*) *Given* r, *decide whether* $(r, w) \leq (r, wx)$ *holds for all* x *and all sufficiently long* w.

(vii) (*Equal size between* PDOL *and* PDTOL *growth infinitely often.*) *Given* s *and* r_P *of which it is known that* $s(n) \leq (r_P, w)$ *holds for all* n *and* w *with* $\lg(w) = n$, *decide whether the equality holds for infinitely many such pairs* (n, w).

(viii) (*Constant level in* DTOL *growth infinitely often.*) *Given* r *of which it is known that* $(r, w) \leq (r, wx)$ *holds for all* w *and* x, *decide whether the equality holds for infinitely many pairs* (x, w).

PROOF. Theorem II.12.1.(i) gives by Lemma 7.2 (respectively Lemma 8.4) the undecidability of (iii) (respectively (iv)). Similarly, Theorem II.12.1.(ii) is utilized to establish the undecidability of (vii) and (viii), Theorem II.12.1.(iii) to establish that of (i) and (ii), and Theorem II.12.1.(iv) to establish that of (v) and (vi). □

As regards the case of one-letter alphabets, problems corresponding to Theorem 5.(i)–(vi) are open, whereas analogies of (vii) and (viii) are shown decidable in the following theorem which is an immediate consequence of Theorem II.12.2.(iii).

Theorem 8.6. *The following two problems are decidable. Given two* DOL *sequences* $r(n)$ *and* $s(n)$, *determine whether or not* $r(n) = s(n)$ *holds for infinitely many values of* n. *Given a* DOL *sequence* $r(n)$, *determine whether or not* $r(n + 1) = r(n)$ *holds for infinitely many* n.

That the problems in one-letter case corresponding to (i)–(vi) in Theorem 8.5 are open is due to the fact that it is not known (and, in our estimation, will be a very difficult problem) whether Theorem II.12.1 holds for one-letter alphabets X, apart from point (ii) which is solved in Theorem II.12.2. In view of Lemma 7.2 and Theorem 7.7, it is easy to see that the decidability of any of the following four problems implies the decidability of the other three problems.

(i) Decide whether the number 0 occurs in a given $\mathbb{Z}$-rational sequence.

115

(ii) Given two DOL sequences $r(n)$ and $s(n)$, decide whether or not $r(n) = s(n)$ holds for some n.

(iii) Given two PDOL sequences $r(n)$ and $s(n)$, decide whether or not $r(n) = s(n)$ holds for some n.

(iv) Given a DOL sequence $r(n)$, decide whether or not $r(n + 1) = r(n)$ holds for some n.

Similar equivalent versions can be given to problems corresponding to Theorem II.12.1.(iii)–(iv) in one-letter case.

We mention, finally, that it is an open problem to extend Theorem 7.5, Corollary 7.8 and Theorem 8.3 to alphabets with more than one letter (or to show that the statements do not hold in this case). One of the difficulties is to find proper generalizations for the decomposition result of Lemma 7.4.

EXERCISES

1. Construct an algorithm which for a given DOL (respectively PDOL) sequence produces a DOL (respectively PDOL) system generating the sequence and with minimal cardinality of the alphabet. (This problem is sometimes referred to as the "cell number minimization problem.")

2. Prove that the following problem (corresponding to Theorem 8.5(iv)) is decidable. Given a PDTOL series r, decide whether

$$(r, w) = (r, wx)$$

holds for some word w and letter x.

3. The basic tool in this section for establishing undecidability results is Theorem II.12.1. Find for this theorem a proof which does not use the undecidability of Hilbert's tenth problem.

Hint: Show first by the method of [E, p. 156] that there is no algorithm which would solve problem (i) for arbitrary alphabets X. Assume then that (i) is decidable for a fixed alphabet containing the letters x and y and derive a contradiction by considering the $\mathbb{Z}$-rational series

$$h(r) + \text{char}((\{x^n, x^{n-1}y, \ldots, xy^{n-1}\}^*)^c),$$

where r is an arbitrary $\mathbb{Z}$-rational series over the alphabet $X = \{x_1, \ldots, x_n\}$, $n \geq 3$, and the homomorphism h is defined by

$$h(x_1) = x^n, \qquad h(x_2) = x^{n-1}y, \ldots, h(x_n) = xy^{n-1}.$$

The problems (ii)–(iv) are treated in the same way.

4. Show that the bound $k_1 + k_2$ given in Theorem 8.1 is the best possible, i.e., given natural numbers k_1 and k_2, construct two DOL systems with alphabets of cardinalities k_1 and k_2 such that the generated sequences are not the same although the first $k_1 + k_2 - 1$ numbers in these sequences are the same.

5. Consider a reduced DOL system with growth matrix M of dimension k. Show that the generated DOL sequence is not polynomially bounded iff some power

M^p with $p \leq 2^k + k - 1$ possesses a diagonal element greater than 1. (Cf. [Ka1].)

6. Give an algorithm for deciding whether or not the ranges of two given DOL growth functions coincide. (Cf. [BN].)

7. Assume that an algorithm is known for finding out whether the number 0 occurs in a given $\mathbb{Z}$-rational sequence. Show that this algorithm can be used to solve each of the following decision problems concerning word sequences. (At present, the decidability status of (ii)–(iv) is open.)

   (i) Given two DOL systems, decide whether or not the generated word sequences differ from each other only in a finite number of terms. (Ultimate equivalence problem for DOL systems.)

   (ii) Given two HDOL systems, decide whether or not the generated word sequences coincide. (Equivalence problem for HDOL systems.)

   (iii) Given two HDOL systems, decide whether or not the generated word sequences differ from each other only in a finite number of terms. (Ultimate equivalence problem for HDOL systems.)

   (iv) Given two HDOL systems with nonsingular growth matrices, decide whether or not the generated word sequences have an empty (respectively finite) intersection.

(Cf. [Ru2,3].)

IV
Algebraic series and context-free languages

In this chapter we will discuss both the general theory of algebraic formal power series and its applications to context-free languages. Since many notions concerning series are very closely related to familiar notions concerning languages, we prefer to present the general theory in connection with applications rather than trying to separate strictly the two things. Perhaps the most significant single result established in this chapter is Shamir's Theorem which gives a characterization similar to the one given in the Representation Theorem of Schützenberger. Shamir's Theorem can also be viewed as a formalized version of the intuitive ideas connected with the notion of a pushdown automaton. The reader will also notice that in many cases, for instance as regards sequences, the algebraic counterpart of the theory developed for rational series is missing.

IV.1 Proper algebraic systems of equations

Unless stated otherwise, A means in this chapter a commutative semiring. We prefer to consider series over a free monoid only, i.e., the family $A\langle\langle X^* \rangle\rangle$, although a number of results remain valid in more general cases. In fact, we often have X^+ instead of X^*.

The following definition introduces a generalization of the notion of a proper linear system discussed in Section II.1. The right sides of the equations may now be arbitrary polynomials. The additional assumption concerning supports, supp $p_i \subseteq (X \cup Z)^+ - Z$, is needed to ensure solvability.

Definition. Let $Z = \{z_1, \ldots, z_n\}$ be an alphabet with $Z \cap X = \emptyset$. An *algebraic system* (with respect to the pair (A, X) and with variables in Z) is a set of equations of the form

$$(1) \qquad\qquad z_i = p_i \qquad i = 1, \ldots, n,$$

where $p_i \in A\langle\langle(X \cup Z)^*\rangle$. The system (1) is termed *proper* iff, for each i and j,

(2) $$(p_i, \lambda) = 0 \quad \text{and} \quad (p_i, z_j) = 0.$$

Let $q \in A\langle\langle(X \cup Z)^*\rangle\rangle$ and $\sigma = (\sigma_1, \ldots, \sigma_n)$, where each σ_i is a quasi-regular series in $A\langle\langle(X \cup Z)^*\rangle\rangle$. We denote by the juxtaposition σq the series in $A\langle\langle(X \cup Z)^*\rangle\rangle$ obtained from q by replacing, for $i = 1, \ldots, n$, simultaneously each occurrence of z_i by σ_i. (Note that σ defines an endomorphism in $A\langle\langle(X \cup Z)^*\rangle\rangle$.) The operator σ is applied to m-tuples of series, as well as to matrices of series, componentwise. If q is a polynomial (or an m-tuple of polynomials), it is not required that the series σ_i are quasiregular.

An n-tuple $\sigma = (\sigma_1, \ldots, \sigma_n)$ of elements of $A\langle\langle X^*\rangle\rangle$ is termed a *solution* of (1) iff $\sigma_i = \sigma p_i$, for $i = 1, \ldots, n$.

Theorem 1.1. *For each proper algebraic system (1), there exists exactly one solution* $\sigma = (\sigma_1, \ldots, \sigma_n)$ *satisfying the condition* $(\sigma_i, \lambda) = 0$, *for* $i = 1, \ldots, n$.

PROOF. Consider the following "restrictions" $R_k s$ of series s, where k is an integer ≥ 0:

$$R_k s = \sum_{\lg(w) \leq k} (s, w) w \qquad (s \in A\langle\langle(X \cup Z)^*\rangle\rangle).$$

The operator R_k is applied to m-tuples of series componentwise.

Denote $p = (p_1, \ldots, p_n)$. We claim that, for any k and any n-tuple $\rho = (\rho_1, \ldots, \rho_n)$ satisfying $(\rho_i, \lambda) = (\rho_i, z_j) = 0$ for all i and j,

(3) $$R_{k+1}(\rho p) = R_{k+1}((R_k \rho) p).$$

In fact, it is obvious that the left side contains at least all the terms appearing on the right side. But because of (2) and our assumption concerning ρ, no contributions to the left side are made by the replacement $(R_{k+1}\rho)p$. Thus, (3) follows.

Define now a sequence of n-tuples as follows:

$$\sigma^0 = (0, \ldots, 0); \qquad \sigma^{j+1} = \sigma^j p, \qquad \text{for } j \geq 0.$$

(The sequence is going to constitute successive approximations for the solution we are looking for.) We prove first that, for any integers k and h,

(4) $$R_k \sigma^k = R_k \sigma^{k+h}.$$

In case $k = 0$, (4) holds true for all h because of (2). Proceeding inductively, we assume that (4) holds true for a fixed value k and all h. By (3) we obtain, for an arbitrary h,

$$R_{k+1}\sigma^{k+1} = R_{k+1}(\sigma^k p) = R_{k+1}((R_k \sigma^k)p)$$
$$= R_{k+1}((R_k \sigma^{k+h})p) = R_{k+1}(\sigma^{k+h}p) = R_{k+1}\sigma^{k+1+h}.$$

119

By (4), we may now conclude that the sequence σ^j converges to a well-defined $\sigma = (\sigma_1, \ldots, \sigma_n)$ with $\sigma_i \in A\langle\langle X^* \rangle\rangle$. Furthermore, $\sigma p = \sigma$ because $R_0(\sigma p) = R_0 \sigma$ and, for any k, we obtain by (3):

$$R_{k+1}(\sigma p) = R_{k+1}((R_k \sigma)p) = R_{k+1}((R_k \sigma^k)p)$$
$$= R_{k+1}(\sigma^k p) = R_{k+1}\sigma^{k+1} = R_{k+1}\sigma.$$

Hence, σ is a solution of (1). Assume that σ' is an arbitrary solution satisfying $(\sigma_i', \lambda) = 0$ for all i. Consequently, $R_0 \sigma = R_0 \sigma'$. Proceeding inductively, we assume that $R_k \sigma = R_k \sigma'$. Using (3) and the fact that σ and σ' are solutions, we obtain

$$R_{k+1}\sigma = R_{k+1}(\sigma p) = R_{k+1}((R_k \sigma)p) = R_{k+1}((R_k \sigma')p) = R_{k+1}(\sigma' p) = R_{k+1}\sigma'.$$

This implies that $\sigma = \sigma'$.   □

Note that the additional assumption made in the statement of Theorem 1.1 is a condition necessary for the uniqueness of the solution. For instance, if $A = \mathbb{N}$ and we consider the system consisting of the single equation $z_1 = z_1 z_1$, then both $\sigma_1 = 0$ and $\sigma_1' = 1$ appear as solutions.

We give now the definitions basic for the considerations in this chapter.

Definition. A quasiregular series in $A\langle\langle X^* \rangle\rangle$ is termed *A-algebraic* iff it is a component of the solution of a proper algebraic system. The family of A-algebraic series is denoted by $A^{\text{alg}}\langle\langle X^* \rangle\rangle$. A language over X is termed *A-algebraic* iff it equals the support of some A-algebraic series.

EXAMPLE 1.1. Choose $A = \mathbb{N}$ and $X = \{x, \bar{x}\}$. The proper algebraic system consisting of the single equation

$$z_1 = xz_1\bar{x} + x\bar{x}$$

defines the series

$$\sum_{n=1}^{\infty} x^n \bar{x}^n$$

which is the characteristic series of the language $\{x^n \bar{x}^n \mid n \geq 1\}$. The support of the series defined by the system

$$z_1 = z_1 z_1 + xz_1\bar{x} + x\bar{x}$$

equals the Dyck language over X. (If x and $\bar{x}$ are viewed as the left and the right parenthesis, respectively, then the Dyck language consists of all sequences of properly nested parentheses.) However, the series is not the characteristic series of the Dyck language. The word $x\bar{x}x\bar{x}x\bar{x}$ is the shortest one in the series with a coefficient > 1.

On the other hand, if we consider the system

$$z_1 = z_2^2 + z_1 z_2$$
$$z_2 = xz_1\bar{x} + xz_2\bar{x} + x\bar{x},$$

we see that the characteristic series of the Dyck language appears as the component of the solution corresponding to z_1. In fact, z_2 corresponds to prime words in the language, i.e., words having no proper initial subword in the language. Every word in the Dyck language can be uniquely represented as a product of prime words. Instead of the system above, we could consider the simpler system

$$z_1 = z_2 + z_1 z_2$$

$$z_2 = x z_1 \bar{x} + x \bar{x}.$$

Although it is not proper, it has a unique solution obtainable by the method of Theorem 1.1. This is due to the fact that the occurrence of the single variable z_2 on the right-hand side is "harmless" and does not lead to infinite sums in the procedure of successive iterations.

EXAMPLE 1.2. Choose $A = \mathbb{N}$ and $X = \{x_0, x_1, \ldots, x_m\}$. Define a homomorphism h of X^* into the additive monoid of integers by

$$h(x_i) = i - 1 \qquad \text{for } i = 0, \ldots, m.$$

By definition, the *Lukasiewicz language* L over X consists of all words w such that $h(w) = -1$ and all proper initial subwords w' of w satisfy $h(w') \geq 0$. Now the characteristic series of the Lukasiewicz language is obtained from the proper algebraic system with the single equation

$$z_1 = x_0 + x_1 z_1 + \cdots + x_m z_1^m.$$

To see this, it suffices to make the following simple observations:

(i) A word w belongs to L^k, $k \geq 1$, exactly in case $h(w) = -k$ and all proper initial subwords w' of w satisfy $h(w') > h(w)$.
(ii) All words of the form $x_k w$, where $0 \leq k \leq m$ and $w \in L^k$, belong to L.
(iii) Every word in L possesses a unique representation in the form $x_k w$, where $0 \leq k \leq m$ and $w \in L^k$.

The examples above already show the interconnection between context-free grammars and the algebraic systems defining algebraic series. This interconnection will now be made explicit.

Definition. Let r be an $\mathbb{N}$-algebraic series defined as the first component of the solution for the equations (1). The context-free grammar G_r *supporting* r is defined by

$$G_r = (Z, X, z_1, F),$$

where for $i = 1, \ldots, n$, the production $z_i \to w$ is in F iff $w \in \text{supp}(p_i)$. Conversely, let

$$G = (\{z_1, \ldots, z_n\}, X, z_1, F)$$

be a context-free grammar such that no production in F has a single nonterminal or the empty word on the right side. The $\mathbb{N}$-algebraic series $r(G)$ *generated* by G is defined as the first component of the solution for the proper algebraic system

$$z_i = p_i \qquad i = 1, \ldots, n,$$

where p_i is the polynomial formed by the right sides of the productions for z_i. (If there are no productions for z_i, the equation reads $z_i = 0$.)

Note that if we begin with a grammar, form the generated series r and, finally, the supporting grammar G_r, we are back in the original grammar. The analogous result does not necessarily hold true if we begin with a series, then go to a grammar and, finally, back to a series because some coefficients may be lost in the first transition. This situation can be avoided if we begin with a system of equations modified according to Lemma 2.5 below.

Theorem 1.2. *The support of an $\mathbb{N}$-algebraic series r equals the language generated by the supporting grammar G_r. Consequently, the language $L(G)$ of a context-free grammar G equals the support of the series $r(G)$ generated by G.*

PROOF. The second sentence follows from the first one by the remark made before the theorem. For the proof of the first sentence, it is useful to keep in mind the fact that the method of constructing successive approximations for the solution in the proof of Theorem 1.1 corresponds to running through derivation trees, "level by level" in a bottom-up fashion.

Assume that r equals the first component of the solution for (1), and consider first the inclusion

(5) $$L(G_r) \subseteq \mathrm{supp}(r).$$

To establish (5), it suffices to prove, for all k, the validity of the following statement $IH(k)$: For $i = 1, \ldots, n$, whenever a word $w \in X^*$ possesses according to G_r a derivation from z_i of length $\leq k$, then w belongs to supp σ_i^k. Here σ^k refers to the sequence of successive approximations constructed in the proof of Theorem 1.1, and σ_i^k is the ith component of σ^k.

By the definition of G_r, $IH(1)$ holds true. We now proceed inductively, assuming that $IH(k)$ holds true. Let $w \in X^*$ (in fact, we can assume $w \in X^+$) possess in G_r a derivation from z_i of length $\leq k + 1$. This derivation can be written as

$$z_i \Rightarrow u_1 z_{i_1} u_2 \cdots u_t z_{i_t} u_{t+1} \Rightarrow^* u_1 w_{i_1} u_2 \cdots u_t w_{i_t} u_{t+1} = w,$$

where each $u_j \in X^*$ and $t \geq 1$. Furthermore, each of the derivations in G_r

$$z_{i_j} \Rightarrow^* w_{i_j} \qquad j = 1, \ldots, t$$

is of length $\leq k$. By $IH(k)$ we now infer that

$$w_{i_j} \in \text{supp } \sigma_{i_j}^k \qquad j = 1, \ldots, t.$$

Since by the definition of G_r,

$$u_1 z_{i_1} u_2 \cdots u_t z_{i_t} u_{t+1} \in \text{supp } p_i$$

and since $\sigma^{k+1} = \sigma^k p$, we now conclude that

$$w \in \text{supp } \sigma_i^{k+1},$$

which completes the induction.

To prove the reverse inclusion

$$\text{supp}(r) \subseteq L(G_r),$$

it suffices to show, for all k, that the following statement $IH(k)$ holds: For $i = 1, \ldots, n$, whenever $w \in \text{supp } \sigma_i^k$ then $z_i \Rightarrow^* w$ according to G_r. (Note that the derivation may be longer than k, cf. exercise 1.3.) $IH(0)$ holds vacuously. Assuming $IH(k)$, we consider a word $w \in \text{supp } \sigma_i^{k+1}$. Thus, there is a word

$$(6) \qquad w' = u_1 z_{i_1} u_2 \cdots u_t z_{i_t} u_{t+1} \in \text{supp } p_i, \qquad u_j \in X^*,$$

such that w can be written as

$$w = u_1 w_{i_1} u_2 \cdots u_t w_{i_t} u_{t+1},$$

where

$$w_{i_j} \in \text{supp } \sigma_{i_j}^k \qquad j = 1, \ldots, t.$$

By (6) $z_i \Rightarrow w'$, and by $IH(k)$, $z_{i_j} \Rightarrow^* w_{i_j}$, for $j = 1, \ldots, t$. Consequently, $z_i \Rightarrow^* w$ which completes the induction in this case. $\qquad \square$

Let A_+ be a positive semiring (defined as in Section II.5). The following lemma is obtained immediately by considering the natural homomorphism of A_+ onto the Boolean semiring $\mathbb{B}$.

Lemma 1.3. *The supports of A_+-algebraic series coincide with the supports of $\mathbb{B}$-algebraic series.*

Combining now Theorem 1.2 with Lemma 1.3, we obtain the following result.

Theorem 1.4. *All of the following statements are equivalent for a language L:*

(i) *L is a λ-free context-free language.*
(ii) *L is $\mathbb{N}$-algebraic.*
(iii) *L is $\mathbb{B}$-algebraic.*
(iv) *L is A_+-algebraic, for all positive semirings A_+.*
(v) *L is A_+-algebraic, for some positive semiring A_+.*

We want to emphasize at this point that the family of $\mathbb{Z}$-algebraic languages contains properly the family of $\mathbb{N}$-algebraic languages. There are even $\mathbb{Z}$-rational series with a non-context-free support, for instance,

$$\sum_{m,n} (m^2 - n)x^m y^n.$$

Some simple results concerning the interrelation between $\mathbb{Z}$-algebraic and $\mathbb{N}$-algebraic series will be established in the next section.

We conclude the present section with some results concerning the ambiguity of context-free languages from the point of view of $\mathbb{N}$-algebraic series.

Theorem 1.5. *The coefficient of each word w in the $\mathbb{N}$-algebraic series $r(G_1)$ generated by a context-free grammar G_1 equals the ambiguity of w according to G_1. Hence, G_1 is unambiguous (respectively of bounded ambiguity) iff the coefficients of $r(G_1)$ are ≤ 1 (respectively bounded).*

PROOF. Consider a context-free grammar

$$G_1 = (\{z_1, \ldots, z_n\}, X, z_1, F)$$

such that no production in F has a single nonterminal or the empty word on the right side. Let $r(G_1)$ be the $\mathbb{N}$-algebraic series generated by G_1. Thus, $r(G_1)$ equals the first component σ_1 of the solution $\sigma = (\sigma_1, \ldots, \sigma_n)$ for the proper algebraic system

$$z_i = p_i \qquad i = 1, \ldots, n,$$

where p_i is the polynomial formed by the right sides of the productions for z_i.

We consider also grammars

$$G_i = (\{z_1, \ldots, z_n\}, X, z_i, F) \qquad i = 2, \ldots, n.$$

Note that it follows by Theorem 1.2 that

$$L(G_i) = \mathrm{supp}(\sigma_i) \qquad i = 1, \ldots, n.$$

For a word $w \in X^+$ and an integer i, $1 \leq i \leq n$, we denote by $\mathrm{amb}(G_i, w)$ the ambiguity of w according to the grammar G_i. Hence, we have to prove that, for all w,

$$\mathrm{amb}(G_1, w) = (\sigma_1, w).$$

We do this by establishing the more general claim: for all i and w,

(7) $$\mathrm{amb}(G_i, w) = (\sigma_i, w).$$

The proof of (7) is by induction on the length of w. We consider again the successive approximations

$$\sigma^j = (\sigma_1^j, \ldots, \sigma_n^j) \qquad j \geq 0$$

and make use of the equation (4). Thus, the coefficient of a word w of length $\leq t$ in σ_i equals the coefficient of w in $\sigma_i^{t_1}$, for any $t_1 \geq t$.

124

Clearly, (7) holds true for $\lg(w) = 1$. (In fact, in the absence of productions $z_i \to z_j$ and $z_i \to \lambda$, the ambiguity of a letter is at most one. On the other hand, the coefficient of w in σ_i is seen from σ_i^1.)

We now assume, inductively, that (7) holds for every i and all words w whose length does not exceed t, $t \geq 1$. Consider from now on a fixed i and a fixed word w of length $t + 1$.

We first compute $\text{amb}(G_i, w)$ in the following way. Let u_j, $j = 1, \ldots, \alpha$, be all the words over the alphabet $\{z_1, \ldots, z_n\} \cup X$ satisfying both of the following conditions: (i) $z_i \Rightarrow u_j$, (ii) $u_j \Rightarrow^* w$. (Thus, z_i yields u_j in one step, and u_j yields w in some number, maybe zero, of steps.) Consider now a fixed u_j and write it in the form

$$u_j = v_1 z_{j_1} v_2 \cdots v_\beta z_{j_\beta} v_{\beta+1}, \qquad 1 \leq j_m \leq n, \, v_m \in X^*.$$

(Thus, β equals the number of occurrences of nonterminals in u_j. Possibly $\beta = 0$.) Let

$$(w_1^{(m)}, \ldots, w_\beta^{(m)}) \qquad m = 1, \ldots, \gamma$$

be all the ordered β-tuples of words such that

$$w = v_1 w_1^{(m)} v_2 \cdots v_\beta w_\beta^{(m)} v_{\beta+1}$$

and

$$z_{j_1} \Rightarrow^* w_1^{(m)}, \ldots, z_{j_\beta} \Rightarrow^* w_\beta^{(m)}.$$

Assume that

$$\text{amb}(G_{j_l}, w_l^{(m)}) = \delta_l^m, \qquad 1 \leq m \leq \gamma, \, 1 \leq l \leq \beta.$$

By our assumptions concerning the grammar G_1, the numbers δ_l^n are finite. Denoting

$$\varepsilon_j = \sum_{m=1}^{\gamma} \prod_{l=1}^{\beta} \delta_l^m$$

we see that

$$\text{amb}(G_i, w) = \sum_{j=1}^{\alpha} \varepsilon_j.$$

Since all words $w_l^{(m)}$ are of length $\leq t$, we infer by the inductive assumption that

$$(\sigma_{j_l}, w_l^{(m)}) = \delta_l^m, \qquad 1 \leq m \leq \gamma, \qquad 1 \leq l \leq \beta.$$

Hence,

$$(\sigma_{j_l}^t, w_l^{(m)}) = \delta_l^m, \qquad 1 \leq m \leq \gamma, \, 1 \leq l \leq \beta.$$

Because $(\sigma_i, w) = (\sigma_i^{t+1}, w)$ and it is easy to see that

$$(\sigma_i^{t+1}, w) = \sum_{j=1}^{\alpha} \varepsilon_j$$

(note that each u_j occurs as a term in p_i), we have completed the inductive proof of (7).

We now obtain the following corollary which corresponds to Theorem 1.4.

Theorem 1.6. *All of the following statements are equivalent for a language L:*

    (i) *L is an unambiguous λ-free context-free language.*
    (ii) *The characteristic series of L is $\mathbb{N}$-algebraic.*
    (iii) *The characteristic series of L is A_+-algebraic, for all positive semirings A_+.*

EXERCISES

1. Show that the characteristic series of the Dyck language over the alphabet $X_t = \{x_1, \ldots, x_t, \bar{x}_1, \ldots, \bar{x}_t\}$, $t \geq 1$, is A-algebraic. Let L_t be the language over X_t consisting of all words w which can be reduced to λ using the relations $x_i \bar{x}_i = \bar{x}_i x_i = \lambda$, for $i = 1, \ldots, t$. Show that the characteristic series of L_t is A-algebraic.

2. Consider the alphabet X_t in the previous exercise. Define a mapping $\rho: X_t^* \to X_t^*$ by

$$\rho(\lambda) = \lambda, \qquad \rho(wx_i) = \rho(w)x_i,$$

$$\rho(w\bar{x}_i) = \begin{cases} \rho(w)\bar{x}_i & \text{if } \rho(w) \notin X_t^* x_i \\ w_1 & \text{if } \rho(w) = w_1 x_i. \end{cases}$$

Fix an element $\gamma \in X_t^*$ such that $\rho(\gamma) = \gamma$, and consider the language $L_\gamma = \{w \mid \rho(w) = \gamma\}$. Prove that the characteristic series of L_γ is A-algebraic. (The mapping ρ will be considered in more detail in Section IV.4.)

3. Consider the proof of Theorem 1.2. Show by an example that, for $w \in \sigma_i^k$, the length of the derivation $z_i \Rightarrow^* w$ may be greater than k. Give an upper bound, as sharp as possible, for the length of this derivation.

4. Verify the statement made in the text concerning the series $\sum (m^2 - n)x^m y^n$. Consider some of the well-known language families between the families of context-free and context-sensitive languages, cf. [Sa1]. To which of these families does the support of the series mentioned belong? (Note that although the answer is easy in some cases, it is open, for instance, as regards the family of matrix languages.)

5. Prove that the family of $\mathbb{N}$-algebraic languages over the alphabet $\{x\}$ equals the family of regular languages over $\{x\}$. (It is not known whether there are nonregular $\mathbb{Z}$-algebraic languages over $\{x\}$.) Show that there are $\mathbb{N}$-algebraic series over $\{x\}$ which are not $\mathbb{N}$-rational.
   Hint: Consider the equation $z_1 = x + z_1^2$.

6. Prove that the $\mathbb{N}$-algebraic series defined by the equation $z_1 = x_1 + z_1 x_2 z_1$ equals

$$\sum_{n=0}^{\infty} \binom{2n}{n}(n + 1)^{-1}(x_1 x_2)^n x_1.$$

7. Construct, for a given $k \geq 1$, a proper algebraic system having more than k solutions, provided the solutions are not required to be quasiregular. Can a proper system have infinitely many solutions in this case?

8. Show that, for a given $\mathbb{R}$-algebraic series r, there is a constant q such that

$$|(r, w)| \leq q^{\lg(w)}$$

holds for all words w. Conclude that there exists a constant q_1 such that

$$\sum_{\lg(w) = n} |(r, w)| \leq q_1^n$$

holds for all n.

IV.2 Reduction theorems

We establish in this section some "normal form" results: every A-algebraic series equals the first component in the solution of a proper algebraic system such that the supports of the right sides p_i in the equations satisfy some additional conditions. In particular, such results can be obtained where the additional conditions resemble the ones in the Chomsky and Greibach normal forms for grammars. At the end of the section, we prove a simple reduction theorem for $\mathbb{Z}$-rational series, as well as some related results.

The proof of the following lemma involves only a straightforward construction of introducing new variables and is, therefore, omitted. The construction is exactly the same as that involving context-free grammars when one eliminates the terminal letters from productions with the exception of productions where a nonterminal yields a terminal.

Lemma 2.1. *Any A-algebraic series equals the first component of the solution for a proper algebraic system*

$$(1) \qquad\qquad z_i = p_i \qquad i = 1, \ldots, n,$$

where

$$\text{supp}(p_i) \subset X \cup ZZ^+, \qquad \text{for } i = 1, \ldots, n.$$

Definition. An algebraic system (1) is in the *quadratic* form iff

$$\text{supp}(p_i) \subseteq X \cup Z^2, \qquad \text{for } i = 1, \ldots, n.$$

The following theorem corresponds to binary Chomsky normal forms for grammars. It is established using Lemma 2.1 and the familiar construction concerning grammars where one introduces new nonterminals to reduce the length of the right sides of the productions to be at most two. Further details are omitted.

Theorem 2.2. *Any A-algebraic series equals the first component in the solution for some algebraic system in quadratic form.*

127

Our next theorem is a useful lemma which will be needed, for instance, in the proof of Shamir's Theorem in Section 4. It corresponds to the language-theoretic result of reducing a given context-free grammar to Greibach normal form.

Theorem 2.3. *Every A-algebraic series over X^* equals the first component in the solution for some algebraic system such that the supports of the right sides of the equations are included in the set*

$$(2) \qquad\qquad X \cup X\bar{Z} \cup X\bar{Z}^2,$$

where $\bar{Z}$ denotes the set of variables in the system.

PROOF. Consider an arbitrary A-algebraic series. By Theorem 2.2, we assume that it is defined by a system in the quadratic form. We write the system in the matrix form

$$(3) \qquad\qquad Z = ZM + P,$$

where

$$Z = (z_1, \ldots, z_n), \qquad P = \left(\sum_j \alpha_j^1 x_j, \ldots, \sum_j \alpha_j^n x_j \right)$$

and M is the $n \times n$ matrix whose (i, j)th entry equals the polynomial

$$\sum_k \alpha_{ik}^j z_k \in A\langle Z^* \rangle.$$

We now introduce n^2 new variables

$$y_{ij} \qquad 1 \le i, j \le n$$

and denote by Y the $n \times n$ matrix whose (i, j)th entry equals y_{ij}. We denote, furthermore, by $M^{(i)}$ the ith row of the matrix M, for $i = 1, \ldots, n$, and similarly by $Y^{(i)}$ the ith row of the matrix Y. Finally, for $i = 1, \ldots, n$, let C_i be the square matrix in $A^{n \times n}$ whose (j, k)th entry equals α_{ij}^k.

Consider the algebraic system with variables z_i and y_{ij}, written in the matrix form

$$(4) \qquad Z = P + PY, \qquad Y^{(i)} = (P + PY)C_i + (P + PY)C_i Y,$$

where $i = 1, \ldots, n$. Clearly, if we write (4) in terms of equations for the variables z_i and y_{ij} (whose collection we denote by $\bar{Z}$), we see that the supports of the right sides of the resulting system are all included in the set (2).

Observe that (4) is obtained by writing (3) in the form

$$(5) \qquad\qquad Z = P + PY, \qquad Y = M + MY$$

and noting that, for all i,

$$M^{(i)} = ZC_i = (P + PY)C_i$$

and

$$Y^{(i)} = M^{(i)} + M^{(i)}Y.$$

Denote by $\sigma = (\sigma_1, \ldots, \sigma_n)$ the solution of (3). The matrix M^+ clearly exists (and is by Corollary II.1.3 an element of $A^{\text{rat}}\langle\langle Z^*\rangle\rangle$). Denote by σ_{ij}, $1 \le i$, $j \le n$, the series appearing in the (i, j)th position of the matrix σM^+. (Here juxtaposition stands for the replacement operator defined in Section 1.) By Theorem 1.1, (4) has a unique solution. It can be readily verified that the $(n + n^2)$-tuple consisting of the series σ_i and σ_{ij} satisfies (5) and, hence, is the solution of (4). $\qquad\square$

The balance of this section investigates interrelations between $\mathbb{Z}$-algebraic and $\mathbb{N}$-algebraic series and similar matters, continuing the discussions begun at the end of the previous section.

As in Section II.8, if A is a subring of $\mathbb{R}$, we denote by A_+ the semiring consisting of the nonnegative numbers in A. The following theorem is analogous to Corollary II.8.2.

Theorem 2.4. *Assume that A is a subring of $\mathbb{R}$. Then every A-algebraic series can be represented (in infinitely many ways) as the difference of two A_+-algebraic series. Consequently, every $\mathbb{Z}$-algebraic series can be represented as the difference of two $\mathbb{N}$-algebraic series.*

PROOF. Assume that the given A-algebraic series r equals the first component of the solution for the system (1). We introduce new variables z_i^+ and z_i^-, $i = 1, \ldots, n$, and replace in (1) z_i everywhere by $z_i^+ - z_i^-$. By applying distributive laws the ith equation of the original system is transformed into the equation

$$z_i^+ - z_i^- = p_i^+ - p_i^-,$$

where both p_i^+ and p_i^- have nonnegative coefficients. Let now r^+ (respectively r^-) be the A_+-algebraic series obtained as the first component of the solution of the proper algebraic system $z_i^+ = p_i^+$, $i = 1, \ldots, n$ (respectively $z_i^- = p_i^-$, $i = 1, \ldots, n$). Then $r = r^+ - r^-$. $\qquad\square$

Lemma 2.5. *Every $\mathbb{N}$-algebraic series equals the first component in the solution for an algebraic system where the coefficients on the right sides are ≤ 1 (after all possible additions have been carried out).*

PROOF. Assume again that the given series is defined by the system (1). By Theorem 2.2, we can assume without loss of generality that

$$\text{supp}(p_i) \subseteq X \cup Z^2, \qquad i = 1, \ldots, n.$$

Let k be the greatest coefficient appearing in some p_i, $i = 1, \ldots, n$. If $k = 1$, there is nothing to prove. Thus, we assume that $k > 1$.

Introduce new variables

$$z_i^j \quad \text{and} \quad y_{x_i}^j, \quad \text{where } j = 1, \ldots, k - 1; x \in X; i = 1, \ldots, n.$$

Define coding homomorphisms h_j, $j = 1, \ldots, k - 1$, on Z^* by

$$h_j(z_i) = z_i^j \qquad i = 1, \ldots, n.$$

129

We now perform the following replacements in each p_i, yielding a new polynomial p_i'. Each term w in p_i with $w \in Z^2$ (respectively $w \in X$) and with a coefficient $\alpha > 1$ is replaced by the sum

$$w + h_1(w) + \cdots + h_{\alpha-1}(w) \qquad \text{(respectively } w + y_w^1 + \cdots + y_w^{\alpha-1}).$$

Clearly, the coefficients in p_i' are ≤ 1. Now the required algebraic system is the following one:

$$z_i = p_i', \qquad z_i^j = p_i', \qquad y_x^j = x,$$

where $i = 1, \ldots, n, j = 1, \ldots, k - 1$, and $x \in X$. Note that although the new system is not necessarily proper, the existence of a unique solution (whose first component equals that in the solution for the original system) obtainable by the method of Theorem 1.1 is immediate. □

Nonproper systems will be discussed in Section 6. Note that Lemma 2.5 is not valid with the additional requirement that the system to be constructed is proper, as seen by considering the simple system

$$z_1 = 2x.$$

By Lemma 2.5 and Theorem 2.4, we now obtain the following result which provides some information concerning the question of what languages can be supports of $\mathbb{Z}$-algebraic series. (As we have seen before, such a language need not be context-free.)

Theorem 2.6. *Let L be the support of some $\mathbb{Z}$-algebraic series. Then there are two context-free grammars G_1 and G_2 with the following property. L consists of all words w such that the ambiguity of w according to G_1 is different from the ambiguity of w according to G_2.*

Because there are inherently ambiguous context-free languages, we get now also the next theorem.

Theorem 2.7. *The characteristic series of an $\mathbb{N}$-algebraic language is not necessarily $\mathbb{N}$-algebraic.*

We point out, finally, that the interconnection between algebraic systems and grammars discussed in the first two sections of this chapter can be naturally extended to concern weighted context-free grammars, weights being elements of the semiring A. (In the weighted grammars considered in the literature, attention is restricted to positive subsemirings of $\mathbb{R}$.) The coefficients in the series generated by a grammar G give the weights of the corresponding words according to G. In this case no information is lost in the transition from an algebraic system to the supporting grammar.

EXERCISES

1. Define the series in exercises 1.1, 1.2 and 1.6 by systems (i) in quadratic form, (ii) in Greibach form (i.e., form obtained from Theorem 2.3).

2. Prove Lemma 2.1 and Theorem 2.2. Give also a detailed verification of the equation (5) needed in the proof of Theorem 2.3.

3. Strengthen Theorem 2.6 in the following way. For the support L of a given $\mathbb{Z}$-algebraic series, one may construct two context-free grammars G_1 and G_2 in the Chomsky normal form (respectively in the Greibach normal form) with the following property. L consists of all words w such that the ambiguity of w according to G_1 is different from the ambiguity of w according to G_2. In contrast to this result, establish the following negative result. It is not always possible to represent a given $\mathbb{Z}$-algebraic series as the difference of two $\mathbb{N}$-algebraic series generated by grammars in the Chomsky (respectively in the Greibach) normal form.

4. Study the applications of Theorem 2.6 for showing that some languages are not $\mathbb{Z}$-algebraic. In particular, prove that $\{a^{2^n} \mid n \geq 0\}$ and $\{a^{n^2} \mid n \geq 1\}$ are not $\mathbb{Z}$-algebraic. (Cf. also exercise 5.8.)

IV.3 Closure properties

In this section we discuss some operations defined for A-algebraic series, and the problem of whether or not the resulting series is still A-algebraic. Results can be applied to establish closure and nonclosure properties of families of A-algebraic languages as well. Further results concerning closure properties are given in exercises 3.1–3.4.

Theorem 3.1. *The family $A^{\mathrm{alg}}\langle\langle X^*\rangle\rangle$ is closed under sum, product and quasi-inverse. If A is a ring then this family is closed also under difference.*

PROOF. Consider product. Let r (respectively r') be the first component in the solution for the system

(1) $z_i = p_i,$ $i = 1, \ldots, n$ (respectively $z_i' = p_i', i = 1, \ldots, n'$).

Then rr' is the component corresponding to z_0 in the solution for the system consisting of all equations (1) and of the additional equation

$$z_0 = p_1 p_1'.$$

The proof for the operations of sum, quasi-inverse and difference is similar, the "initial" equation being in these cases

$$z_0 = p_1 + p_1', \qquad z_0 = p_1 + z_1 z_0, \qquad z_0 = p_1 - p_1',$$

respectively.   □

Considering supports, we get from Theorem 3.1 the result that the family of context-free languages is closed under union, catenation and Kleene +.

This conclusion cannot be made on the basis of Theorem 3.1 for $\mathbb{Z}$-algebraic languages.

We investigate next closure under various homomorphisms, both as regards the semiring A and the monoid X^*.

Theorem 3.2. *Let $h\colon A \to A'$ be a semiring homomorphism. If $r \in A^{\mathrm{alg}}\langle\langle X^*\rangle\rangle$ then $hr \in A'^{\mathrm{alg}}\langle\langle X^*\rangle\rangle$.*

PROOF. Let r be the first component in the solution for the proper algebraic system $z_i = p_i$, $i = 1, \ldots, n$. Clearly, the system $z_i = hp_i$, $i = 1, \ldots, n$, is proper. But since the coefficients in the components of the solution for a proper algebraic system are constructed by semiring operations from the coefficients in the equations, we conclude that hr equals the first component of the solution for the latter system. A detailed verification can be based on the restriction operator R_k considered in Section 1. $\qquad\square$

Turning into the discussion of monoid homomorphisms, we note first that erasing homomorphisms do not necessarily map algebraic series into algebraic series because of the simple reason that the possibly existing image is not necessarily quasiregular. However, this is only a minor difficulty compared to summability difficulties caused, for instance, by projections. Even under strong summability assumptions concerning A, no result corresponding to Theorem II.4.6 is known for algebraic series. A result in this direction is Theorem 6.4 below.

EXAMPLE 3.1. Choose $A = \mathbb{N}$, and consider the $\mathbb{N}$-algebraic series

$$r = x_1 + \sum_{n \geq 1} x_2^n$$

and the endomorphism h of $\{x_1, x_2\}^*$ defined by $h(x_1) = \lambda$, $h(x_2) = x_2$. Then hr is not quasiregular. For the series

$$r_1 = \sum_{n \geq 1} (x_1^n + x_2^n),$$

$h(r_1)$ is not even defined. (In fact, considering the system of equations formed as in the proof of Theorem 3.2, we are led to the impossible equation $z_1 = 1 + z_1$.)

However, the following result can be obtained.

Theorem 3.3. *Let h be a nonerasing homomorphism of X^* into Y^*. If $r \in A^{\mathrm{alg}}\langle\langle X^*\rangle\rangle$ then $hr \in A^{\mathrm{alg}}\langle\langle Y^*\rangle\rangle$.*

PROOF. The theorem is established in the same way as the preceding one. It suffices to notice that the new system $z_i = hp_i$ is proper because h is non-erasing. $\qquad\square$

Theorem 3.4. *Let h be a substitution defined on X (and extended to $A\langle\langle X^* \rangle\rangle$) such that, for each $x \in X$, hx is an A-algebraic series in $A\langle\langle Y^* \rangle\rangle$. If r belongs to $A^{\mathrm{alg}}\langle\langle X^* \rangle\rangle$, then hr belongs to $A^{\mathrm{alg}}\langle\langle Y^* \rangle\rangle$.*

PROOF. Assume that r is the first component in the solution of the proper algebraic system

$$(2) \qquad\qquad z_i = p_i, \qquad i = 1, \ldots, n.$$

Furthermore, for $x \in X$, assume that hx is the first component in the solution of the proper algebraic system

$$(3) \qquad\qquad z_i^x = p_i^x, \qquad i = 1, \ldots, m_x.$$

Now hr is the component corresponding to z_1 in the solution for the proper algebraic system constructed in the following way. The system consists of all equations (3), where x ranges over the alphabet X, and of the equations (2) modified in such a way that in each p_i every letter $x \in X$ is replaced by p_1^x. □

The mapping h considered in Theorem 3.4 is a special case of a regulated algebraic transduction, a notion which will be considered in Section 7. The proof of the theorem is essentially the same as the proof of the fact that the family of context-free languages is closed under substitution. In the latter proof, the substituted languages may contain λ because situations like the one in Example 3.1 cannot arise in the case of languages. Theorem 3.4 can also be viewed as a generalization of Theorem 1.1, asserting the solvability also in the case where algebraic series may appear as coefficients.

We conclude this section with some results concerning closure under different types of products. As regards Hadamard product, we have the result that the Hadamard product of two A-algebraic series is not necessarily A-algebraic. This is illustrated by the following example, cf. also exercise 3.5.

EXAMPLE 3.2. Choose $A = \mathbb{N}$ and $X = \{x_1, x_2, x_3\}$. Let r (respectively r') be the first component in the solution for the proper algebraic system

$$z_1 = z_1 x_3 + z_2 x_3$$
$$z_2 = x_1 z_2 x_2 + x_1 x_2$$

(respectively the system

$$z_1 = x_1 z_1 + x_1 z_2$$
$$z_2 = x_2 z_2 x_3 + x_2 x_3).$$

Clearly,

$$r = \sum_{m,n \geq 1} x_1^m x_2^m x_3^n \quad \text{and} \quad r' = \sum_{m,n \geq 1} x_1^m x_2^n x_3^n.$$

If the Hadamard product

$$r \odot r' = \sum_{n \geq 1} x_1^n x_2^n x_3^n$$

were $\mathbb{N}$-algebraic, then the language $\{x_1^n x_2^n x_3^n \mid n \geq 1\}$ would be context-free.

The following weaker closure property can be established.

Theorem 3.5. *The Hadamard product of an A-rational and an A-algebraic series is A-algebraic.*

PROOF. Note first that the Hadamard product is commutative because we have assumed A to be commutative. Consider an A-rational series r_1 and an A-algebraic series r_2 over X^*. Let r_2 be the first component in the solution for a proper algebraic system $z_i = p_i$, $i = 1, \ldots, n$. Let μ be a representation of X^* into $A^{m \times m}$ such that, for all $w \in X^+$,

$$(r_1, w) = (\mu(w))_{1m}.$$

We shall construct a proper algebraic system S such that $r_1 \odot r_2$ equals one component in its solution.

We introduce $n \cdot m^2$ new variables

$$z_i^{jk} \qquad 1 \leq i \leq n; 1 \leq j, k \leq m.$$

Denote by Z_1 the collection of all those variables z_i^{jk} and by M_i the $m \times m$ matrix whose (j, k)th entry equals z_i^{jk}. For each i, j, k in their appropriate ranges, we now construct a polynomial p_i^{jk} in $A\langle (X \cup Z_1)^* \rangle$ as follows. We replace in p_i each letter z_t by the matrix M_t and each letter $x \in X$ by the matrix $(\mu x)x$. (Note that we are, in fact, defining a regulated rational transduction.) These replacements and performing the additions and multiplications involved in p_i transform the original p_i into an $m \times m$ matrix. The polynomial p_i^{jk} is the (j, k)th entry in this matrix. The system S is now defined by

$$z_i^{jk} = p_i^{jk} \qquad 1 \leq i \leq n; 1 \leq j, k \leq m.$$

Clearly, S is proper. Moreover, it is not difficult to see that the component r in its solution corresponding to z_i^{jk} satisfies, for all $w \in X^*$,

$$(r, w) = (\mu w)_{jk} \cdot (s_i, w),$$

where s_i is the component corresponding to z_i in the original system. Consequently, the component corresponding to z_1^{1m} equals $r_1 \odot r_2$. $\qquad \square$

We illustrate the construction in the above proof by the following example.

EXAMPLE 3.3. Choose $A = \mathbb{Z}$ and $X = \{x_1, x_2\}$. Let r_1 be defined by the representation μ, where

$$\mu x_1 = \begin{pmatrix} 1 & 1 \\ 0 & 1 \end{pmatrix} \quad \text{and} \quad \mu x_2 = \begin{pmatrix} -1 & 0 \\ 2 & 1 \end{pmatrix},$$

such that for all w,

$$(r_1, w) = (\mu w)_{12}.$$

Let r_2 be defined by the system consisting of the single equation

$$z = x_1 z x_2 - x_1 x_2.$$

Following the proof of Theorem 3.5, we obtain first

$$\begin{pmatrix} z^{11} & z^{12} \\ z^{21} & z^{22} \end{pmatrix} = \begin{pmatrix} x_1 & x_1 \\ 0 & x_1 \end{pmatrix} \begin{pmatrix} z^{11} & z^{12} \\ z^{21} & z^{22} \end{pmatrix} \begin{pmatrix} -x_2 & 0 \\ 2x_2 & x_2 \end{pmatrix} - \begin{pmatrix} x_1 & x_1 \\ 0 & x_1 \end{pmatrix} \begin{pmatrix} -x_2 & 0 \\ 2x_2 & x_2 \end{pmatrix},$$

which gives the proper algebraic system

$$z^{11} = -x_1 z^{11} x_2 - x_1 z^{21} x_2 + 2x_1 z^{12} x_2 + 2x_1 z^{22} x_2 - x_1 x_2$$

$$z^{21} = -x_1 z^{21} x_2 + 2x_1 z^{22} x_2 - 2x_1 x_2$$

$$z^{12} = x_1 z^{12} x_2 + x_1 z^{22} x_2 - x_1 x_2$$

$$z^{22} = x_1 z^{22} x_2 - x_1 x_2.$$

In this particular case (because of the representation μ), the Hadamard product is determined by the two last equations only, yielding

$$r_1 \odot r_2 = \sum_{n=1}^{\infty} - n x_1^n x_2^n.$$

As a corollary of Theorem 3.5 we get the result that the intersection of a context-free and a regular language is context-free.

The Hurwitz product (also referred to as the shuffle product) $r \amalg s$ of two series r and s was defined in exercise II.4.6. Note that the Hurwitz product is associative, commutative and distributive (with respect to addition). The Hurwitz product of two A-algebraic series need not be A-algebraic. This is seen similarly as in Example 3.2. However, we are again able to obtain the following weaker result.

Theorem 3.6. *The Hurwitz product of an A-rational and an A-algebraic series is A-algebraic.*

PROOF. Let r (respectively s) be an A-rational (respectively A-algebraic) series over X. As in the definition of Hurwitz product, consider the auxiliary alphabet $\bar{X} = \{\bar{x} \mid x \in X\}$. Define two substitutions h_1 and h_2 on X^* by

$$h_1(x) = x\left(\sum_{\bar{w} \in \bar{X}^*} \bar{w}\right), \qquad h_2(x) = \left(\sum_{w \in X^*} w\right)\bar{x}, \qquad \text{for all } x \in X.$$

By Theorem II.4.2 (respectively Theorem 3.4), the series $r' = h_1(r)$ (respectively $s' = h_2(s)$) is A-rational (respectively A-algebraic). Let now h be the coding homomorphism defined by

$$h(x) = h(\bar{x}) = x, \qquad \text{for all } x \in X.$$

Now it is easily verified that

$$r \amalg s = h(r' \odot s').$$

Theorem 3.6 now follows by Theorems 3.5 and 3.3. $\qquad\square$

Exactly the same argument can be used in solving exercise II.4.6. Considering supports, one obtains the corollary that the shuffle product of a regular and a context-free (respectively regular) language is context-free (respectively regular).

EXERCISES

1. Show that the family of A-algebraic series is a rationally closed semiring (and, in addition, a ring if A is a ring) which contains all quasiregular A-rational series.

2. Show that the family of A-algebraic series is closed under inverse (monoid) homomorphism. Study conditions under which it is closed under inverse semiring homomorphism.

3. Define the mirror image $mi(r)$ of a series r by

$$(mi(r), w) = (r, mi(w)).$$

Show that the family of A-algebraic series is closed under mirror image.

4. Consider quasiregular series r in $\mathbb{B}\langle\langle X^* \rangle\rangle$. Define the "complement" r^C of r to be the quasiregular series satisfying, for all nonempty words w,

$$(r^C, w) = \begin{cases} 1 & \text{if } (r, w) = 0 \\ 0 & \text{if } (r, w) = 1. \end{cases}$$

Construct a $\mathbb{B}$-algebraic series r such that r^C is not $\mathbb{B}$-algebraic.

5. Show that the series

$$r = \sum_{n=1}^{\infty} \binom{2n}{n} x^n$$

is $\mathbb{N}$-algebraic. Show that the Hadamard square of $1 + r$ equals

$$\frac{2}{\pi} \int_0^{\pi/2} d\varphi / (1 - 4x(2 \sin \varphi)^2)^{1/2}.$$

Hint: Considering the solution r_1 of $z_1 = x + 2xz_1 + xz_1^2$, it is seen that $r = 2r_1^+$. Note also that

$$\int_0^{\pi/2} \sin^{2n} \varphi \, d\varphi = \binom{2n}{n} \cdot \frac{\pi}{2} \Big/ 2^{2n}.$$

This result gives another argument of showing that A-algebraic series are not closed under Hadamard product.

6. Consider an $\mathbb{N}$-algebraic series r over the alphabet $\{x_1, \ldots, x_m\}$ generated by an unambiguous context-free grammar G. Let the homomorphism h be defined

by $h(x_i) = x$, for $i = 1, \ldots, m$. Then, for each j, the coefficient of x^j in $h(r)$ equals the number of words of length j in $L(G)$. The series $h(r)$, viewed as a function in the complex variable x, is termed the *structure generating function* of G (or of $L(G)$).

Show that the structure generating functions of the grammars

$$G_1 = (\{S\}, \{a, b\}, S, \{S \rightarrow aS^2, S \rightarrow b\}),$$

$$G_2 = (\{S\}, \{a, b, (\;,\;)\}, S, \{S \rightarrow (SaS), S \rightarrow b\})$$

are, respectively,

$$f_1(x) = (1 - \sqrt{1 - 4x^2})/2x = \sum_{n=0}^{\infty} (2n)! \, x^{2n+1}/n! \, (n+1)!$$

$$f_2(x) = (1 - \sqrt{1 - 4x^4})/2x^3 = \sum_{n=0}^{\infty} (2n)! \, x^{4n+1}/n! \, (n+1)!$$

What are the radii of convergence of these two series? Note that G_1 (respectively G_2) generates the well-formed formulas of the implicational propositional calculus in one variable in Polish prefix (respectively parenthesis) notation.

7. Show that the structure generating function of an unambiguous nonexpansive grammar is a rational function. (Cf. [Ku] and [KM].) Use this result to give examples of context-free languages which cannot be generated by an unambiguous nonexpansive grammar. (In particular, $L(G_1)$ and $L(G_2)$ of the previous exercise are such languages.) The converse of this result is open, i.e., it is not known whether the structure generating function of an unambiguous language, which cannot be generated by an unambiguous nonexpansive grammar, is always nonrational.

8. Prove some of the main results concerning the wedge operator of [Gi] (e.g., the results in Section 5.5 of [Gi]) using Hurwitz product.

IV.4 Theorems of Shamir and Chomsky–Schützenberger

In this section we shall discuss some basic methods for computing the coefficients in an algebraic power series. The method given in Theorem 1.1 is an iterative one consisting of successive approximations. The procedures discussed in this section are, at least in some sense, noniterative. There are two basic results. The first one (Theorem 4.1, also referred to as Shamir's Theorem) uses a homomorphism of the free monoid into a multiplicative monoid of polynomials. The second one (Theorem 4.5, also referred to as the Chomsky–Schützenberger Theorem) produces the coefficients of a given algebraic series by a homomorphism from the characteristic series of the intersection between a Dyck language and a regular language.

From the point of view of formal language theory, methods for computing the coefficients in an algebraic power series can be used for determining the number of derivations of a word according to a given context-free grammar.

Definition. Consider the alphabet

$$Y = Y_1 \cup \bar{Y}_1, \qquad \bar{Y}_1 = \{\bar{y} \mid y \in Y_1\}, \qquad Y_1 \cap \bar{Y}_1 = \varnothing.$$

The *involutive monoid* $M(Y)$ (also called the "free half-group") is the monoid generated by Y with the defining relations

$$y\bar{y} = \lambda, \qquad \text{for all } y \in Y_1.$$

The *Dyck mapping* ρ of Y^* into itself is defined by

$$\rho(\lambda) = \lambda,$$

$$\rho(wy) = \rho(w)y, \qquad \text{for all } w \in Y^*, y \in Y_1,$$

$$\rho(w\bar{y}) = \begin{cases} \rho(w)\bar{y} & \text{if } \rho(w) \notin Y^*y, \\ w_1 & \text{if } \rho(w) = w_1 y. \end{cases}$$

Note that the relation E_ρ on Y^* defined by

$$w E_\rho w' \quad \text{iff} \quad \rho(w) = \rho(w')$$

is a congruence, the factor monoid Y^*/E_ρ being isomorphic to $M(Y)$.

Theorem 4.1. *Let r be a series in $A^{\mathrm{alg}}\langle\langle X^*\rangle\rangle$. Then there exist an alphabet $Y = Y_1 \cup \bar{Y}_1$, a representation h of X^+ into $A\langle M(Y)\rangle$ and an element γ of $M(Y)$ such that, for every $w \in X^+$,*

(1) $$(r, w) = (h(w), \gamma).$$

Moreover, h may be chosen in such a way that the condition

$$\mathrm{supp}(h(x)) \subseteq \bar{Y}_1 Y_1^2 \cup \bar{Y}_1 Y_1 \cup \bar{Y}_1$$

is satisfied for all $x \in X$.

PROOF. By Theorem 2.3, we assume that $r = \sigma_1$, where $\sigma = (\sigma_1, \ldots, \sigma_n)$ is the solution for the system

$$z_i = p_i \qquad i = 1, \ldots, n,$$

where for all i, denoting $Z = \{z_1, \ldots, z_n\}$,

(2) $$\mathrm{supp}(p_i) \subseteq XZ^2 \cup XZ \cup X.$$

We define

$$Y_1 = \{y_1, \ldots, y_n\}, \qquad \bar{Y}_1 = \{\bar{y} \mid y \in Y_1\}, \qquad Y = Y_1 \cup \bar{Y}_1.$$

The representation h of X^+ into $A\langle M(Y)\rangle$ is now defined by, for $x \in X$,

$$h(x) = \sum_{i,j,k} \{\alpha^i_{jk} \bar{y}_i y_k y_j \mid \alpha^i_{jk} = (p_i, xz_j z_k)\}$$

$$+ \sum_{i,j} \{\alpha^i_j \bar{y}_i y_j \mid \alpha^i_j = (p_i, xz_j)\} + \sum_i \{\alpha^i \bar{y}_i \mid \alpha^i = (p_i, x)\}.$$

We choose $\gamma = \bar{y}_1$. To establish (1) we prove the more general result

(3) $$(\sigma_i, w) = (h(w), \bar{y}_i), \qquad i = 1, \ldots, n.$$

(Note that h satisfies the condition concerning the supports of $h(x)$. Note also that the coefficients α depend also on x, so we should actually write, for instance, $\alpha_{jk}^i(x)$. However, no confusion should arise because of our usage of the simpler notation.)

The proof of (3) is based on the fact that the generation process (according to Theorem 1.1) of the coefficients of words w in the series σ_i corresponds to reductions in the sense of the Dyck mapping ρ in $h(w)$. The proof is by induction on $\lg(w)$.

Assume that $\lg(w) = 1$, i.e., $w = x \in X$. Then

$$(\sigma_i, w) = (p_i, x) = \alpha^i = (h(w), \bar{y}_i).$$

We now make the inductive hypothesis that (3) holds for all words w satisfying $\lg(w) \leq t$, where $t \geq 1$. Consider a word $w = xw_1$ of length $t + 1$. Thus, $\lg(w_1) = t$. By (2), we obtain

$$(\sigma_i, w) = (\sigma_i, xw_1) = \sum_{\substack{j,k \\ w_1 = u_1 u_2}} \alpha_{jk}^i(\sigma_j, u_1)(\sigma_k, u_2) + \sum_j \alpha_j^i(\sigma_j, w_1).$$

Hence, we may write by the inductive hypothesis

(4) $$(\sigma_i, w) = \sum_{\substack{j,k \\ w_1 = u_1 u_2}} \alpha_{jk}^i(h(u_1), \bar{y}_j)(h(u_2), \bar{y}_k) + \sum_j \alpha_j^i(h(w_1), \bar{y}_j).$$

On the other hand, we have

(5) $$(h(w), \bar{y}_i) = (h(x)h(w_1), \bar{y}_i).$$

Using (4) and (5), we now complete the inductive step as follows. By (5) and the definition of $h(x)$, we look for such terms in $h(w_1)$ which cancel (in the sense of the Dyck mapping) with $h(x)$ to yield $\bar{y}_i$. Writing the first sum on the right side of (4) in the form

$$\sum_{j,k} \alpha_{jk}^i \left(\sum_{w_1 = u_1 u_2} (h(u_1), \bar{y}_j)(h(u_2), \bar{y}_k) \right),$$

we see that to complete the inductive step it suffices to establish the equation

(6) $$(h(w_1), \bar{y}_j \bar{y}_k) = \sum_{w_1 = u_1 u_2} (h(u_1), \bar{y}_j)(h(u_2), \bar{y}_k).$$

(We assume that $\lg(w_1) \geq 2$ because, otherwise, the inductive step can be completed using only the second sum on the right side of (4).) Writing w_1 as a product of t letters, we see that

(7) $$h(w_1) = \Sigma_1 \cdots \Sigma_t,$$

where each of the Σ's is a sum of terms of the form $\bar{y}_{i_1} y_{k_1} y_{j_1}$, $\bar{y}_{i_1} y_{j_1}$ or $\bar{y}_{i_1}$, provided with some coefficients. We now apply the distributive law on the right-hand side of (7), and after that reduce the individual terms in the sense of the Dyck mapping. Because barred letters occur in terms of the Σ's in (7) only at the beginning, we see that the coefficient of $\bar{y}_j \bar{y}_k$ in $h(w_1)$ is obtained

139

by (i) considering all decompositions $w_1 = u_1 u_2$ (with $u_1 \neq \lambda$ and $u_2 \neq \lambda$) and (ii) summing up the products $(h(u_1), \bar{y}_j)(h(u_2), \bar{y}_k)$ obtained from each decomposition. This shows that (6) holds true.

(An alternative way to establish (6) is via the following sequence of equations:

$$\sum_{w_1 = u_1 u_2} (h(u_1), \bar{y}_j)(h(u_2), \bar{y}_k) = \sum_{w_1 = u_1 u_2} (\sigma_j, u_1)(\sigma_k, u_2) = (\sigma_j \sigma_k, w_1) = (h(w_1), \bar{y}_j \bar{y}_k).$$

Here the first equation follows by the inductive hypothesis, the second by the definition of the product, and the third by an inductive argument similar to the main induction.)

Having established (6), we can now complete the inductive step leading to the validity of (3) by (4) and (5) and the definition of $h(x)$, as already indicated. Note that the last sum in the definition of $h(x)$ need not be considered because $w_1 \neq \lambda$. $\qquad\qquad\square$

We illustrate the construction by some examples about $\mathbb{N}$-algebraic series.

EXAMPLE 4.1. The system consisting of the single equation

$$z = x_0 + x_1 z + x_2 z^2$$

generates the characteristic series of the Lukasiewicz language over $X = \{x_0, x_1, x_2\}$ (cf. Example 1.2). Following the notations of Theorem 4.1, we have in this case

$$Y = \{y_1, \bar{y}_1\}.$$

The representation h of X^+ into $\mathbb{N}\langle M(Y) \rangle$ is defined by

$$h(x_0) = \bar{y}_1, \qquad h(x_1) = \bar{y}_1 y_1, \qquad h(x_2) = \bar{y}_1 y_1 y_1.$$

Thus, the values of $h(w)$ are in this case always monomials and $(h(w), \bar{y}_1)$ equals either 1 or 0, depending on whether or not the monomial in question is reduced to $\bar{y}_1$ in the sense of the Dyck mapping, for instance,

$$\rho(h(x_2 x_0 x_2 x_2 x_0 x_0 x_1 x_0 x_0))$$
$$= \rho(\bar{y}_1 y_1 y_1 \bar{y}_1 \bar{y}_1 y_1 y_1 \bar{y}_1 y_1 y_1 \bar{y}_1 y_1 y_1 \bar{y}_1 \bar{y}_1 \bar{y}_1 y_1 \bar{y}_1 \bar{y}_1) = \bar{y}_1.$$

The representation h gives a pretty good idea of the properties of the Lukasiewicz language. For instance, no word beginning with x_0 or $x_1 x_0$, with the exception of these words themselves, can be in the language.

EXAMPLE 4.2. Consider the following system consisting of two equations

$$z_1 = 3x_1 z_1 z_2 z_2 + 2x_2 z_1 z_2 + x_1$$
$$z_2 = 4x_2 z_1 z_1 + 5x_1 z_2 + 6x_2.$$

(Note that supp(p_1) is not exactly of the form considered in the proof of

Theorem 4.1. However, the same construction applies in all cases where the supports are included in XZ^*.) We have now

$$Y = \{y_1, y_2, \bar{y}_1, \bar{y}_2\},$$

$$h(x_1) = 3\bar{y}_1 y_2 y_2 y_1 + \bar{y}_1 + 5\bar{y}_2 y_2,$$

$$h(x_2) = 2\bar{y}_1 y_2 y_1 + 4\bar{y}_2 y_1 y_1 + 6\bar{y}_2.$$

Let us compute the coefficient of the word $x_1 x_1 x_1 x_2 x_2$ in the series corresponding to z_1. (It equals the weight of the word $x_1 x_1 x_1 x_2 x_2$ according to the weighted grammar with nonterminals z_1 and z_2, initial letter z_1, and the six weighted productions obtained from the given equations for z_1 and z_2.) By Theorem 4.1, this coefficient is obtained as the coefficient of $\bar{y}_1$ in $h(x_1 x_1 x_1 x_2 x_2)$ when the reductions corresponding to the Dyck mapping have been made. Thus, we have to compute the coefficient of $\bar{y}_1$ in

$$(3\bar{y}_1 y_2 y_2 y_1 + \bar{y}_1 + 5\bar{y}_2 y_2)^3 (2\bar{y}_1 y_2 y_1 + 4\bar{y}_2 y_1 y_1 + 6\bar{y}_2)^2.$$

Before applying the reductions, there will be 243 terms in the resulting polynomial. (This shows clearly that, although the method given by Shamir's Theorem for computing the coefficients is in some sense noniterative, the combinatorial flavor of the ordinary iterative procedure is reflected in the form and complexity of the polynomials involved.) However, since we are only interested in the coefficient of $\bar{y}_1$, it suffices to consider the product

$$(3\bar{y}_1 y_2 y_2 y_1)(\bar{y}_1)(5\bar{y}_2 y_2)(6\bar{y}_2)(6\bar{y}_2),$$

which shows that the coefficient we are looking for equals 540.

Instead of the involutive monoid $M(Y)$, we can also state Theorem 4.1 in terms of the free group $G(Y_1)$ generated by Y_1. (We may visualize $\bar{Y}_1$ as the set of inverses of the letters in Y_1.) Although this may be more elegant mathematically, it does not in general yield a simpler method for computing the coefficients in an algebraic series.

Theorem 4.2. *Let r be a series in $A^{\mathrm{alg}}\langle\langle X^* \rangle\rangle$. Then there exist an alphabet Y_1, a representation h of X^+ into $A\langle G(Y_1)\rangle$ and an element γ of $G(Y_1)$ such that, for every $w \in X^+$,*

(8) $\qquad\qquad\qquad (r, w) = (h(w), \gamma).$

Moreover, h may be chosen in such a way that the condition

$$\mathrm{supp}(h(x)) \subseteq \bar{Y}_1 Y_1^4 \cup \bar{Y}_1 Y_1^2 \cup \bar{Y}_1 Y_1 \cup \bar{Y}_1$$

is satisfied for all $x \in X$.

PROOF. The argument runs along the lines of the proofs of Theorems 2.3 and 4.1. Rather than giving all the details, we only give an outline.

Modifying Theorem 2.3, we claim first that every A-algebraic series $\bar{r}$ over X^* is generated by a system with variables in Z_1 in which the supports of the right sides are included in the set

(9) $\qquad\qquad X \cup XX \cup XZ_1 X \cup XZ_1 XZ_1 X.$

To see this, we first construct for $\bar{r}$ according to Theorem 2.3 a system S_1 in which the supports of the right sides are included in the set

$$X \cup XZ \cup XZ^2.$$

By symmetry, we then construct for $\bar{r}$ another system S_2 (with the same variables) in which the supports of the right sides are included in the set

$$X \cup ZX \cup Z^2X.$$

Substituting right sides of the equations of S_2 for the corresponding variables on the right sides of the equations of S_1 (in monomials of the form $\alpha x z_j z_k$ only the last variable z_k is substituted for), we obtain a system S_3 for $\bar{r}$ in which the supports of the right sides are included in the set

$$X \cup X^2 \cup XZX \cup XZ^2X \cup XZ^3X.$$

We let now Z_1 be the alphabet consisting of the letters of Z and ordered pairs, triples, quadruples, quintuples and sixtuples of the letters of Z. (The intuitive meaning of a quadruple (z_i, z_j, z_k, z_l), for instance, is the product $\sigma_i \sigma_j \sigma_k \sigma_l$ of the corresponding series.) Using systems S_1, S_2 and S_3, one can now construct a system for $\bar{r}$ with variables in Z_1 such that the supports of the right sides of the equations are included in (9). How this is done, is seen from the following table, in which the first column gives an element of Z_1, the second column indicates how the right side of the equation for this element is constructed from the right sides of equations in S_1, S_2, S_3, and the third column tells in which set the support of the constructed right side is included.

z_i	S_3	$X \cup X^2 \cup XZ_1X$
(z_i, z_j)	S_1S_2	$X^2 \cup XZ_1X$
(z_i, z_j, z_k)	$S_1z_jS_2$	XZ_1X
(z_i, z_j, z_k, z_l)	$S_1z_jz_kS_2$	XZ_1X
$(z_i, z_j, z_k, z_l, z_m)$	$S_1z_jS_1z_lS_2$	XZ_1XZ_1X
$(z_i, z_j, z_k, z_l, z_m, z_n)$	$S_1z_jz_kS_1z_mS_2$	XZ_1XZ_1X

Having established our claim concerning the modified version of Theorem 2.3, we may now assume that the given algebraic series r equals the first component in the solution of the system

$$z_i = \sum_x \alpha_x^i x + \sum_{x,x'} \alpha_{xx'}^i xx' + \sum_{j,x,x'} \alpha_{xjx'}^i xz_jx'$$
$$+ \sum_{j,k,x,x',x''} \alpha_{xjx'kx''}^i xz_jx'z_kx'', \qquad i = 1, \ldots, n.$$

We define now

$$Z = \{z_1, \ldots, z_n\}, \qquad Y_1 = X \cup Z,$$

and consider the free group $G(Y_1)$ generated by Y_1. (The inverses of the generating elements are denoted by bars.) The representation h of X^+ into $A\langle G(Y_1)\rangle$ is now defined, for $x \in X$, by

$$h(x) = \bar{x} + \sum_i \alpha_x^i \bar{z}_i + \sum_{i,x'} \alpha_{xx'}^{'i} \bar{z}_i x'$$

$$+ \sum_{i,j,x'} \alpha_{xjx'}^i \bar{z}_i x' z_j + \sum_{i,j,k,x',x''} \alpha_{xjx'kx''}^i \bar{z}_i x'' z_k x' z_j.$$

We choose $\gamma = \bar{z}_1$. The proof of the validity of (8) is now carried out as in connection with Theorem 4.1 by establishing inductively the more general result

$$(\sigma_i, w) = (h(w), \bar{z}_i), \qquad i = 1, \ldots, n.$$

The basis of induction consists of words of length 1 and 2, and the inductive step is carried out by writing $w = x w_1 x''$ and using the equation

$$(\sigma_i, w) = (\sigma_i, x w_1 x'') = \sum_j \alpha_{xjx''}^i (\sigma_j, w_1) + \sum_{\substack{j,k \\ w_1 = u_1 x' u_2}} \alpha_{xjx'kx''}^i (\sigma_j, u_1)(\sigma_k, u_2). \qquad \square$$

As a corollary concerning grammars, we can interpret the result about the supports being included in the set (9) in the following way.

Theorem 4.3. *Every λ-free context-free language is generated by a context-free grammar such that the right side of every production belongs to the set*

$$V_T \cup V_T^2 \cup V_T V_N V_T \cup V_T V_N V_T V_N V_T,$$

where V_T denotes the terminal and V_N the nonterminal alphabet.

The form given for context-free grammars in Theorem 4.3 is referred to as the "Greibach–Nivat normal form". The transition to the Greibach–Nivat normal form (as well as the transition to the Greibach normal form, resulting from the proof of Theorem 2.3) preserves the ambiguity of every word. Another language-theoretic observation is that the construction in the proof of Theorem 4.1 is essentially a specification of a pushdown automaton with one state which accepts the language by the empty stack according to a grammar in the Greibach normal form.

Using a suitable encoding, one can prove a stronger version of Theorem 4.2, where the alphabet Y_1 consists of two letters only.

We shall now prove the converse of Shamir's Theorem.

Theorem 4.4. *Assume that r is a quasiregular series in $A\langle\langle X^*\rangle\rangle$ such that there exist an alphabet $Y = Y_1 \cup \bar{Y}_1$, a representation h of X^+ into $A\langle M(Y)\rangle$ satisfying for every $x \in X$*

(10) $$(h(x), \lambda) = 0, \qquad h(x) \neq 0,$$

and an element γ of $M(Y)$ with the property that

$$(r, w) = (h(w), \gamma)$$

is satisfied for every $w \in X^+$. Then r is A-algebraic.

143

PROOF. Let L_γ consists of all words w over Y such that $\rho(w) = \gamma$. Then the characteristic series r_1 of L_γ is A-algebraic. (Cf. Example 1.1 and exercise 1.2.) We consider now the alphabet X_1 whose letters are pairs (w, x), where $w \in Y^+$ and $x \in X$, defined as follows. A pair (w, x) belongs to X_1 iff w belongs to $\operatorname{supp}(h(x))$. Consider the series r_2 in $A\langle\langle X_1^* \rangle\rangle$ such that, for an arbitrary word $(w_1, x_1) \cdots (w_k, x_k)$,

$$(r_2, (w_1, x_1) \cdots (w_k, x_k)) = (h(x_1), w_1) \cdots (h(x_k), w_k).$$

Clearly, $r_2 \in A^{\text{rat}}\langle\langle X_1^* \rangle\rangle$ and $\operatorname{supp}(r_2) = X_1^+$. Consider also the series r_3 in $A\langle\langle X_1^* \rangle\rangle$ such that, for an arbitrary word $(w_1, x_1) \cdots (w_k, x_k)$,

$$(r_3, (w_1, x_1) \cdots (w_k, x_k)) = (r_1, w_1 \cdots w_k).$$

It is easy to see, by modifying the system generating r_1, that r_3 is A-algebraic. Let now h_1 be the coding homomorphism of X_1^* into X^* defined by

$$h_1(w, x) = x.$$

We obtain

$$r = h_1(r_2 \odot r_3).$$

This shows, by Theorems 3.3 and 3.5, that r is A-algebraic. □

In exactly the same way one can prove the converse of Theorem 4.2, only the definition of r_1 has to be modified accordingly. One can obtain also a stronger version of these two converses, where one considers representations

$$h: X^+ \to (A\langle M(Y) \rangle)^{m \times m} \quad \text{or} \quad h: X^+ \to (A\langle G(Y_1) \rangle)^{m \times m}$$

(with a restriction analogous to (10) concerning supports). If the coefficients of a series r are computed from

$$(r, w) = (h(w)_{1m}, \gamma),$$

then r is A-algebraic.

We conclude this section with the Chomsky–Schützenberger Theorem.

Theorem 4.5. *Let r be an A-algebraic series in $A\langle\langle X^* \rangle\rangle$. Then there exist an alphabet*

$$Y = Y_1 \cup \overline{Y}_1, \qquad \overline{Y}_1 = \{\bar{y} \mid y \in Y_1\}, \qquad Y_1 \cap \overline{Y}_1 = \varnothing,$$

and a regular language R over Y such that

(11) $$r = h(\operatorname{char}(D \cap R)),$$

where D is the Dyck language over Y and h is an alphabetical homomorphism such that, for every $y \in Y$, $h(y)$ equals either an element of X or an element of A (multiplied by λ).

PROOF. Assume that r equals the first component σ_1 in the solution $\sigma = (\sigma_1, \ldots, \sigma_n)$ of a proper algebraic system $z_i = p_i$, $i = 1, \ldots, n$. By Theorem 2.2, we assume that the system is of the form

(12) $$z_i = \sum_{j,k} \alpha_{jk}^i z_j z_k + \sum_j \alpha_j^i x_j, \qquad i = 1, \ldots, n.$$

Define

$$Y_1 = \{y_{jk}^i \mid \alpha_{jk}^i \neq 0\} \cup \{x_j^i \mid \alpha_j^i \neq 0\},$$
$$\bar{Y}_1 = \{\bar{y} \mid y \in Y_1\}, \qquad Y = Y_1 \cup \bar{Y}_1.$$

It is clear that if $\sigma' = (\sigma_1', \ldots, \sigma_n')$ is the solution of the system modified from (12)

(13) $$z_i = \sum_{j,k} \alpha_{jk}^i y_{jk}^i z_j \bar{y}_{jk}^i z_k + \sum_j \alpha_j^i x_j^i \bar{x}_j^i, \qquad i = 1, \ldots, n,$$

and h_1 is the homomorphism on Y^* defined by

$$h_1(x_j^i) = x_j, \qquad h_1(y_{jk}^i) = h_1(\bar{y}_{jk}^i) = h_1(\bar{x}_j^i) = \lambda,$$

then $\sigma = h_1(\sigma')$. (Although h_1 is erasing, the languages

$$L_{v,i} = \{w \mid h_1(w) = v, \, w \in \mathrm{supp}(\sigma_i')\}$$

are finite. Therefore, no difficulties arise with respect to summability. The same remark applies to the homomorphism h.)

Let now R be the regular language over Y whose characteristic series equals the first component in the solution of the system

(14) $$z_i = \sum_{j,k} y_{jk}^i z_j + \sum_{t,j,k} x_t^i \bar{x}_t^i \bar{y}_{jk}^i z_k + \sum_t x_t^i \bar{x}_t^i,$$

where $i = 1, \ldots, n$. Let D be the Dyck language over Y and h the homomorphism defined by

$$h(y_{jk}^i) = \alpha_{jk}^i \cdot \lambda, \qquad h(\bar{y}_{jk}^i) = \lambda, \qquad h(x_j^i) = x_j, \qquad h(\bar{x}_j^i) = \alpha_j^i \cdot \lambda.$$

We omit the detailed verification of the fact that (11) holds true for D, R and h defined above. In fact, the proof (by induction on the length of the generation process) of the weaker result that both sides of (11) have the same support is the same as the corresponding argument in language theory (cf. [Sa1, pp. 69–71]). To obtain the stronger result that also the coefficients coincide, one has to add to this argument a comparison between (13) and the system resulting from (14) by providing the first sum on the right side with the coefficient α_{jk}^i and the other two sums with the coefficient α_t^i. ☐

Theorem 4.5 has the language-theoretic corollary (also referred to as the Chomsky–Schützenberger Theorem) that every context-free language L can be represented in the form

(15) $$L = h(D \cap R),$$

for some Dyck language D, regular language R and homomorphism h. Also the converse of this language-theoretic corollary holds true: every language of the form (15) is context-free. As regards power series, $h(\text{char}(D \cap R))$ need not be even defined if h is erasing. We return to this question (mentioned already several times earlier) in Section 6.

EXERCISES

1. Make yourself clear by a case analysis why it suffices in Example 4.2 to consider the product indicated in the computation of the coefficient of $x_1^3 x_2^2$. What conclusion can be made concerning the derivation of $x_1^3 x_2^2$ according to the corresponding weighted grammar?

2. Give new proofs for closure results concerning the family of A-algebraic series using Shamir's Theorem. Consider, in particular, inverse homomorphism and the Hadamard product of rational and algebraic series.

3. Give a representation according to Theorem 4.2 to the series in Examples 4.1 and 4.2.

4. Study what conditions a grammar has to satisfy in order to generate a series for which $h(w)$ in Shamir's Theorem is a monomial for all words w.

5. Formulate and prove the converse of Theorem 4.2 (analogous to Theorem 4.4).

6. Strengthen Theorem 4.2 by showing that it is always possible to use the free group generated by two elements. (Cf. [Ja2].)

7. Prove the following stronger converse of Shamir's Theorem. Assume that the coefficients of a quasiregular series r are computed from

$$(r, w) = (h(w)_{1m}, \gamma),$$

where $h: X^+ \to (A\langle M(Y)\rangle)^{m \times m}$ is a representation, then r is A-algebraic. (Cf. [Ja1]. The result holds true also if the involutive monoid is replaced by the free group.)

8. Give another proof for the Theorem of Chomsky–Schützenberger starting with a system in the form of Theorem 2.3 (instead of quadratic form). In what way does the regular language R obtained now differ from the one obtained in the proof in the text? (This observation will be needed in the proof of Theorem 7.4.)

9. We have not discussed power series in connection with languages more general than context-free. We now exhibit one possible way of associating a power series with an arbitrary type 0 language. The method is in some sense related to Shamir's Theorem.

   Consider a type 0 grammar $G = (V_N, X, S, F)$, where all productions in F are of the three types $A \to BC$, $AB \to C$, $A \to a$ (capital letters are nonterminals, small letters terminals). Every (λ-free) recursively enumerable language can be generated by such a grammar. Introduce, for each nonterminal A in V_N, two new letters y_A and $\bar{y}_A$. Denote by Y the collection of

146

these new letters. Consider the context-free grammar $G' = (V_N, X \cup Y, S, F')$, where F' is obtained as follows. All productions of the types $A \to BC$ and $A \to a$ belonging to F are taken into F'. For each production $AB \to C$ in F, the production $A \to Cy_B$ is taken into F'. Finally, all productions $A \to \bar{y}_A$ are taken into F'. Let r' be the $\mathbb{B}$-algebraic series generated by G'.

Let ρ be the Dyck mapping on Y^*. Extend it in the natural way to $\mathbb{B}\langle\langle(X \cup Y)^*\rangle\rangle$. Let r be the series in $\mathbb{B}\langle\langle X^*\rangle\rangle$ obtained from $\rho(r')$ by omitting all terms containing letters of Y. Prove that r is the characteristic series of $L(G)$.

Modify the construction in such a way that the number of different derivations of a word can be seen from the coefficient in r. Extend then the construction to weighted type 0 grammars. (In both of these tasks you have to modify the given grammar in such a way that no word has infinitely many derivations.)

10. Using the previous exercise, show that every type 0 language L_0 can be expressed in the form

$$L_0 = \rho(L) \cap X^*,$$

where L is a context-free language and ρ is the Dyck mapping. (This result is due to Stanat, cf. [Sta].)

IV.5 Commuting variables and decidability

Denote by $c(X^*)$ the free commutative monoid generated by the alphabet X. Our considerations in this section deal with formal power series in $A\langle\langle c(X^*)\rangle\rangle$. Although this is a side issue in our general theory, it gives rise to some interesting decidability results for context-free languages. These results are obtained because some powerful tools become applicable for series with commuting variables. Such series can be viewed as ordinary Taylor expansions.

If X consists of one letter only, then clearly $X^* = c(X^*)$. Indeed, for language-theoretic applications it would suffice to consider series over one-letter alphabet, i.e., algebraic sequences. However, Theorem 5.1 is given for arbitrary alphabets.

Given a series r in $A\langle\langle X^*\rangle\rangle$, we define the *commutative variant* $c(r)$ of r to be the series in $A\langle\langle c(X^*)\rangle\rangle$, obtained from r by applying the natural homomorphism h_c (mapping X^* into $c(X^*)$).

EXAMPLE 5.1. Let r be the characteristic series of the language $\{a, b\}^*$. (We assume that $A = \mathbb{N}$.) Then

$$c(r) = \sum \psi(m, n)a^m b^n,$$

where $\psi(m, n)$ equals the number of words over $\{a, b\}$ whose Parikh vector is (m, n). (It is easy to see that $\psi(m, n)$ equals the binomial coefficient $\binom{m+n}{m}$.)

We will show in this section that in certain cases it is decidable whether the commutative variants $c(r_1)$ and $c(r_2)$ coincide although it is not decidable whether r_1 and r_2 coincide. We restrict our attention to the case $A = \mathbb{N}$.

Theorem 5.1. *It is decidable of two given $\mathbb{N}$-algebraic series r_1 and r_2 whether or not $c(r_1) = c(r_2)$.*

PROOF. The proof uses some basic facts concerning Taylor expansions, as well as the decidability of the elementary theory of real numbers.

Note first that the commutative variant $c(r)$ of an $\mathbb{N}$-algebraic series r, viewed as a Taylor expansion, has a positive radius of convergence. This follows because (cf. exercise 1.8) there is a number M such that, for all $n \geq 1$ and all words w of length n,

$$(c(r), w) \leq M^n.$$

We need two simple facts concerning Taylor expansions and implicitly defined functions. In the first place, consider two Taylor series s_1 and s_2 with variables from $X = \{x_1, \ldots, x_m\}$. Assume that both s_1 and s_2 converge when $|x_i| < \varepsilon$, for $i = 1, \ldots, m$, and that they define the same function within this domain. Then s_1 and s_2 coincide.

Secondly, consider a proper algebraic system with respect to $(\mathbb{N}, X)$ and with variables in $Z = \{z_1, \ldots, z_n\}$:

(1) $$z_i = p_i \qquad i = 1, \ldots, n.$$

We view this system as an implicit definition of the vector $(z_1, \ldots, z_n)$ in terms of the real-valued vector $(x_1, \ldots, x_m)$. Writing (1) in the form

$$q_i = p_i - z_i = 0 \qquad i = 1, \ldots, n$$

and noting that

$$\left(\frac{\partial q_i}{\partial z_j}\right)_{0,\ldots,0} = \begin{cases} -1 & \text{for } i = j, \\ 0 & \text{otherwise,} \end{cases}$$

we conclude that, for some $\varepsilon > 0$, (1) defines $(z_1, \ldots, z_n)$ uniquely as a function of $(x_1, \ldots, x_m)$ in the domain $|x_i| < \varepsilon$, $i = 1, \ldots, m$, $|z_j| < \varepsilon$, $j = 1, \ldots, n$.

After these preliminary remarks, consider now two $\mathbb{N}$-algebraic series r_1 and r_2, defined as the first components in the solutions for the proper algebraic systems

(2) $$z_i = p_i, i = 1, \ldots, n, \quad \text{and} \quad z_i' = p_i', i = 1, \ldots, n'.$$

We may assume that both r_1 and r_2 are series in $\mathbb{N}^{\text{alg}}\langle\langle X^* \rangle\rangle$ with $X = \{x_1, \ldots, x_m\}$. Denote

$$Q = Q(x_1, \ldots, x_m, z_1, \ldots, z_n, z_1', \ldots, z_{n'}')$$

$$= \sum_{i=1}^{n} (z_i - p_i)^2 + \sum_{i=1}^{n'} (z_i' - p_i')^2.$$

Thus, we view Q as a polynomial in the variables x_i, z_j and z_j'. Intuitively, Q can be considered as the conjunction of all of the equations (2). In what follows, Q is considered to be a polynomial in the real variables x_i, z_j and z'_j. We denote, furthermore, by $P(\varepsilon)$ the conjunction of the inequalities

$$|x_i| < \varepsilon, i = 1, \ldots, m; \qquad |z_j| < \varepsilon, j = 1, \ldots, n; \qquad |z'_j| < \varepsilon, j = 1, \ldots, n'.$$

Consider now the following statement

(3) $(\exists \varepsilon > 0)(\forall x_1, \ldots, x_m, z_1, \ldots, z_n, z'_1, \ldots, z'_{n'})[(P(\varepsilon) \wedge Q = 0) \to z_1 = z'_1].$

Clearly, (3) is a statement in the elementary theory of real numbers and, hence, its validity is decidable by the well-known result of Tarski (cf., for instance, [J]). Moreover, $c(r_1) = c(r_2)$ holds true exactly in case (3) is valid. This is seen by the results established earlier in this proof as follows. Both $c(r_1)$ and $c(r_2)$ have a positive radius of convergence. Within this radius, they define the same function exactly in case they coincide. On the other hand, in a small enough neighborhood of 0, the function defined by $c(r_1)$ (respectively $c(r_2)$) is implicitly represented by z_1 (respectively z'_1) in (2). Thus, the existence of an $\varepsilon > 0$ as in (3) is equivalent to $c(r_1)$ coinciding with $c(r_2)$. $\square$

The proof of Theorem 5.1 is one of the few instances where in the theory of formal power series we actually make use of the function defined as the sum of the series. Using Theorem 5.1, one can obtain a number of decidability results for context-free languages.

Theorem 5.2. *Assume that G is an unambiguous context-free grammar and that G_1 is a context-free grammar of which it is known that $L(G_1) = L(G)$. Then it is decidable whether or not G_1 is unambiguous.*

Theorem 5.3. *Assume that G_1 and G_2 are given unambiguous context-free grammars of which it is known that one of the languages $L(G_1)$ and $L(G_2)$ is contained in the other. Then it is decidable whether or not $L(G_1) = L(G_2)$.*

Theorems 5.2 and 5.3 are immediate consequences of Theorem 5.1. They are instances of relative decision procedures, i.e., decision procedures with an oracle: the given information constitutes in itself an undecidable property.

A number of similar results are valid for cases where one has information about the degree of ambiguity. For instance, Theorem 5.3 remains valid if G_1 and G_2 are grammars generating each word with the same degree of ambiguity k. Also the following theorem is an immediate consequence of Theorem 5.1.

Theorem 5.4. *It is decidable whether or not two $\mathbb{N}$-algebraic series over $X = \{x\}$ coincide. Given two weighted context-free grammars G_1 and G_2, it is decidable whether or not, for all n, the sum of the weights associated to words of length n according to G_1 equals the corresponding sum according to G_2.*

149

Theorem 5.5. *Given an unambiguous grammar G and a regular language R, it is decidable whether or not $L(G) = R$.*

PROOF. The theorem is reduced to Theorem 5.3 because it is possible to construct an unambiguous grammar for the language $L(G) \cap R$. Clearly, $L(G) = R$ iff $L(G) \cap R = L(G)$ and $L(G) \cap R = R$. □

It is well known that it is decidable whether or not a given regular and a given deterministic context-free language are equal. The proof of this result uses the fact that deterministic context-free languages are closed under complementation. Theorem 5.5 gives a stronger result because the family of unambiguous context-free languages includes strictly the family of deterministic context-free languages. Note also that the unambiguous context-free languages are not closed under complementation. Indeed, no proof is known for Theorem 5.5 which uses only standard formal language theory.

The theory of *A-algebraic sequences*, i.e., sequences of coefficients in series belonging to $A^{\text{alg}}\langle\langle\{x\}^*\rangle\rangle$ falls within the subject matter of this section. However, as we have already pointed out, no comprehensive theory corresponding to the theory of *A-rational* sequences developed in Sections II.9 and II.10 is known for *A*-algebraic sequences. Some results are mentioned in the remainder of this section. Further material is given in exercises 5.6–5.8.

A series $r \in A\langle\langle c(X^*)\rangle\rangle$ with $X = \{x_1, \ldots, x_m\}$ can be written in the form

$$r = \sum r(k_1, \ldots, k_m) x_1^{k_1} \cdots x_m^{k_m}.$$

The *diagonal Dr* of r is the series in $A\langle\langle c(\{x\}^*)\rangle\rangle = A\langle\langle\{x\}^*\rangle\rangle$ defined by

$$Dr = \sum_{k \geq 0} r(k, \ldots, k) x^k.$$

Theorem 5.6. *The diagonal of a rational series r in $A\langle\langle c(\{x_1, x_2\}^*)\rangle\rangle$ is an algebraic series (belonging to $A^{\text{alg}}\langle\langle\{x\}^*\rangle\rangle$).*

PROOF. Let h_c be the natural homomorphism of $\{x_1, x_2\}^*$ into $c(\{x_1, x_2\}^*)$. Clearly, there exists a series $r' \in A^{\text{rat}}\langle\langle\{x_1, x_2\}^*\rangle\rangle$ such that $r = h_c r'$. The characteristic series s of the language L over $\{x_1, x_2\}^*$, consisting of all words where the number of occurrences of x_1 equals that of x_2, is *A*-algebraic (cf. exercise 1.1). Considering now the homomorphism h_1 defined by

$$h_1(x_1) = h_1(x_2) = x,$$

we see that

$$Dr = h_1 h_c(r' \odot s),$$

which by Theorems 3.3 and 3.5 completes the proof. □

One can show that Theorem 5.6 is no longer valid if one considers diagonals of rational series in three variables. (The intuitive reason behind this result is that the series in $A\langle\langle\{x_1, x_2, x_3\}^*\rangle\rangle$ corresponding to s in the proof above is not *A*-algebraic.) However, if A is a finite field, then the diagonal of a rational series in arbitrarily many (commuting) variables is an algebraic series. Moreover, in this case also the converse of Theorem 5.6 is valid: every A-algebraic series in one variable can be represented as the diagonal of a rational series in two (commuting) variables. For these results, the reader is referred to [Fü]. The results can be generalized to arbitrary perfect fields, cf. [Fl2].

EXERCISES

1. Assume that G and G' are context-free grammars whose degree of ambiguity equals 2 and that $L(G') \subseteq L(G)$. Assume, furthermore, that the set of words in $L(G)$ (respectively $L(G')$) with ambiguity 2 according to G (respectively G') is generated by a given unambiguous grammar G_1 (respectively G_1'). Show that it is decidable whether or not $L(G) = L(G')$.

2. The previous exercise is analogous to Theorem 5.3 above. Formulate and prove results analogous to Theorems 5.2 and 5.5. Formulate and prove also analogous results starting with grammars whose degree of ambiguity exceeds 2.

3. Prove that it is decidable whether or not the commutative variants of two given $\mathbb{Z}$-algebraic series coincide.

4. Show that for the given language-theoretic applications (Theorems 5.2, 5.3, 5.5) it suffices to prove Theorem 5.1 only for one-letter alphabets.

5. Show that there are $\mathbb{B}$-rational series r (referred to as series of type 1) such that the equation $r = r'$ is undecidable for a given $\mathbb{B}$-algebraic series r', and that there also are $\mathbb{B}$-rational series r (series of type 2) such that the equation $r = r'$ is decidable for a given $\mathbb{B}$-algebraic series r'. Is it decidable whether a given $\mathbb{B}$-rational series is of type 1 or 2?

6. Show that every K-algebraic series over the one-letter alphabet $\{x\}$, where K is a subfield of $\mathbb{R}$, satisfies a generating equation of the form

$$a_0(x)z^m + a_1(x)z^{m-1} + \cdots + a_m(x) = 0, \qquad a_0(x) \neq 0,$$

where each $a_i(x)$ is a polynomial in $K\langle\langle\{x\}^*\rangle\rangle$. (The best way to do this is to use Tarski's elimination techniques, cf. [J].)

7. Prove directly by the previous exercise that it is decidable whether or not a given $\mathbb{Z}$-algebraic series over the alphabet $\{x\}$ is identically zero. (As a consequence, note by exercise 5.4 that, in fact, exercise 5.6 suffices for proving the language-theoretic applications of this section.)

8. Exercise 5.6 is very useful because it shows that, in case of a one-letter alphabet, an algebraic series can be considered to define an algebraic function in the sense of classical complex analysis. As an example of this, prove that no series

$$\sum_{i=0}^{\infty} a_i x^{k_i}, \qquad a_i \text{ real}, k_i \text{ natural}, \lim_{i \to \infty} k_i/i = \infty$$

is $\mathbb{R}$-algebraic.
Hint: Use the Gap Theorem of Fabry, cf. [Di]. Conclude that the languages of exercise 2.4 are not $\mathbb{Z}$-algebraic and not even $\mathbb{R}$-algebraic.

IV.6 Generalizations of proper systems: Fatou extensions

The algebraic systems of equations defined in Section 1

(1) $$z_i = p_i \qquad i = 1, \ldots, n$$

are often referred to in the literature as "algebraic constructible" systems. This term suggests the way of constructing the solution by means of successive approximations. The condition

(2) $$(p_i, \lambda) = 0 \quad \text{and} \quad (p_i, z_j) = 0$$

is a technical restriction to ensure the convergence of the sequence of successive approximations. In this section, we discuss more general cases, in particular, systems which do not satisfy condition (2). At the end of the section, we return to proper systems and discuss Fatou extensions in the sense of algebraic series.

System (1) is only a very special case of the general algebraic system

(3) $$p_i = q_i \qquad i = 1, \ldots, n,$$

where both p_i and q_i belong to $A\langle (X \cup Z)^* \rangle$. However, very little can be said of the general system (3) in case of noncommuting variables, even if some quite restrictive assumptions are made. Moreover, from the point of view of language-theoretic applications, (3) is much too general. Languages which are not even recursively enumerable may appear as supports of solutions, as seen from the following simple example.

EXAMPLE 6.1. All series are solutions for the system $z_1 = z_1$. Choose next $A = \mathbb{B}$, $X = \{x\}$, and consider the system

$$x + xz_1 = z_1 = z_1 z_2 + z_2.$$

While the solution for z_1 is the unique one

$$z_1 = \sum_{n=1}^{\infty} x^n,$$

any series r_2 with the properties

$$(r_2, \lambda) = 0, \qquad (r_2, x) = 1$$

is a solution for z_2.

To restrict the range of solutions, we shall introduce in this section the notion of a strong solution.

We want to emphasize at this point that, in case of noncommuting variables, usual elimination techniques are very seldom applicable. Thus, solutions of (3) cannot in general be represented as solutions of single equations of the form

$$\alpha_0 z_1^k + \alpha_1 z_1^{k-1} + \cdots + \alpha_k = 0.$$

(In some cases this is possible, cf. exercise 5.6.) However, as we have already pointed out, in the noncommutative case and with language-theoretic applications in mind. System (1) is the natural type of system of algebraic equations to be considered. With restrictions (2) and with certain additional assumptions concerning A, we have seen that (1) corresponds in a natural way to context-free grammars. Let the following serve as an example of the fact that, even in the case of (1) with (2) satisfied, rather strange languages may turn out to be A-algebraic if A does not satisfy the additional assumptions.

EXAMPLE 6.2. Let A be a field of characteristic $p > 0$. Let $X = \{x\}$, and consider the proper algebraic system consisting of the single equation

$$z_1 = x + z_1^p.$$

The solution is

$$z_1 = \sum_{n \geq 0} x^{p^n},$$

and the support of the solution is $L = \{x^{p^n} \mid n \geq 0\}$. One can prove that L is not A-algebraic if A is a field of characteristic 0.

We now turn to the discussion of conditions (2) which, as already pointed out, are technical restrictions to ensure the convergence of the sequence of successive approximations. We can always "force" conditions (2) to be satisfied by introducing a new letter y to the alphabet X and adding y to appropriate places in the polynomials p_i (i.e., terms αz_j and $\alpha \cdot \lambda$ appearing in p_i are replaced by $\alpha y z_j$ and αy, respectively). The resulting system has a unique solution whose components belong to $A^{\mathrm{alg}}\langle\langle(X \cup \{y\})^*\rangle\rangle$. However, we cannot in general apply to the solution the homomorphism h which erases y and leaves letters of X fixed because of the summability difficulties discussed earlier in this chapter.

The following example shows that if one of the conditions (2) is not satisfied then it is possible that the system has no solution.

EXAMPLE 6.3. Assume that $A = \mathbb{N}$ and $X = \{x\}$. The system consisting of the single equation

$$z_1 = z_1 z_1 + \lambda \qquad \text{(respectively } z_1 = z_1 + x)$$

which does not satisfy the first (respectively the second) of the conditions (2) has no solution. This follows because if b is the coefficient of λ (respectively x) in a solution then b must satisfy

$$b = b^2 + 1 \qquad \text{(respectively } b = b + 1)$$

which is impossible in $\mathbb{N}$.

153

On the other hand, Example 6.1 shows that if conditions (2) are not satisfied then in many cases almost any series is a solution for the system. To avoid this situation, we now single out the solutions obtained by the method of successive approximations of Theorem 1.1. This method is well motivated also from the point of view of formal language theory because it is essentially the same as the fixed-point definition of context-free languages. It also resembles the method of minimal fixed-points in semantics.

Definition. Consider an algebraic system (1) and form the sequence of n-tuples

$$(4) \qquad \sigma^0 = (0, \ldots, 0) = (\sigma_1^0, \ldots, \sigma_n^0),$$

$$\sigma^{j+1} = \sigma^j p = (\sigma_1^{j+1}, \ldots, \sigma_n^{j+1}), j \geq 0,$$

(as in the proof of Theorem 1.1). If this sequence converges to the n-tuple $\sigma = (\sigma_1, \ldots, \sigma_n)$ then the latter is referred to as the *strong solution* of (1).

THEOREM 6.1. *Every strong solution s also a solution. Strong solutions (when they exist) are unique. Every proper algebraic system has a strong solution.*

PROOF. The second sentence follows by the definition, and the third sentence by Theorem 1.1. To prove the first sentence, assume that we are dealing with a system (1) such that the sequence (4) converges. Consider the restriction operator R_k introduced in the proof of Theorem 1.1. The convergence of (4) implies that, for any k, there exists an integer $m(k)$ such that

$$(5) \qquad R_k(\sigma^{m(k)+h}) = R_k(\sigma^{m(k)})$$

holds for all h. The equation $\sigma p = \sigma$ is now a consequence of (5). □

The next theorem gives a sufficient condition concerning the question of when the second of the restrictions (2) can be relaxed.

Theorem 6.2. *Assume that A is a ring, and consider an algebraic system (1) satisfying the first of the conditions (2). Let M be the square matrix formed by the coefficients of the z_j's in p_i. If the matrix $I - M$ is invertible in A, then the system possesses a unique solution in quasiregular series.*

PROOF. Write (1) in the matrix form

$$Z = MZ + Q,$$

where $Q = (q_1, \ldots, q_n)$, and none of the q_i's contains terms with a single variable z_j. By the assumption, we may now replace (1) with the proper system

$$Z = (I - M)^{-1}Q. \qquad □$$

Note that the solution obtained in Theorem 6.2 is not necessarily a strong one, cf. exercise 6.3.

We say that a series r in $A\langle\langle X^* \rangle\rangle$ is A-*semi-algebraic* iff

$$r = (r, \lambda)\lambda + r',$$

where r' is A-algebraic.

In the special case of the Boolean semiring, we can easily establish the following theorem, for instance, along the lines of the proofs of Theorems 3.2 and 3.3.

Theorem 6.3. *The homomorphic image of a* $\mathbb{B}$-*algebraic series* (*under a monoid homomorphism*) *is a* $\mathbb{B}$-*semi-algebraic series.*

It is a consequence of Theorem 6.3 that the strong solution of a $\mathbb{B}$-algebraic system (whenever one exists) consists of $\mathbb{B}$-semi-algebraic series. We do not know to what extent this result can be generalized, for instance, whether it holds for $\mathbb{Z}$-algebraic systems as well. The following theorem solves the problem for $\mathbb{N}$-algebraic systems.

Theorem 6.4. *The components of the strong solution* (*provided one exists*) *of the system* (1), *where* $A = \mathbb{N}$, *are* $\mathbb{N}$-*semi-algebraic series.*

PROOF. We consider first the semiring $\mathbb{N}^{(\infty)}$ defined as in Section II.4. If we are dealing with an algebraic system (1) with $A = \mathbb{N}^{(\infty)}$, it is clear that the sequence of n-tuples (4) satisfies $\sigma^j \leq \sigma^{j+1}$, for all j. Moreover, for each i and each word w, $\lim_{j \to \infty}(\sigma_i^j, w)$ exists. Let $\sigma = (\sigma_1, \ldots, \sigma_n)$ be the n-tuple of series satisfying, for each w and i,

$$(\sigma_i, w) = \lim_{j \to \infty}(\sigma_i^j, w).$$

Then, clearly, σ is a solution of (1). Furthermore, it is minimal in the sense that an arbitrary solution σ' satisfies $\sigma \leq \sigma'$.

(Note that the minimal solution is not necessarily a strong solution. The system $z_1 = z_1 + 1$ has the minimal solution $\sigma_1 = \infty$ which is not a strong solution. On the other hand, a strong solution is always also minimal.)

The minimal solution σ can be written in the form

(6) $\qquad \sigma = \rho + \tau, \qquad \rho = (\rho_1, \ldots, \rho_n), \qquad \tau = (\tau_1, \ldots, \tau_n),$

where $\mathrm{supp}(\rho_i) \subseteq \{\lambda\}$ and $\lambda \notin \mathrm{supp}(\tau_i)$. This implies that τ is the minimal solution of a system of the form

$$z_i = q_i \qquad i = 1, \ldots, n,$$

where each q_i is a quasiregular polynomial in variables z_j (and x_j). We separate from q_i the terms involving only single variables z_j, and write at the same time the whole system in the matrix form:

(7) $\qquad\qquad\qquad Z = QZ + P(Z).$

(Thus, the support of each component in $P(Z)$ is contained in $(X \cup Z)^+ - Z$.)

155

We now claim that τ equals the solution of the proper system

(8) $$Z = (I + Q^+)P(Z).$$

In fact, by (7),

$$\tau = Q\tau + P(\tau) = Q^2\tau + QP(\tau) + P(\tau) = \cdots$$
$$= Q^{j+1}\tau + Q^jP(\tau) + \cdots + P(\tau) \geq Q^jP(\tau) + \cdots + P(\tau),$$

whence

(9) $$\tau \geq (I + Q^+)P(\tau).$$

On the other hand, τ is the minimal solution of (7). Let us consider the sequence $\tau^0, \tau^1, \ldots$ corresponding to (4). Clearly,

$$\tau^0 \leq (I + Q^+)P(\tau^0).$$

Assuming that

$$\tau^j \leq (I + Q^+)P(\tau^j),$$

we infer

$$\tau^{j+1} = Q\tau^j + P(\tau^j) \leq Q(I + Q^+)P(\tau^j) + P(\tau^j)$$
$$= (I + Q^+)P(\tau^j) \leq (I + Q^+)P(\tau^{j+1}).$$

This implies that

$$\tau \leq (I + Q^+)P(\tau)$$

which together with (9) shows that τ equals the solution of the proper system (8).

If (6) equals the strong solution of (1) with $A = \mathbb{N}$, then τ equals the solution of the proper system obtained from (8) by replacing all coefficients ∞ with 0's. This follows because in this case there are no coefficients ∞ in τ. $\qquad\square$

The final conclusion in the proof above was based on a simple Fatou property. We now define the notion of a Fatou extension similarly as in Section II.6.

Definition. Let A be a subsemiring of B. We say that B is a *Fatou extension* of A iff

$$A\langle\langle X^*\rangle\rangle \cap B^{\mathrm{alg}}\langle\langle X^*\rangle\rangle = A^{\mathrm{alg}}\langle\langle X^*\rangle\rangle,$$

for all alphabets X.

The proof of the following theorem is similar to the proof of Lemma II.6.6.

Theorem 6.5. *Assume that K_1 is an algebraic extension field of the field K and r_1 belongs to $K_1^{\mathrm{alg}}\langle\langle X^*\rangle\rangle$. Then there is an element θ algebraic with respect to K such that r_1 can be written in the form*

$$r_1 = \sum_{l=0}^{m-1} \theta^l r_{1l},$$

where each of the series r_{1l} belongs to $K^{\mathrm{alg}}\langle\langle X^*\rangle\rangle$. Consequently, an algebraic extension field of a field is always a Fatou extension.

PROOF. By Theorem 2.2, we assume that r_1 equals the first component in the solution $(r_1, \ldots, r_n)$ for the system

$$z_i = \sum_{j,k} \alpha^i_{jk} z_j z_k + \sum_j \alpha^i_j x_j, \qquad i = 1, \ldots, n,$$

where the α's are elements of K_1. We express these (finitely many) α's in terms of one generator θ:

$$\alpha^i_{jk} = \sum_{t=0}^{m-1} \beta^i_{jkt}\theta^t, \qquad \alpha^i_j = \sum_{t=0}^{m-1} \beta^i_{jt}\theta^t,$$

where the β's are elements of K. We also express all powers of θ in the form

$$\theta^j = \sum_{t=0}^{m-1} \gamma^t_j \theta^t,$$

where the γ's belong to K.

We introduce now new variables

$$z_{il}, \qquad i = 1, \ldots, n, \, l = 0, \ldots, m-1,$$

and consider the system

$$z_{il} = \sum_{j,k,t,u,v} \beta^i_{jkt} \cdot \gamma^l_{t+u+v} z_{ju} z_{kv} + \sum_j \beta^i_{jl} x_j.$$

Denoting by r_{il} the component in the solution of this system corresponding to z_{il}, we see that, for all i,

$$r_i = \sum_{l=0}^{m-1} \theta^l r_{il}. \qquad \Box$$

Also our last theorem deals with a Fatou property. It is often referred to as Eisenstein's Theorem and is similar to Lemma II.6.5.

Theorem 6.6. *Let A be an integral domain and K its quotient field. If $r \in K^{\mathrm{alg}}\langle\langle X^*\rangle\rangle$, there exists an element $\alpha \in A$, $\alpha \neq 0$. such that the series r_1 resulting from r by substituting every $x \in X$ with αx is in $A^{\mathrm{alg}}\langle\langle X^*\rangle\rangle$. If K is a subfield of $\mathbb{R}$, the statement remains valid if A is replaced by A_+ and K by K_+.*

PROOF. The theorem follows immediately by Theorem 2.3. We construct a system for r such that the supports of the right sides are included in the set (2) mentioned in the statement of Theorem 2.3. We may then choose α to be the product (or any multiple of the product) of the denominators of the coefficients appearing on the right sides. $\qquad \Box$

EXERCISES

1. Prove that the family of $\mathbb{Z}$-semi-algebraic series (over the alphabet X) is a rationally closed ring containing all $\mathbb{Z}$-rational series.

2. Extend the results about Hadamard and Hurwitz product established in Section 3 to concern A-semi-algebraic series.

3. Give examples where the solution obtained from Theorem 6.2 is not a strong one. (A simple example is $z_1 = \frac{1}{2}z_1 + x$.) State conditions for A under which the solution will always be a strong one.

4. Assume that a $\mathbb{Z}$-algebraic system $z_i = p_i$, $i = 1, \ldots, n$, where $(p_i, \lambda) = 0$, possesses a strong solution. Does it follow that the matrix $I - M$ (cf. Theorem 6.2) is invertible?

5. Assume that an A-algebraic system possesses a strong solution r. Can the system have other solutions r' with $(r', \lambda) = (r, \lambda)$?

IV.7 Algebraic transductions

We have already considered rational transductions in Chapter III.1, where the main emphasis was on regulated rational transductions. We now discuss the corresponding algebraic notions. Again, attention will be focused on regulated algebraic transductions. More general types of transductions will be only briefly mentioned. The reason for this is twofold. The more general transductions will be only partial mappings, and usually no *a priori* conditions can be given concerning the question of when the image of a given series under a given transduction will be defined. (This holds true unless very strong summability assumptions are made with respect to A.) Secondly, the more general transductions are closely linked with the theory of algebraic series over products of free monoids, a topic not discussed above (although we have pointed out that many of our results hold in this more general case as well).

We denote by $A^{\text{semi-alg}}\langle\langle X^* \rangle\rangle$ the family of all A-semi-algebraic series over X^*. The notion of a regulated representation is defined as in Section II.11. The following lemma is analogous to Lemma II.11.5. For our purposes it suffices to consider the case where there is only one coefficient domain involved, namely, our commutative semiring A.

Lemma 7.1. *Assume that*

$$r \in A^{\text{semi-alg}}\langle\langle X^* \rangle\rangle$$

and

$$\mu: X^* \to (A^{\text{semi-alg}}\langle\langle Y^* \rangle\rangle)^{m \times m}$$

is a regulated representation. Then the entries of $\mu r = \sum (r, w)\mu w$ belong to $A^{\text{semi-alg}}\langle\langle Y^* \rangle\rangle$.

PROOF. We assume without loss of generality that r is A-algebraic. For if

$r = (r, \lambda) \cdot \lambda + r'$, where r' is an A-algebraic series for which the statement holds, then it clearly holds for r as well.

Suppose first that the matrices μx, where $x \in X$, have A-algebraic entries. We argue exactly as in the proof of Lemma II.11.5: Replacing each variable z_i in the system $z_i = p_i$, $i = 1, \ldots, n$, defining r by the matrix

$$\begin{pmatrix} z_{i11} & \cdots & z_{i1m} \\ \vdots & & \vdots \\ z_{im1} & \cdots & z_{imm} \end{pmatrix}$$

we obtain an algebraic system for the entries of μr. (Hence, in this case, the entries of r are even A-algebraic.)

In the general case, we suppose that all of the matrices μw with $\lg w = k$ ($k \geq 1$) have quasiregular entries. Let $y_1, \ldots, y_l$ be the words of X^k and let $h: Y_1^* = \{y_1, \ldots, y_l\}^* \to X^*$ be the natural homomorphism. It is easy to see (for instance, cf. exercise 3.2) that, for any word w, the series

$$r_w = \sum_{v \in Y_1^*} (r, whv) v$$

is A-algebraic. By the first part of the proof, this implies that the entries of

$$\mu r_w = \sum (r, whv) \mu (hv)$$

are A-algebraic. Consequently, the entries of

$$\mu r = \sum_{\lg w < k} \mu w \cdot \mu r_w$$

are A-semi-algebraic. $\qquad\qquad\square$

Definition. A mapping $\tau: A\langle\langle X^* \rangle\rangle \to A\langle\langle Y^* \rangle\rangle$ is termed a *regulated semi-algebraic transduction* iff

(1) $$\tau s = (s, \lambda) r_0 + \sum_{w \neq \lambda} (s, w)(\mu w)_{1m},$$

where $r_0 \in A^{\text{semi-alg}}\langle\langle Y^* \rangle\rangle$ and $\mu: X^* \to (A^{\text{semi-alg}}\langle\langle Y^* \rangle\rangle)^{m \times m}$ is a regulated representation. If, moreover, the series r_0 as well as all entries in the matrices μx, for $x \in X$, are A-algebraic, then τ is referred to as a *regulated algebraic transduction*.

The following theorem is now an immediate consequence of Lemma 7.1 (and, as regards algebraic series, the first part of its proof).

Theorem 7.2. *A regulated semi-algebraic (respectively regulated algebraic) transduction always maps a semi-algebraic (respectively an algebraic) series into a semi-algebraic (respectively an algebraic) series.*

Definition. If A is a complete commutative semiring, the mapping τ defined by (1) is referred to as an *algebraic-rational transduction*.

Theorem 7.3. *Let A be a complete commutative semiring. Then every algebraic-rational transduction τ has a factorization $\tau = p\sigma$, where p is a projection and σ is a regulated semi-algebraic transduction.*

PROOF. We proceed exactly as in the proof of Theorem III.1.4: We add a new letter $\bar{y}$ to Y, multiply the coefficients of λ in all entries of μw by $\bar{y}$ obtaining, thus, a regulated semi-algebraic representation χ which together with r_0 defines a regulated semi-algebraic transduction σ. Finally, p is defined to be the projection which erases $\bar{y}$ and keeps other letters of Y fixed. $\qquad\square$

Theorem 7.3 shows that, as regards algebraic-rational transductions, we are back in our old problems concerning erasing homomorphisms applied to algebraic series. For instance, it is not known whether or not an algebraic-rational transduction maps a semi-algebraic series into a semi-algebraic series.

One can also consider (for complete commutative semirings A) transductions τ defined by

$$\tau s = \psi((\varphi^{-1}s) \odot r),$$

where r is a given semi-algebraic series, and ψ and φ are homomorphisms. Such "algebraic transductions" are analogous to rational transductions in the form of Theorem III.1.3.(iii). They correspond to algebraic series over $X^* \otimes Y^*$ (cf. exercise 7.3). They do not in general map a semi-algebraic series into a semi-algebraic one, a fact due to the nonclosure of the family of algebraic series under Hadamard product (for instance, in case of the semiring $\mathbb{N}^{(\infty)}$). From results like this some well-known language-theoretic results about pushdown transducer mappings can be obtained.

As regards algebraic series and regulated rational transductions, we still mention the following result which is an immediate consequence of exercises 4.8 and 7.4.

Theorem 7.4. *For every A-algebraic series r, there is an alphabet $Y = Y_1 \cup \bar{Y}_1$ and a regulated rational transduction τ such that*

$$r = \tau(\mathrm{char}(D)),$$

where D is the Dyck language over Y.

The notion of a regulated rational cone of series was briefly discussed in Section III.1, where it was also pointed out that the family of pairs (X, r), where $r \in A^{\mathrm{rat}}\langle\langle X^* \rangle\rangle$, forms a regulated rational cone. The same result holds true also with respect to algebraic series. Moreover, it is not difficult to see that both of these cones are *principal*. (The cone *generated* by a family S of series is the smallest cone containing S. A cone is *principal* iff it is generated by a family with a single member.) As regards algebraic series, this principality result is a consequence of Theorem 7.4.

On the other hand, one can construct an infinite hierarchy of nonprincipal (regulated rational) cones such that, for each cone C in this hierarchy, the family of the supports of the series in C equals the family of context-free languages. The essential feature in this construction is to consider $\mathbb{N}$-algebraic series r such that the subseries of r obtained by omitting words whose coefficient exceeds a certain bound is $\mathbb{N}$-rational, cf. [Ja1].

Some results about ambiguity can also be obtained along these lines. For instance, one can study the ambiguity of a generator for the cone of context-free languages. The following theorem indicates how one can reduce the ambiguity of a generator. We state the theorem in a slightly more general set up.

Theorem 7.5. *Assume that* $\tau: \mathbb{N}\langle\langle X^* \rangle\rangle \to \mathbb{N}\langle\langle Y^* \rangle\rangle$ *is a regulated rational transduction and that r and s are series satisfying $\tau(r) = s$. Assume, furthermore, that the coefficients in s do not exceed a fixed integer k. Then there is a regular language R such that*

$$(2) \qquad \tau(r) = \tau(r \odot \mathrm{char}(R)) = s$$

and the coefficients in $r \odot \mathrm{char}(R)$ do not exceed k. Consequently, if s is unambiguous (i.e., the coefficients in s are ≤ 1) then there is a regular language R such that (2) holds and $r \odot \mathrm{char}(R)$ is unambiguous.

PROOF. Express τ in the form

$$\tau r = (r, \lambda) r_0 + \sum_{w \neq \lambda} (r, w)(\mu w)_{1m},$$

where $r_0 \in \mathbb{N}^{\mathrm{rat}}\langle\langle Y^* \rangle\rangle$ and $\mu: X^* \to (\mathbb{N}^{\mathrm{rat}}\langle\langle Y^* \rangle\rangle)^{m \times m}$ is a regulated representation. Clearly, the language

$$R = \{w \in X^+ \mid (\mu w)_{1m} \neq 0\}$$

is regular. It is also immediate by our assumption concerning s that R satisfies (2) and that the coefficients in $r \odot \mathrm{char}(R)$ do not exceed k. $\qquad \square$

EXERCISES

1. Express some of the operations considered in Section 3 (such as product and substitution by quasiregular series) as regulated semi-algebraic transductions.

2. Show that if A equals $\mathbb{B}$, $\mathbb{N}^{(\infty)}$ or $\mathbb{R}^{(\infty)}$, then an algebraic-rational transduction maps a semi-algebraic series into a semi-algebraic series.

3. Establish a correspondence between algebraic transductions defined by

$$\tau s = \psi((\varphi^{-1} s) \odot r)$$

and algebraic series over $X^* \otimes Y^*$. (Cf. Section III.1, especially Theorem III.1.3.)

4. A series r in $A\langle\langle(X \cup Y)^* \rangle\rangle$ is termed "X-limited" iff there is a natural number k such that no word belonging to the support of r possesses a subword

of length $> k$ belonging to X^*. Let h be the homomorphism (projection) defined by

$$h(x) = \begin{cases} \lambda & \text{if } x \in X \\ x & \text{if } x \in Y. \end{cases}$$

Assuming that $r \in A^{\text{rat}}\langle\langle (X \cup Y)^* \rangle\rangle$ is X-limited, prove that the mapping

$$\tau(s) = h(s \odot r)$$

is a regulated rational transduction. (Cf. [Ja1].)

5. Extend the Dyck mapping ρ over Y^* in the natural way to the family $\mathbb{B}\langle\langle Y^* \rangle\rangle$. Show that $\rho(r)$ is not in general $\mathbb{B}$-semi-algebraic, for a $\mathbb{B}$-semi-algebraic series r. (Cf. exercise 4.9.)

6. Consider exercise II.4.5. Let $\gamma: X^* \to 2^{X^*}$ be the mapping which associates to a word w all words equivalent to w. Extend γ in the natural way to languages over X. Prove that $\gamma(L)$ is context-free if L is context-free. (Cf. [Fl1], where also the transcendental nature of γ, viewed as a transduction, is discussed.)

7. Show that every regulated rational cone contains all rational series.

8. Consider the principal regulated rational cone generated by the A-semi-algebraic series

$$r = \sum \{ w \mid w \in \{x, y\}^*, w = mi(w) \}$$

("palindrome series"). Characterize the family of languages appearing as supports of the series in this cone.

9. Let r_1 be the characteristic series of the Dyck language over $\{x_1, \bar{x}_1\}$, and r_2 the characteristic series of the language L_1 defined in exercise 1.1. Show that r_1 and r_2 determine the same principal regulated rational cone.

10. Show that every principal regulated rational cone is an A-module. (A is assumed to be a ring.)

Historical and bibliographical remarks

In many cases it is very difficult to trace down the origin of a specific result presented in this book: the line of development might on one hand emerge from classical analysis and, on the other hand, from algebra and theory of automata. Therefore, we are quite aware of the fact that the subsequent remarks are rather scattered and incomplete. The list of references following the remarks is not intended to be a bibliography of the field. Many of the listed references, especially [Bec] and [Fl1], contain bibliographies which might be of further aid.

The theory of rational (respectively algebraic) formal power series in the sense treated in this book was originated in [Sch1]–[Sch3] (respectively [CS]). These papers contain the basic notions, as well as some of the main results.

Most of the material in Sections II.1–II.2 is from [Sch2], although we have tried to avoid the cumbersome matrix calculations of [Sch2]. The Representation Theorem goes back to the work of Jungen. Exercises 2.4 and 2.5 are based on the paper by Richard, [Ri]. As regards Section II.3, Theorem 3.1 is from [Ja1], most of the remaining material being modified from [Fl1]. The reader is referred also to [CP]. The idea of closure under Hadamard product goes back to Jungen, and is presented also in [Sch2]. Projections were considered in [Fl1], and exercise 4.5 is due to Schützenberger, cf. [Fl1]. Section II.5 is classical automata theory, cf. also [Sch3]. The classical result of Fatou deals with $\mathbb{Q}$ as an extension of $\mathbb{Z}$ in the one-letter case. Theorem 6.3 is due to Fliess, [Fl1]. For material related to Section II.6, we refer the reader also to [Sch3] and [Ben]. Lemma 7.7 is from [Ja1]. Theorem 8.4 is new; in the proof ideas of J. Karhumäki were helpful. Theorem 8.6 is from [E], although our proof is entirely different. Most of Section II.9 is classical analysis, going probably back to Weierstrass. Lemma 9.10 is known as the Skolem–Mahler–Lech Theorem, cf. [Le]. Lemma 9.11 is due to Mahler, [Ma]. Section II.10

163

is from [Be1] and [So3], Theorem 10.5 was proved independently also in [KOE]. The treatment of regulated representations in Section II.11 is from [Ja1]. Theorem 12.1 can be inferred from the results in [Pa], a weaker version (where the cardinality of the alphabet is not fixed) is contained in [E]. Theorem 12.2.(iii) appears also in [BM]. Theorem 12.4 is from [So3].

As regards the rational transductions presented in Section III.1, we refer to [EM] and [Ni] as early papers in this area. Our main concern are regulated transductions which have been discussed in [Ja1]. Section III.2 is mostly classical automata theory, cf. especially [Sch3]. The material from Section III.3 is from [Tu]; Turakainen has also suggested exercise 3.2. The results in Section III.4 are due to Turakainen, Fliess and Soittola, cf. [Pa], [Fl1] and [Sol]. Theorem 4.7 is essentially from [PDD]. Section III.5 is from [Sol], some of the results being proposed in [Fl1] as open problems. Section III.6 is from [Be2]. [Sz] and [PS] are the first papers concerning growth functions. The important Theorems 7.5 and 7.7 are from [So4]. The solution of the synthesis problem and Theorem 8.3 are from [So3] and [So4], cf. also [So2]. Theorem 8.5 is from [Sa2].

As already mentioned, [CS] contains the basic notions concerning algebraic series. More comprehensive treatments of the topic are contained in [Ni] and [Ja1], and to some extent also in [Fl1] and [Sh2]. Reduction theorems are treated in [Ni], Theorem 2.3 was established for grammars first in [Gr]. Closure properties belong partly to classical formal language theory; they are treated also in [Fl1]. Theorem 3.5 is from [Sch2]. Theorem 4.1 was established in [Sh1], our proof is a modification from [Ni]. Theorem 4.2 belongs to Nivat, cf. [Ja1] and [Ja2]. Theorem 4.4 is from [Sh1], cf. also [Sh2] and [Ja2]. The original version of Theorem 4.5 appears in [CS]. The material in Section IV.5 up to Theorem 5.5 is essentially from [Se]. The remainder of the section comes from [Fü] and [Fl1]. The notion of a semi-algebraic series is from [Ni]. Theorem 6.4 was obtained by analyzing an argument in [Ja1]. (The proof of a stronger statement appearing as Theorem 2 in [Ni, p. 407] is clearly wrong.) The material in Section IV.7 is essentially from [Ja1].

References

[Bec]   H. Becker, Formale Potenzreihen und Formale Sprachen. Mitteilungen der GMD, Bonn, Nr. 20 (1972).

[Ben]   B. Benzaghou, Algèbres de Hadamard. *Bull. Soc. Math. France, 98* (1970), pp. 209–252.

[Be1]   J. Berstel, Sur les pôles et le quotient de Hadamard de séries $\mathbb{N}$-rationnelles. *C.R. Acad. Sci. Paris, 272,* série A (1971), pp. 1079–1081.

[Be2]   J. Berstel, Contribution à l'étude des propriétés arithmétiques des langages formels. Thèse de doctorat d'état, Université Paris, VII (1972).

[BM]   J. Berstel and M. Mignotte, Deux propriétés décidables des suites récurrentes linéaires. Séminaire d'Informatique, Univ. Louis Pasteur, Strasbourg (1975).

[BN]   J. Berstel and M. Nielsen, The growth range equivalence problem for DOL systems is decidable. In A. Lindenmayer and G. Rozenberg (ed.), *Automata, Languages, Development*, North-Holland, Amsterdam (1976), pp. 161–178.

[CP]   J. W. Carlyle and A. Paz, Realizations by stochastic finite automata, *J. Computer and System Sciences,* 5 (1971), pp. 26–40.

[CS]   N. Chomsky and M. P. Schützenberger, The algebraic theory of context-free languages. In P. Braffort and D. Hirschberg (ed.), *Computer Programming and Formal Systems*, North-Holland, Amsterdam (1963), pp. 118–161.

[Di]   A. Dinghas, *Vorlesungen über Funktionentheorie.* Springer-Verlag, Berlin (1961).

[E]   S. Eilenberg, *Automata, Languages, and Machines*, Vol. A. Academic Press, New York (1974).

[ES]   S. Eilenberg and M. P. Schützenberger, Rational sets in commutative monoids. *J. Algebra, 13* (1969), pp. 173–191.

[EM]   C. C. Elgot and J. Mezei, On relations defined by generalized finite automata. *I.B.M. J. Res. Develop., 9* (1965), pp. 47–68.

[Fl1]   M. Fliess, Sur certaines familles de séries formelles. Thèse de doctorat d'état, Université Paris, VII (1972).

[Fl2]   M. Fliess, Sur divers produits de séries formelles. *Bull. Soc. math. France, 102* (1974), pp. 181–191.

[Fü]   H. Fürstenberg, Algebraic functions over finite fields. *J. Algebra, 7* (1967), pp. 271–277.

[Gi]   S. Ginsburg, *Algebraic and Automata-Theoretic Properties of Formal Languages.* North-Holland, Amsterdam (1975).

[Gr]   S. Greibach, A new normal-form theorem for context-free phrase structure grammars. *J. Assoc. Comput. Mach., 12* (1965), pp. 42–52.

[Ja1]   G. Jacob, Représentations et substitutions matricielles dans la théorie algébrique des transductions. Thèse de doctorat d'état, Université Paris, VII (1975).

[Ja2]   G. Jacob, Sur un théorème de Shamir. *Information and Control, 27* (1975), pp. 218–261.

[J]   N. Jacobson, *Basic Algebra* I. W. H. Freeman and Company, San Francisco (1974).

[Ka1]   J. Karhumäki, On length sets of L systems. Licenciate Thesis, Univ. of Turku (1974).

[Ka2]   J. Karhumäki, Two theorems concerning recognizable N-subsets of σ^*. *Theoretical Computer Science, 1* (1976), pp. 317–323.

[KOE]   T. Katayama, M. Okamoto and H. Enomoto, Characterization of the structure generating functions of regular sets. Submitted for publication.

[Ku]   W. Kuich, On the entropy of context-free languages. *Information and Control, 16* (1970), pp. 173–200.

[KM]   W. Kuich and H. Maurer, The structure generating function and entropy of tuple languages. *Information and Control, 19* (1971), pp. 195–203.

[La]   S. Lang, *Algebra.* Addison-Wesley, Reading, Mass. (1965).

[Le]   C. Lech, A note on recurring series. *Arkiv. Mat., 2* (1953), pp. 417–421.

[Ma]   K. Mahler, On the Taylor coefficients of rational functions. *Proc. Cambridge Philos. Soc., 52* (1956), pp. 39–48.

[NRSS] M. Nielsen, G. Rozenberg, A. Salomaa and S. Skyum, Nonterminals, homomorphisms and codings in different variations of OL systems, I and II. *Acta Informatica, 3* (1974), pp. 357–364, and *4* (1974), pp. 87–106.

[Ni]   M. Nivat, Transductions des langages de Chomsky. *Ann. Inst. Fourier, 18* (1968), pp. 339–455.

[Pa]   A. Paz, *Introduction to Probabilistic Automata.* Academic Press, New York (1971).

[PS]   A. Paz and A. Salomaa, Integral sequential word functions and growth equivalence of Lindenmayer systems. *Information and Control, 23* (1973), pp. 313–343.

[PDD]   Phan Dinh Dieu, Necessary condition for stochastic languages. *Elektronische Informationsverarbeitung und Kybernetik, 8* (1972), pp. 575–587.

[Ri]   J. Richard, Représentations matricielles des séries rationnelles en variables non commutatives. *C.R. Acad. Sci. Paris, 270,* série A (1970), (1970), pp. 224–227.

[Ru1]   K. Ruohonen, On the synthesis of DOL growth, *Ann. Acad. Scient. Fennicae, Ser. A I,* Vol. 1 (1975), pp. 143–154.

[Ru2]   K. Ruohonen, Zeros of $\mathbb{Z}$-rational functions and DOL equivalence. *Theoretical Computer Science, 3* (1976), pp. 283–292.

[Ru3]   K. Ruohonen, On some decidability problems for HDOL systems with nonsingular Parikh matrices. Submitted for publication.

[Sa1]   A. Salomaa, *Formal Languages.* Academic Press, New York (1973).

[Sa2]   A. Salomaa, Undecidable problems concerning growth in information-less Lindenmayer systems. *Elektronische Informationsverarbeitung und Kybernetik, 12* (1976), pp. 331–335.

[Sch1] M. P. Schützenberger, Un problème de la théorie des automates. Séminaire Dubreil-Pisot, 13e année (1959–1960), no. 3, Inst. H. Poincaré, Paris (1960).

[Sch2] M. P. Schützenberger, On a theorem of R. Jungen. *Proc. Amer. Math. Soc., 13* (1962), pp. 885–890.

[Sch3] M. P. Schützenberger, On the definition of a family of automata. *Information and Control, 4* (1961), pp. 245–270.

[Se]   A. L. Semenov, Algoritmitšeskie problemy dlja stepennykh rjadov i kontekstnosvobodnykh grammatik. *Doklady Akad. Nauk SSSR, 212* (1973), pp. 50–52.

[Sh1]   E. Shamir, A representation theorem for algebraic and context-free power series in noncommuting variables. *Information and Control, 11* (1967), pp. 239–254.

[Sh2]   E. Shamir, Algebraic, rational, and context-free power series in non-commuting variables. In M. Arbib (ed.), *Algebraic Theory of Machines, Languages, and Semigroups*, Academic Press, New York (1968), pp. 329–341.

[So1]   M. Soittola, On stochastic and ℚ-stochastic languages. *Ann. Acad. Scient. Fennicae, Ser. A I*, Dissertationes 7 (1976).

[So2]   M. Soittola, On DOL synthesis problem. In A. Lindenmayer and G. Rozenberg (ed.), *Automata, Languages, Development*, North-Holland, Amsterdam (1976), pp. 313–321.

[So3]   M. Soittola, Positive rational sequences. *Theoretical Computer Science, 2* (1976), pp. 317–322.

[So4]   M. Soittola, Remarks on DOL growth sequences. Revue Francaise d'Automatique, *Informatique et Recherche Operationnelle, Ser. Rouge, 10* (1976), pp. 23–34.

[Sta]   D. F. Stanat, A homomorphism theorem for weighted context-free grammars. *J. Computer and System Sciences, 6* (1972), pp. 217–232.

[St]   K. B. Stolarsky, *Algebraic Numbers and Diophantine Approximation*. Marcel Dekker, Inc., New York (1974).

[Sz]   A. Szilard, Growth functions of Lindenmayer systems. Computer Science Department, University of Western Ontario Technical Report No. 4 (1971).

[Tu]   P. Turakainen, Generalized automata and stochastic languages. *Proc. Amer. Math. Soc., 21* (1969), pp. 303–309.

Index

Texts and Monographs
in Computer Science

The Design of Well-Structured and Correct Programs
By **S. Alagić** and **M. A. Arbib**
1978. approx. 260p. approx. 68 illus. cloth

Chess Skill in Man and Machine
Edited by **P. W. Frey**
1977. xi, 217p. 55 illus. cloth

Design of Digital Computers
An Introduction
Second Revised Edition
By **H. W. Gschwind** and **E. J. McCluskey**
1975. ix, 548p. 375 illus. cloth

The Origins of Digital Computers
Selected Papers
Second Edition
Edited by **B. Randell**
1975. xvi, 464p. 120 illus. cloth

Adaptive Information Processing
An Introductory Survey
By **J. R. Sampson**
1976. x, 214p. 83 illus. cloth

Computer Science from Springer-Verlag

Compiler Construction
An Advanced Course
Second Edition
Edited by **F. L. Bauer** and **J. Eickel**
1976. xiv, 638p. 123 illus. 2 tables. paper
(Springer Study Edition)

This text consists of papers carefully prepared by a group of experts for a workshop on compiler construction held in Munich in 1974 and repeated in 1975. The second edition contains an addendum by A. P. Ershov to the contribution by F. L. Bauer, as well as a new paper by D. Gries on "Error Recovery and Correction—An Introduction to the Literature."

Software Engineering
An Advanced Course
Edited by **F. L. Bauer**
1977. xii, 545p. paper
(Springer Study Edition)

Proceedings of an Advanced Course on Software Engineering, organized by the Mathematical Institute of the Technical University of Munich and the Leibniz Computing Center of the Bavarian Academy of Sciences, March, 1972.

MICROCOMPUTER
Problem Solving Using PASCAL
By **K. L. Bowles**
1977. x, 563p. paper

This text introduces problem solving and structured programming using the PASCAL language, extended with built-in functions for graphics. Designed for a one-quarter/semester curriculum at the sophomore/junior level, this book serves a dual purpose: to teach students an organized approach to solving problems, and to introduce them to the computer and its applications, which may be of use later in their chosen professions.

PASCAL
User Manual and Report
Second Edition
By **K. Jensen** and **N. Wirth**
1978. viii, 167p. paper
(Springer Study Edition)

This book is divided into two parts: the User Manual and the Revised Report. The Manual is directed at those who have previously acquired some familiarity with computer programming, and who wish to become acquainted with PASCAL. Many examples demonstrate the various features of this language. Tables and syntax specifications are included in the appendix. The Report serves as a concise and ultimate reference for both programmers and implementors. By defining Standard PASCAL, the book provides a common base for various implementations of the language.